The Fraser Institute

The Fraser Institute is an independent Canadian economic and social research and educational organization. It has as its objective the redirection of public attention to the role of competitive markets in providing for the well-being of Canadians. Where markets work, the Institute's interest lies in trying to discover prospects for improvement. Where markets do not work, its interest lies in finding the reasons. Where competitive markets have been replaced by government control, the interest of the Institute lies in documenting objectively the nature of the improvement or deterioration resulting from government intervention.

The Fraser Institute is a national, federally-chartered, non-profit organization financed by the sale of its publications and the contributions of its members.

Orders for publications and membership enquiries should be addressed to:

THE FRASER INSTITUTE
626 Bute Street
Vancouver, British Columbia
Canada V6E 3M1

Telephone (604) 688-0221

PUBLIC PROPERTY?

THE HABITAT DEBATE CONTINUED

PUBLIC PROPERTY?

THE HABITAT DEBATE CONTINUED

ESSAYS ON
THE PRICE, OWNERSHIP
AND GOVERNMENT OF LAND

Edited by
LAWRENCE B. SMITH
Associate Chairman, Department of
Political Economy, University of Toronto
and
MICHAEL WALKER
Research and Editorial Director,
The Fraser Institute, Vancouver

THE FRASER INSTITUTE
1977

Canadian Cataloguing in Publication Data
Main entry under title:
Public property?

Includes bibliographies.
ISBN 0-88975-017-3 bd.
ISBN 0-88975-014-9 pa.

1. Land—Addresses, essays, lectures.
2. Land—Canada—Addresses, essays, lectures.
3. Real property—Prices—Addresses, essays, lectures. I. Smith, Lawrence Berk, 1939-
II. Walker, Michael, 1945- III. Fraser Institute, Vancouver, B.C.
HD111.P82 333.7'0971 C77-002134-4

Printed in Canada.

Contents

PREFACE

Lawrence B. Smith, *Professor of Economics, Associate Chairman, Department of Political Economy, University of Toronto*

Michael Walker, *Research and Editorial Director, The Fraser Institute*

THE LAND MARKET: HOW IT WORKS

David Nowlan, *Professor of Economics, University of Toronto*

THE IMPACT OF GOVERNMENT POLICIES ON THE SUPPLY AND PRICE OF LAND FOR URBAN DEVELOPMENT

Larry R.G. Martin, *Associate Professor, School of Urban and Regional Planning, University of Waterloo*

GOVERNMENT OWNERSHIP AND THE PRICE OF LAND

Stanley W. Hamilton, *Associate Professor of Urban Land Economics, Acting Dean, Faculty of Commerce and Business Administration, University of British Columbia*

David E. Baxter, *Assistant Professor, Faculty of Commerce and Business Administration, University of British Columbia*

PUBLIC LAND BANKING AND THE PRICE OF LAND

Jack Carr, *Associate Professor of Economics, University of Toronto*

Lawrence B. Smith, *Professor of Economics, Associate Chairman, Department of Political Economy, University of Toronto*

OWNERSHIP CONCENTRATION IN THE URBAN LAND MARKET: ANALYTICAL FOUNDATIONS AND EMPIRICAL EVIDENCE

James R. Markusen, *Assistant Professor of Economics, University of Western Ontario*

David T. Scheffman, *Associate Professor of Economics, University of Western Ontario*

THE ECONOMIC IMPLICATIONS OF FOREIGN OWNERSHIP OF CANADIAN LAND

Stuart McFadyen, *Associate Professor, Faculty of Business Administration and Commerce, University of Alberta*

Robert Hobart, *Economist, Ministry of State for Urban Affairs*

HOUSING AND LAND PRICES IN CANADA AND THE U.S.

Michael A. Goldberg, *Professor and Chairman, Urban Land Economics Division, Faculty of Commerce and Business Administration, University of British Columbia*

Preface

During the last decade increasing attention has been devoted to the role of land and the factors affecting land prices in Canada. To a large extent this attention has occurred because much of the increase in the price of single family homes has been attributed to land inflation. However, land markets have also come under scrutiny because their organization is thought to affect the distribution of income and wealth and to influence the allocation of land between competing uses.

THE HIGH PRICE OF LAND?

The primary concern of most commentators on land is the high cost of land. Although most commentators feel that the price of land is too high this view is not universally held, especially by farmers who view their farmland as their primary asset and who feel that economic conditions and policies often combine to hold down the value of their farms.

Most commentators, however, refer not to the price of farmland but to the price of land on the urban fringe which would normally be shifted into urban use as development proceeds, and would be the base for future industrial and residential growth. Commentators who feel the price of this land is too high offer a variety of explanations.

Monopolists and speculators

One explanation, offered predominantly by a group that might be called social reformers, places the blame for the high price of land on monopolistic developers who, they claim, acquire land and withhold it from the market, driving up the price and artificially creating shortages, or on speculators who perform similar gymnastics with the price of land.

This view is not substantiated by careful research. Professors Markusen and Scheffman, reporting on their extensive original research into the structure of ownership in the Toronto area (reputedly the most concentrated), conclude that "... even when linkages among companies are taken into consideration, concentration of ownership in the Toronto region was far too low to imply market power." The authors further conclude that this finding "leaves social critics such as Lewis (1972) and Lorimer (1976) without a factual basis for their explanation of the recent land price boom." In commenting on monopoly power, Professor Nowlan says there is "... on balance little reason to believe that such power is a very important feature of Canadian urban land markets."

The role of the speculator in the process of land price inflation is also examined in the volume. In their paper, Professors Carr and Smith demonstrate that "speculation may alter the price of land at any point in time ... but (it) will not affect the long-run equilibrium level of land prices." In addition, since speculators can only make money by buying land when the price is low (i.e. when the demand for land is low) and selling when the price is high (i.e. when the supply is low), they tend to act as a counterbalance in moderating price fluctuations.

Government intervention

A second explanation, offered predominantly by developers and builders, places the blame for the high price of land mainly on government intervention and regulation in the market. This group feels that the myriad of development regulations and the extraordinarily long delays in obtaining development permissions and building approvals are responsible for less land being developed. Further, because these delays increase the holding period of land by developers before it can be used, they lead to higher costs for the developer and hence a higher price of land.

The papers by Martin, Markusen and Scheffman, and Nowlan offer evidence on this view. Professor Martin concludes that "public land planning policies . . . restrict the supply of non-urban land for conversion." Citing work by Flowers (1976), Martin notes, for example, that the *average* time taken to gain subdivision approval in the City of Mississauga was 22 months. The delays were caused by "the complexity of the process, . . . the shortage of competent municipal staff, . . . intentional stalling by public bodies in order to exact concessions from developers . . . and . . . *the complete absence of sweet reason . . ." Martin's examination of the impact of government controls leads him to conclude ". . . Clearly, governments' continuing contribution to land supply restrictions and increasing land price is unjustified and is in conflict with the public interest." Nowlan is led to the same sort of conclusion about zoning regulations since ". . . it is not always easy to establish that their application has furthered the public interest."*

Fiscal fracas

A third explanation, offered predominantly by academics and planners, focuses upon the impediments created in the market by the financial arrangements associated with urban development, such as the distribution of tax revenues between the provinces and the municipalities. While the latter bear the brunt of the financial burden associated with urban growth, they often do not have the resources required to sustain it. As a result, municipalities are often opposed to increasing the supply of development land and reluctant to supply sufficient water, sewers and other services to increase the supply of developable land ahead of the demand.

In the opinion of Professors Markusen and Scheffman, problems of this sort in combination with a burst in demand triggered by inflationary expectations and increased relative tax advantages for homeownership were responsible for the boom in land prices in Ontario during the early seventies.

First, "because much of the increase in demand was unanticipated, subdivision applications (which are now taking at least three years to process) were not made at the proper point in time. Second, a number of the municipalities surrounding Metro Toronto were moving towards no-growth policies in this period, which resulted in the slowing down or outright killing of many existing subdivision applications. Third, a lack of proper planning left large areas of land without trunk servicing facilities, especially sewers, that were essential for new construction. Thus the red tape of the subdivision approval process and the lack of trunk servicing facilities left the development industry little scope to respond to the surge in demand."

The maldistribution of taxing powers and spending responsibilities is examined by Professor Martin and found to be responsible for many of the anomalies in the supply of housing. One consequence of this mismatch is that the cost of servicing "has been shifted from the municipality to the developer and thus to the new homebuyer, as opposed to all homeowners . . ." The extent to which municipalities require service installation by developers in many cases exceeds any realistic need and in "some metropolitan areas excessive municipal servicing demands can only be regarded as exclusionary." That is, municipalities are driven by the lack of an appropriate tax base to impose requirements on new developments that can only effectively price the developments off the market. Moreover, the intervention of more senior levels of government may not provide the answer either since "the tendency of senior governments' policies to emphasize housing demand subsidies in preference to land and housing supply has contributed to a relative increase in housing demand and has ignored the concomitant adverse fiscal impact upon local government."

If the price of land is too high in the sense of being above the level that would exist in the absence of any of the imperfections described above, the price could be reduced if the imperfection or imperfections were removed. However, a prerequisite for reducing the price is the identification of the imperfection(s) responsible, and this requires detailed economic analysis. Unfortunately, all too often rhetoric and philosophy have been offered rather than analysis, and consequently the level of knowledge and accomplishment in this area is often wanting.

Are prices too high?

In his provocative paper, which analyzes the difference between land prices in Canada and in the U.S., Professor Goldberg suggests that "higher prices (in Canada) signal healthy cities not government and industry bumbling" and that instead of bemoaning high prices in Canadian cities, we should "glory in the knowledge that Canadian core areas are in demand, and are healthy." In other words, although housing and land prices may be somewhat lower in the U.S., that fact is not unrelated to the notorious condition of U.S. cities. Viewed as a symptom of urban blight, lower prices seem much less attractive. Moreover, as Professor Goldberg points out, "recent high prices should have taught us that housing, land and housing materials are in short supply. They are scarce resources. As such they should be treated with care, not frittered away through prodigal policies . . . High prices from both an economic and environmental point of view, while unpleasant, are warranted if we are to maintain a reasonable standard of living in a world of finite resources."

THE ROLE FOR GOVERNMENT INTERVENTION

The Habitat resolutions

One of the consequences of the increased attention devoted to land by the press and the public has been the recent surge in government intervention into the land markets in Canada. This intervention has taken a variety of forms, from controls on foreign investment through discriminatory transfer taxes and direct prohibitions, to discriminatory taxes imposed on gains realized on land, to outright government ownership. Not only have both federal and provincial governments imposed such controls but a federal-provincial delegation endorsed a highly interventionist set of recommendations for national action adopted at the United Nations Conference on Human Settlements (Habitat Conference), held in Vancouver. These recommendations included the views that

> "land, because of its unique nature and the crucial role it plays in human settlements, cannot be treated as an ordinary asset, controlled by individuals and subject to the pressures and inefficiencies of the market;
>
> "private land ownership . . . may become a major obstacle in the planning and implementation of development schemes;
>
> "public control of land use is . . . . indispensible to its protection as an asset and the achievement of the long-term objectives of human settlements policies and strategies; and
>
> "the unearned increment resulting from the rise in land values . . . must be subject to appropriate recapture by public bodies (the community), unless the situation calls for other additional measures such as new patterns of ownership."[1]

Unfortunately, much recent government intervention and support of an interventionist position seems to have been undertaken without the benefit of rigorous economic analysis, since such analysis has only recently been completed. Consequently, the purpose of this volume is to present in a non-technical way the results of recent economic analysis which the Fraser Institute hopes will generate further research and form the basis for enlightened public opinion and government policies in Canada.

The general view pervading the research reported here is that the market mechanism, although imperfect, works reasonably well in allocating land between alternative uses. There is little evidence of market failure or excessively high prices of land due to market imperfections and, as the Nowlan paper shows, the price of land is an important mechanism in rationing a scarce resource and allocating "each parcel of land into its most valuable use."

On the other hand, the operation of the market mechanism does not mean the exclusion of government. Quite the contrary, public intervention is justified to remedy externality problems and imperfections in the allocative mechanism which sometimes arise in a free market system. Consequently, although the pervading theme of the work in this volume is the value of the market mechanism, a recurring refrain throughout the book is the role to be played by government in removing market imperfections, increasing economic efficiency and compensating where necessary for economic externalities. However, the type of intervention suggested as appropriate is designed to improve the functioning of the market mechanism, and not to replace it by a non-market system nor inhibit it by excessive constraints.

The nature of government intervention is a very serious issue because of the large scale on which it is presently undertaken in Canada and because excessive intervention or controls can seriously inhibit the operation of the market and create more problems than they solve. The problems associated with some forms of government intervention, such as public ownership via land banks, increased land use controls, and prohibitions on foreign ownership, are discussed in detail in a number of papers.

The impact of interventions like those suggested by the Habitat resolutions is thoroughly analyzed in the Baxter and Hamilton paper by examining the implications of public ownership of land. The Hamilton and Baxter paper shows that public land ownership "will not resolve the allocation of increases in property values," "will not necessarily result in improved planning," "will not result in a lowering or stabilization of land values unless a steady flow of land, ripe for development where and when required, is made available" and will "offer no advantages over our present system in terms of monitoring supply."

Moreover, as Hamilton and Baxter note, the issue is not unrestricted private ownership versus government control since at present "private landowners are not free to do as they wish with their land or to charge the prices they wish for use of their land . . . the private 'owner' of a parcel of land is . . . more akin to a long-term tenant than an owner in the general sense of the word . . ."

Owners are greatly constrained by public and private restrictions through both law and market operation. Further reducing the rights of users, and of owners of interests in land,is not an efficient or equitable method to achieve social goals of equity and efficient use of scarce resources.

The Carr-Smith paper analyzes the effects of public landownership via landbanking on the price of land, and concludes that "arguments that it will reduce the price . . . are all unfounded." The McFadyen-Hobart paper evaluates alien landownership controls and concludes that existing controls on foreign landownership are probably harmful since "foreign investment on the present scale appears to provide benefits which more than offset the costs," and that "additional prohibitions or regulatory measures are costly in terms of both administrative and compliance costs and in terms of potential retaliatory measures."

Policy 're-think' required

Taken as a whole the research reported in this book clearly indicates that further large scale government intervention in the land markets runs the risk of reducing the efficiency of the markets and leading to a less beneficial allocation of scarce land between its various competing uses. The papers suggest that government regulation and controls have in some instances distorted the response of the supply of land to demand pressures contributing significant upward pressure on the price of land. On the other hand, the papers (especially the Nowlan and Martin papers) suggest that failure to intervene constructively in the provision of adequate primary and secondary services in advance of need constrains the availability of usable land and contributes to the misallocation of resources. These points taken together and buttressed by the evidence provided in the other papers, suggest that all levels of government should re-appraise their existing programmes and policies impinging on the land area from the viewpoint of their economic consequences, and that they should seriously consider the economic implications of any further incursions in the area before initiating new policies. The example of senior levels of government stimulating the demand for housing while junior levels of government are restricting the supply is only the most obvious case where policy 're-think' is called for.

The papers also suggest that our governments should reassess their acceptance of the recommendations of the Habitat Conference, because there is little evidence to justify their unqualified support.

If such strong evidence exists that additional large scale intervention in land markets by public ownership, discriminatory taxes, or prohibitions on uses and ownership, is likely to be detrimental to our basic direct objectives for land and should be undertaken with extreme caution, then how can we explain the continuing pressure for such intervention? There appear to be two possible explanations. The first explanation is that the lack of economic analysis in the past has allowed many myths and misconceptions to dominate our thinking, and consequently such pressure is simply a reflection of our ignorance of the functioning of the land market and our failure to appreciate the full economic implications of introducing distortions in this market.

The second explanation is more complicated since it focuses on social rather than economic reasons. This explanation holds that those exerting pressure for increased intervention feel that "the distribution of benefits from current methods of urban and other growth and development are inequitable"[2] and consequently increased government intervention is required to provide "social justice' and to appropriate for the public increments in land values. In other words, this explanation is that increased public intervention in land markets is urged as a means of redistributing income and wealth. However, there is little doubt among economists that if a redistribution of wealth is desired it should be done in such a way as to minimize its effects on the efficiency of the economy, and that is accomplished by policies that redistribute wealth directly, and not indirectly through policies such as increased intervention in land markets. Furthermore, policies of this sort are unlikely to achieve the desired goal as is demonstrated by Hamilton and Baxter and Carr and Smith.

Because the appropriate use of land is vital for our continuing prosperity and standard of living the Fraser Institute believes it is important to increase our understanding of the land market and the effects of various proposals respecting it. It is our hope in this book to raise the level of understanding about land markets and to correct many misconceptions that currently exist with respect to land and proposals affecting land. The views presented here, while often differing in emphasis and perspective, all reinforce the view that an increased awareness of the operation and importance of land markets is desirable, and is required before any new policy initiatives are taken in this area. Moreover, the papers indicate that some restructuring or dismantling of existing programmes affecting land may be appropriate for the well-being of the nation.

The Fraser Institute has been pleased to support the work reported in this volume. However, owing to the independence of the authors, the views expressed by them may or may not conform severally or collectively with those of the members of the Institute.

Lawrence B. Smith **June 1977**

Michael Walker

Notes and References

[1]United Nations *Report of Habitat: United Nations Conference on Human Settlements* (United Nations: New York, 1976) pp. 61, 65.

[2]D. Kehoe, et. al. "Public Land Ownership and Planning: Policy, Objectives, and Strategy" in D. Kehoe et. al. (editors) *Public Landownership: Programmes for Evaluation* (D.C. Heath: Lexington, Mass. 1976) p. 35.

Flowers, D., "The Cost of Housing in Ontario," Unpublished paper, University of Waterloo, 1976 (mimeograph).

Lewis, D., *The Corporate Welfare Bums*, James Lewis and Samuel, Toronto, 1972.

Lorimer, J., "Their Land, Your Money," *Weekend Magazine*, May 22, 1976.

The Land Market: How it Works

DAVID M. NOWLAN

Professor of Economics
University of Toronto

THE AUTHOR

David M. Nowlan received his B.Sc. degree in engineering from Queen's University in 1958, at which time he was awarded a Rhodes Scholarship. He received his B.A. degree from Oxford in 1960, and his M.A. and Ph.D. degrees in economics from the University of Toronto in 1963 and 1965, respectively. He is Professor of Economics at the University of Toronto and also a Research Associate for the Institute for Policy Analysis. He has been an economist with the Government of Canada, a member of the Metropolitan Toronto Planning Board and is a Registered Professional Engineer.

Among his publications, Professor Nowlan lists: *The Demand for Energy in the Atlantic Provinces, 1950-1980*, published by the Queen's Printer in 1962; "Land Policy in the Central City: A Toronto Perspective" in *The Management of Land for Urban Development*, Conference Proceedings of the Canadian Council on Urban and Regional Research, April, 1974; *Development Control Policies: Their Purpose and Economic Implications*, published by the City of Toronto Planning Board in 1975; "Value and the Use of Land: The Public Connection," published in *Urban Forum*, Fall, 1976.

The Land Market: How it Works

DAVID M. NOWLAN*

Professor of Economics
University of Toronto

I. INTRODUCTION: THE IDEA OF A MARKET

Some writers reject the very idea of a market in land. The matter was put quite bluntly by a group of planning consultants reporting to the City of Toronto Planning Board in 1975. "We dispute the proposition," they wrote at the beginning of their analysis, "that there exists a market in land."[1] Others cautiously accept the existence of a land market, but firmly believe that it is not like other markets. Professor R.W.G. Bryant, the author of *Land: Private Property, Public Control*, argues, for example, that "land is not a product. The laws of supply and demand cannot operate satisfactorily in the land market, because the supply side has a built-in element of monopoly . . . the supply is fixed by nature."[2]

Any analysis that starts with these premises is clearly not going to find the private market a very satisfactory device for allocating land uses. However, the premises are not well-founded. Neither the existence of a land market, nor even the possibility of competitive selling in that market, is precluded by a fixed overall supply of land.

*In preparing this essay, I have taken advantage of helpful comments by my colleagues, Larry Smith, Michael Denny, Jack Carr, and Larry Bourne, all of whom kindly read a first draft.

Fixed supply a 'catch'?

In fact, everything that has economic value to us—everything that has a price, from Picassos through bauxite ore to medical doctors—is in fixed supply at any given time. The supply of some things can, of course, be varied more readily than others, but, ultimately, only by adjusting the use of resources that are themselves firmly fixed in supply. We can, for example, increase the supply of potatoes by allocating more of our fixed stock of land to potato farming. In this case, a private market can help allocate the land to potato growing, just as a market can help allocate potatoes to consumers. A resource like land may be fixed in total supply, but the amount available for any one use is not fixed, and some social device, like a private market, is needed to determine how much of the fixed supply gets used for each separate purpose.

All that is needed for the existence of a land market is the opportunity for individuals or corporations to buy and sell rights or entitlements to the use of land. Such an entitlement gives the individual an exclusive right either to use the property or to receive income from its use. If these rights are permitted by law, and if they are both enforceable and exchangeable, then there will exist a market in land—or, more accurately, a market in land rights—with the price of land serving to determine both who uses various parcels of land and, within various legal constraints, what those uses will be.

Finding the most valuable use

This market-determined price places a value on the scarcity or uniqueness of different pieces of land. By means of these scarcity-value prices the market directs each parcel of land into its most valuable use. If land of any given quality were available in unlimited supply, then the market would be unimportant; indeed, it would cease to exist. But it is precisely the limitation on natural supply that creates the market and makes its workings so important to us.

It is not the fault of the market if we all do not get as much land as we would like, in the places we would like. That limitation is a consequence of land's scarcity. On the other hand, the simple existence of a private market is no guarantee that land will be placed in its most efficient or most generally desirable use. An unregulated private market might readily permit a noisy tavern in the midst of a quiet residential community; and fragmented landownership can work against the creation of a new centre of mixed but complementary land uses.

Restrictions on rights

In an attempt to overcome these kinds of market-directed, land-allocation problems we have developed in our society enormously complex regulatory structures with which to surround the land-rights market. These take the form of official plans, zoning by-laws and subdivision controls, among many others.[3] Such regulations naturally affect the outcome of the allocation process, but they do not fundamentally alter the workings of the private land-rights market; they simply serve to define the product that is being bought and sold. For example, an exclusive ownership or leasehold right over a parcel of land may not, because of government regulation, include the right to erect a commercial building, or to surround the property by a fence higher than six feet. This kind of regulation may affect the use of land and the market price of the rights that are bought and sold, but the nature of the market process is not altered. The market can continue to allocate uses and distribute land among owners within the boundaries established by these regulatory constraints.†

Of course, it is an open question whether many of these constraints are socially beneficial. For example, one common, although notorious, form of zoning regulation establishes minimum residential lot sizes. This is widely believed to have contributed both to high house prices and inefficiently sprawling suburbs. Whether the private market without that particular regulation would produce cheaper housing and better designed cities can be answered only through a careful study and understanding of the way in which the market works.

†Editors' Note: An extensive discussion of the concept of ownership as it applies to land is to be found in the paper by Professors Hamilton and Baxter–chapter three in this volume.

Mechanism a must

However, the main point to be understood is that society has to have some basic mechanism, whether regulated or not, to determine how the fixed supply of land within its jurisdiction will be used and who the users will be. Clearly, the private market is not the only mechanism that could be conceived for this purpose. We could battle over land and barricade our holdings against intruders; or, as in some societies, use long-standing custom to dictate how land should be used. Alternatively, we could assign land through lotteries, or have it distributed authoritatively by a Chief Land Allocator.

Naturally, it is none of these whimsical alternatives that we generally have in mind when the merits of private-market allocations are debated. Rather, the prime alternative to the private market is some—usually unspecified or only vaguely specified—political or bureaucratic method of allocation. While the land-allocation process in centrally planned economies might be thought to provide a working model for this alternative, the fact that the other major means of production in those societies are also publicly owned and administratively allocated makes it difficult if not impossible to graft their means of land administration onto our government institutions. Alternative processes of publicly administered land allocation in our society would necessarily have to connect at many points with market prices and private incentives. We have already experienced some of the problems of this connection, in the unintended wealth transfers bestowed upon individuals who have been able to re-sell building lots (in Saskatchewan) and homes (in Ontario) purchased, as a result of government policy, at below market prices.†

†Editors' Note: The two problem areas referred to are the AHOP housing scheme in Ontario and the land bank scheme in Saskatoon. In the former case, original purchasers of the housing were able to buy a single-family dwelling at prices below the market. As the market price of these units rose (substantially in most cases) some of the original purchasers sold the units at the now much higher market price and realized a capital gain. In the case of the land bank in Saskatoon, initial purchasers were able to buy land at a price that was held, by the land bank, below the true 'scarcity value' of the land. Having secured ownership of the rights to the

We really understand very poorly the various administrative devices that might replace the market, but one thing about any political or bureaucratic alternative seems certain: that it would be much more complicated than the market, and ultimately, therefore, more difficult to control. As the next sections of this essay show, the market mechanism is quite simple, although the land-allocation problems it has to deal with can be very complex.

II. HOW CAPITAL VALUE IS DETERMINED — THE PRICE OF LAND

When land (with or without buildings), or a lease on land is bought and sold, what is being exchanged is an entitlement either to a stream of income from the property or to enjoyment of the land through personal use. A capital asset is being exchanged, the market price of which is based on the value of future net benefits that the asset is expected to generate.

Discounting the future

Suppose, for example, that a piece of property is expected to produce net income (i.e. gross income less all operating expenditures) of $100 a year, and that this income is expected to last for an indefinitely long period into the future. (For the moment, price inflation is assumed away.) How might we, as potential purchasers, decide how much to pay for this asset? The total amount of money that it would generate for us is enormously large—$100 a year multiplied by an indefinitely large number of years. But clearly, the asset is not worth an unlimited sum of money. It is not worth $100 today to get $100 twenty years hence, or even one year from

---

land people then resold the rights to the land at their true 'scarcity value' as reflected in market prices.

The moral of this story is that attempts to artificially maintain the price of a product below the market price or true 'scarcity value' will inevitably founder as long as freedom of exchange is permitted. Market price is not a fiction and policies which regard it as such, rather than as a reflection in the main of the community's preferences, are bound to be frustrated.

now. We know that to get $100 from a savings bank account at the end of a year, we need only deposit about $93 today. To get $100 back after twenty years (at today's rate of interest) we need deposit only $25 or so.

On the basis of the latter example, we know that the most we should pay for an asset yielding a single payment of $100 in twenty years is $25. The reason is that we can invest $25 in a bank account and receive $100 in twenty years because of accumulated interest. Looking at it another way, the $100 payment in twenty years' time is today 'worth' only $25 because the $100 is largely an accumulation of interest. The process of calculating the present value of a future payment in this way is referred to as 'discounting' the future payment. The extent to which a future payment is reduced or discounted to arrive at a present value depends on the rate of interest obtainable on money invested at the time when the present value is being calculated.

Since there are alternative interest-bearing or profitable ways of investing money in assets, the future income from landed property must be discounted at a rate that reflects the value to us of those alternatives.[4] Suppose we simply say that the rate of interest on alternative investments is r (so that, if the rate were 8 per cent a year, r would be 0.08). Then, the capital value, V, of $100 a year for an indefinitely long number of years, with each year's net earnings discounted back to the present at an annual rate r, is given by the formula:

$$V = \frac{100}{1+r} + \frac{100}{(1+r)^2} + \ldots + \frac{100}{(1+r)^n} + \ldots$$

With constant annual earnings, this particular present property value is nice and easy to calculate. V is equal to $\$\left[\frac{100}{r}\right]$. If future net income is discounted at 5 per cent a year (r = 0.05), the present asset value of an entitlement to this income is $\$\left[\frac{100}{0.05}\right]$, or $2,000. If 8 per cent is used as the annual discount rate, the value of the piece of property will be $1,250.

Normally, a parcel of land would not be expected to yield a constant flow of net earnings over future years, even if inflationary factors were not built into the calculation. Improvements to the property might be required in one year but not in others; an owner, or potential owner, might be thinking of putting up new buildings, which would require a heavy capital outlay for a year or so sometime in the future but which would raise net income flows afterwards; or a person might simply intend to hold an empty piece of land, to pay taxes for a few years, or a development levy, and then to sell it to someone else.

All of these possibilities may be handled simply by permitting the expected net income to vary from year to year. Let R_1 stand for the net income of the first year. R_2 for the net income of the second year, and so on. (Each year's income should be thought of as being received at the end of the year.) Let V_1 be the capital value of the property now, at the beginning of the first year. Then we have:[5]

$$V_1 = \frac{R_1}{1+r} + \frac{R_2}{(1+r)^2} + \frac{R_3}{(1+r)^3} + \ldots + \frac{R_n}{(1+r)^n} + \ldots$$

The R's in the above formula could be either positive or negative. There is no way to reduce this present-value calculation to the simple relationship between V and r that we used before, but the principle behind the calculation has not changed. If, for example, a potential purchaser of a piece of land believed that the land could be sold in four years for \$250 (and that four years hence would be the best time to sell), and if taxes of \$20 a year had to be paid until it was sold, and if his annual alternative earnings rate was 6 per cent, then the present value of the property to him would be:

$$V_1 = \frac{-20}{1+.06} + \frac{-20}{(1+.06)^2} + \frac{-20}{(1+.06)^3} + \frac{(250-20)}{(1+.06)^4} = \$130$$

It is not hard to see that different people might value the same piece of land differently. They might have different expectations about the size of the net income stream, or they might discount future earnings at different rates. Indeed, if the property is not to be re-sold or rented out, but used by the owner, then the annual R values are some implicit, personal valuations of net benefits to be received from the property, and could clearly vary greatly from one person to the next. (For example, people assign different values to the view, to the proximity of trees, water, etc.) Thus, present valuations of a property may differ, but we can say that the market price of any actual sale must lie at or above the present value to the seller, and at or below the present value to the buyer.

III. RISING CAPITAL VALUES: THE MECHANICS OF LAND PRICE INCREASES

This basic connection between the present capital value of a piece of property and the income flows (or sale price) that it is expected to generate, may now be used to help us understand the very important role of capital gains in the economics of land markets.

Suppose that a piece of land is being held vacant, for development later on, or perhaps for resale after subdivision or zoning approvals have been obtained. Under these circumstances, the property will not be expected to earn any revenue for the next several years, so today's market value of the property will have been determined by discounting back to the present the property's expected future annual earnings, or expected future sale value. If expectations about the timing and magnitude of the future revenues do not change, then a year from now these expected revenues will be closer in time, and so discounted less heavily. As a result, the market value of the property will be higher next year than it is today. A person buying the property today and intending to sell it next year, will expect to earn this capital gain over the year.

In this example, the increase in capital value took the place of net revenue from the property in a year in which there was no revenue. A property owner must expect to receive each year an annual rate of return equivalent to the rate of return expected on alternative investments, but this return may take the form of either a capital gain or a flow of money earnings, or some combination of the two. Given commonly-held expectations about the kind of revenue ultimately to be obtained from a piece of property, buyers and sellers in the market will adjust today's price until it is at such a level that purchase of the property at that price will be expected to yield a standard annual rate of return.

If the standard rate of return on investment is, say, 12 per cent and if current revenue from the property is zero, then the value of the property must be rising at 12 per cent annually, simply as a condition of holding wealth or property in land. This means that an unimproved property earning no current revenue must be priced today at about half the market price that is expected six years from now, and a quarter the price expected twelve years hence. If expectations are met, and this property does double in capital value every six years, it will still return the owner no more than any equivalent asset is expected to yield. If current net earnings from an unimproved site are negative, the capital value of landed property must rise even faster than the market rate of return.

For the sake of a numerically concrete example, suppose that the current net operating cost of some site is 3 per cent of capital value, and that the market rate of return on similar assets is, as before, 12 per cent. Capital value must then be expected to rise at 15 per cent annually, a rate that would quadruple the property's price every ten years. Far from being a manifest evil, this rapid price rise would simply reflect the force of compound interest acting on annual asset earnings that happened to accrue to the landed property owner in the form of unrealized or unliquified capital gain.

IV. HOW THE MARKET DETERMINES USE

In the examples used so far, the expected revenue from a parcel of land has been given; and implicitly, therefore, so has the use. But how does the market determine this use, with its corresponding stream of revenue? This is the question that we turn to now.

Consider an acre of vacant urban land that has the potential of being used for any one of three different projects: (A) an apartment building; (B) townhouses; or (C) an office building. Each alternative would require capital spending for construction (the amount of which would depend on the size of the project), and each would generate a stream of net income or net benefits.

Any one of a number of potential developers of this acre of land, including the present owner, agree more or less, on the costs of putting up each alternative, and on the net revenue stream that each project would generate if the dwelling or office units were rented out at market prices. For the various amounts of capital spending (a figure that includes construction costs, architectural fees, developer's profit margins, and so on) shown in column (1) of Table 1, the generally accepted net annual revenue figure for each of the three alternatives are shown in column (2).

If we suppose that the net income flows in column (2) are expected to continue at the same (constant price) level for a long time, then we may capitalize them simply by dividing by the annual (real) rate of discount. This has been done, using a 5 per cent annual discount rate, with the results shown in column (3). Each of these capital values is the estimated present value of the land with a certain type and size of building or buildings on it. If the cost of building the structure is now deducted from this total property value, we will be left with an estimate of the value of land for a variety of uses and building intensities. Such a calculation yields the land values shown in column (4).

It is clear that the value of the land today, before development, depends entirely on the kind of development that is contemplated. Some developments—say a $600,000 apartment building, alternative A—would yield just enough net revenue to pay for the construction of the building. If the acre of land were, for some reason, forced to be used in this way, its value would be zero.

TABLE 1
Alternative Land Use Schemes
(costs and revenues in $000's)

(1) Capital Spending (all alternatives)	(2) Net Annual Income (alternatives)			(3) Capital Value of Net Income (alternatives)			(4) Value of Land (alternatives)		
	A	B	C	A	B	C	A	B	C
$ 400	$ 18	$ 35	$ 15	$ 360	$ 700	$ 300	$-40	$300	$-100
600	30	49	25	600	980	500	0	380	-100
800	45	62	44	900	1240	880	100	440	80
1000	60	70	61	1200	1400	1220	200	400	220
1200	75	78	75	1500	1560	1500	300	360	300
1400	90	85	88	1800	1700	1760	400	300	360
1600	98	92	100	1960	1840	2000	360	240	400
1800	105	99	112	2100	1980	2240	300	180	440
2000	110	105	124	2200	2100	2480	200	100	480
2200	115	110	131	2300	2200	2620	100	0	420
2400	120	115	139	2400	2300	2780	0	-100	380

Notes:

1. Alternative A is an apartment building; B is a set of townhouses; and C is an office building.
2. The annual income streams in column (2) are discounted at 5 per cent per year to yield the capital values shown in column (3).
3. The value of land in column (4) is computed by subtracting the capital cost in column (1) from the corresponding capital value in column (3).

Most valuable use

Looking over the figures in column (4), we see that for each alternative there is a best-size development—a development, that is, that maximizes the present value of the land. If an apartment building is to go on the site, a $1,400,000 building will leave the largest residual value to the land—$400,000 in this case. For other alternatives, the best land values are created by $800,000 worth of townhouses, yielding a land value of $440,000, or a $2,000,000 office tower, with a corresponding land value of $480,000. Because of construction technologies and different rental prices for units built at different densities, bigger or smaller projects than these yield smaller land values.

With all of the organizational costs of developing the land included under 'capital spending' in column (1), there is no reason for any present or future owner of this site not to contemplate using the land in such a way that it's value is maximized. If all the alternatives were legally permitted, this value is maximized by developing a $2,000,000 office building on the site. On the assumption that the present owner and potential owners all know this and agree on the figures in Table 1, the $480,000 maximum achievable land value will be, in fact, the market price of this acre of land. There is no reason for the present owner to take less, because he could develop the land and create an income stream that had, to him, exactly that capital value. At the same time, no potential buyer will pay more, because it is impossible to develop in such a way that the land can be made more valuable than $480,000.

As long as there are some potential developers of this site who are aware of the value of the best alternative, the market-produced price for the land will keep the site from being used in less valuable ways. An apartment developer, for example, who knows nothing about office buildings but who agrees with the alternative A figures in Table 1, will find that he cannot pay more than $400,000 for the land. A market price higher than this precludes apartment development, just as a market price higher than $440,000 precludes townhouse development.

This example also helps show how it is true both that land value determines use and that use determines value. Public discussion of land development frequently flaps around in confusion over this relationship of value to use. But the structure of market-determined cause and effect is really quite simple. It is potential use that determines the highest value, which then becomes market price. This market price, in turn, precludes uses other than the one which creates the highest value.

Best use and by-law restrictions

Suppose that, before this land is developed, a by-law is passed restricting its use to residential only. With alternative

C, the office building, no longer legally feasible, the best use now becomes alternative B, a townhouse development with a capital intensity of $800,000. Land value is reduced from $480,000 to $440,000, a value that still will keep an apartment building from going on the site. If a new owner had paid $480,000 for the land just before the by-law was passed, that owner would suffer a capital loss of $40,000. But the fact that $480,000 had been paid for the site will not keep the new 'best' use, the townhouses, from being developed, even though the value of the land is reduced. An old, and now irrelevant, value can never determine the current, market-allocated use. Current value determines use, not past value.

Different opinions and highest value

Before turning to other matters, one further comment may be warranted. By assuming that a number of potential developers all agree on the figures in Table 1, we have, of course, simplified matters, and so have been able to arrive at a single market price. In reality, different people will tend to have different ideas about costs and revenues, and even about the types of projects that might be developed. Suppose there are half-a-dozen prospective buyers for this acre of land, each one of whom has a different estimate of the highest value. If there is competitive bidding for property with potential buyers able to adjust their bids as other bids become known, the land will in the end be sold to the developer who has the highest estimate of its value—provided that this estimate is above the value of the land to the original owner. But the successful purchaser may not have to pay his full estimated value; all he has to do is outbid the potential buyer who has the next highest estimate of value. If the new owner did indeed get the land for less than his estimated value, and if his figures turn out to be correct, then he will have made a capital gain on his new asset. In such a case, the observed market price of the land will be below its 'true' value. However, the asking price of the new owner would be at the 'true' or highest value.

V. DEVELOPMENT TIMING

In the last section, the examples of alternative development schemes all ignored the possibility that it might be better to delay development rather than to proceed now with today's best alternative. Ignoring this enabled us more easily to concentrate on the way in which the market selected among alternative kinds of use and various intensities of use. In this section, we turn to examine this question of development timing, which is the third dimension of the general land-allocation problem.

Suppose we again take as an example an acre of vacant urban land, one that is best suited (or zoned) for residential purposes. If rental accommodation were built today on this land, it would be most profitable to build an $800,000 building which would be expected to yield a net revenue stream of $60,000. This is shown as alternative A in Table 2.

Market conditions

Although this alternative is definitely the best (we suppose) if development had to take place today, changing market conditions expected in the future might mean that quite a different size and type of project would be the best to build if development were delayed. Given generally agreed-upon expectations about the future costs of construction and about the market value of rental accommodation, something like alternative B might be best if development were delayed for six years. This alternative consists of a $1,600,000 building yielding a continuing net revenue stream of $110,000 a year.

Yet a third alternative might be to use the land in some temporary way (perhaps as a mini-golf course) and later undertake an even more intensive residential development — something like alternative C in Table 2, with an initial outlay of $200,000 followed by nine years of $30,000 net annual revenue and then by a $2,400,000 development in the tenth year, a development which would be expected to yield a continuing net revenue stream of $150,000 a year.

TABLE 2
Alternative Development Timing
(costs and revenues in $000's)

Year	Alternatives (A minus entry indicates the cost of development; other entries show annual net revenue) A	B	C
0 (now)	$-800	$ 0	$ -200
1	60	0	30
2	60	0	30
3	60	0	30
4	60	0	30
5	60	0	30
6	60	-1,600	30
7	60	110	30
8	60	110	30
9	60	110	30
10	60	110	-2,400
11	60	110	150
12	60	110	150
.	.	.	.
.	.	.	.
.	.	.	.
Present Value of the Undeveloped Property:			
with r = .04	$700	$909	$931
with r = .05	400	448	382
with r = .06	200	162	116

Notes:

1. Alternative A represents immediate development of this parcel of land to the most profitable current use; alternative B represents delayed development to a higher density use; and C represents a temporary use for 10 years, followed by an even larger development.
2. Present values are the positive and negative income streams discounted to the beginning of year one. With r standing for the rate of discount, these are the appropriate formulas for present value (V_1):

For alternative A, $V_1 = -800 + \frac{60}{r}$;

For alternative B, $V_1 = \left(-1{,}600 + \frac{110}{r}\right)\left(\frac{1}{1+r}\right)^6$;

For alternative C, $V_1 = -200 + \frac{30}{r}\left[1 - \left(\frac{1}{1+r}\right)^9\right] + \left[-2{,}400 + \frac{150}{r}\right]\left(\frac{1}{1+r}\right)^{10}$

Each of these development alternatives implies a certain present value for the acre of vacant land. If the appropriate discount rate is 5 per cent a year, then, as the figures at the bottom of Table 2 indicate, alternative B would maximize the land's present worth. A developer contemplating this alternative could outbid others who had in mind either of the other alternatives. Once again, the market price of land will tend towards its maximum value—at least, this will happen if there is general agreement about the costs and revenues associated with the various alternatives. This market price will preclude all but the single, 'best-value' alternative.

Signals from financial markets

In general, different discount rates will lead the market to rank the alternatives differently, and to choose something different as the best development pattern.[6] As the figures in Table 2 show, if the annual discount rate drops to 4 per cent, alternative C becomes best; if the rate were at 6 per cent, alternative A would be best.

Private developers take their discount-rate signals from the investment or money market. If the general level of interest rate rises, this says to land developers that society is discounting future costs and earnings more heavily. Smaller present streams of income rise in value relative to larger, later ones, while present costs come to weigh more heavily than later costs. In terms of our present example, a rising annual discount rate, from 5 per cent to 6 per cent, will result in early-development alternative A being chosen over later-development alternative B.

If the market discount rate falls to 4 per cent a year, later revenues become relatively more important and the land development market moves to alternative C as the best use for this acre of vacant land.

At first blush, it may seem unlikely that it would ever be in society's interest to leave land vacant if it were approved and available for development, even though, as we have seen, the market might dictate just such a delayed-development alternative. A little reflection, however, should be sufficient to convince us that it would hardly be in society's interest to develop now all of our developable land. How would we decide what pattern and density of land uses to establish? Would we build small houses on large lots, so that they could all be filled now, although they would necessarily be overcrowded later on? Or, should we build dense housing on small lots that would be empty or extravagantly used now, and filled up later on? More importantly, what social warrant would ever exist to assign our resources to the massive development effort that would be required?

Use of other resources

Just like land, the skilled manpower, machinery and raw materials necessary for development are scarce. Any of these scarce resources assigned to one task are not available for other jobs. By taking account of the resource costs of development in determining the best pattern of land use, the market is allocating not only scarce land but also these other scarce resources. More than that, by bringing expected revenues into the calculation, the market is taking account of how much we value the products of development. If office space rents are low this year, but expected to rise several years from now, this suggests that society is not desperate for office space now, but may become so later on. The market responds by not diverting scarce resources into relatively unnecessary office development this year. Instead, land may be used in some other way, or held until there is more justification for directing resources towards office development.[7]

In actual patterns of property development, we frequently observe vacant land being held for later development. This is a phenomenon as common in the centre of large cities as on their suburban fringe. The commercial centre of the City of Toronto, for example, with its land completely urbanized and, one might have thought, 'fully developed', shows a pattern of land use that many will find surprising: in the mid-1970s only a little over ten per cent of all downtown commercial properties were developed up to their maximum allowable amount of floor area, and over one-half of the properties had less than twenty per cent of the building area that they were legally permitted to have.[8]

The point is not that the land use pattern determined by the market is necessarily the best, but that any reasonably efficient pattern that might be determined outside the market—by bureaucrats, say, administering publicly-owned land—will exhibit the same basic features as the market-determined pattern. At any point in time, some land will be heavily developed, some less developed, and some vacant, being held for later development. If a government land administrator were to calculate, using good economic principles, the best time to develop some publicly-owned piece of land, and if he used the same development cost and expected revenue information that the market used, then he would come up with basically the same result as the market. The rule for the government and for the market is this: develop in such a way and at such a time that the present value of the land is maximized. Of course, the land administrator would come up with a different result than the market if he used different cost and different expected-revenue or benefit figures, which perhaps he would do if there were costs and benefits to development not taken into account by the market. This possibility will be raised again in the last section.

VI. DEMAND AND SUPPLY

The value-maximizing, net-revenue stream that a parcel of land is capable of producing depends on both the physical structure placed on the land and the rental or market price that the building space is expected to command. Revenue, in other words, has both a quantity and a price component.

So far, we have concentrated on quantity and timing decisions, and implicitly assumed that dwelling unit or commercial space prices were simply given parameters to the land developer. Each individual developer or land holder may well have a different expectation about the pattern of future prices, but none can personally influence that pattern. This is, of course, a standard feature of competitive markets—indeed, the inability of individuals to influence prices defines a competitive market.

However, as every student of elementary economics knows, buyers and sellers, taken all together in competitive markets, do determine price. Individuals, in turn, respond to this market-determined price, with buyers generally wanting to buy more at lower prices and sellers wanting to sell less, and vice versa at higher prices.

Supply response

To understand how this mechanism works in the land market, consider the principles of development timing discussed in the last section. Individuals in the market balance the expected cost of development (now or in the future) against the pattern of net revenue the development is expected to generate, in order to arrive at some notion of the best time to develop. If some future time for development has initially been decided upon, and then a current, or soon-expected, upsurge in demand takes place for the final product of the development (residential units, perhaps, or offices), prices and net revenues close to the present time will be expected to rise above the initial estimates. This will cause development-timing plans to be revised, with the result that (as long as later expected net revenue has not changed from the initial estimate) the property will be developed earlier. In other words, a higher current price for the product of the development will lead to a larger supply of land for immediate development. Conversely, a lower current price for the final product (with later expected prices remaining constant) will result in less land being made available currently for development.

From the principles by which capital values are established, it should be clear that if net benefits rise in early years and stay constant in later years, the whole capital value of that stream of benefits will rise; and if immediate net benefits fall, the capital value will also fall. Thus, a typical competitive supply relationship is established between the price of land (the capital value) and the amount of land that is made available for development: higher current land prices (brought about by higher market prices for the products of land development) lead to a larger current supply of land and lower prices to less supply.

Demand factors

On the demand side, we have seen how higher land prices preclude various uses. The lower the price of any parcel of land, the larger the number of uses for the land that may profitably be contemplated. It follows that the demand for developable property is inversely related to the price of property—the lower the price, the higher the demand.

To illustrate this interaction of supply and demand, suppose we think of the development of residential land in and around some large urban area. At any given time, the urban area has a certain, fixed residential population. There is nonetheless a demand for new residential acreage. The bulk of this new demand arises from net in-migration pressures but is augmented by sociological changes within the existing population. For example, if households are formed by persons earlier in their lives and if households tend, on average, to have fewer members, the housing demand of a population of unchanged size will increase. The extent to which these salient sources of demand are reflected in demand for developable land is determined by the price of new land for development—the lower the price, the higher the demand.

Price adjustment

Lower prices create a larger demand for new land, but elicit a smaller supply. Higher prices cut back some of the demand and draw forth a larger supply of land for current development. Normally, we would expect property prices to adjust up or down so as to equate this current migrant demand for developable residential land with the current supply.[9] However, because additional influences on the price and quantity of developing suburban land must be taken into account, the market mechanism is a little more complicated.

Adjustments to price

The urban area will have a huge stock of land already in residential use, and a price-related demand for land on the part of existing residents. Aside entirely from the sociological changes referred to above, the existing population will tend to want more land, to spread out a bit more and live less densely, at lower land prices. Conversely, existing residents will tend to conserve land as land prices rise, by converting dwellings from single-family to multiple-family use or by tearing down low-density dwellings and replacing them with higher-density townhouses or apartments.

In addition, therefore, to the new demand and new supply, there is a given supply of existing land and a price-responsive demand among the existing population. At some price, the existing supply and existing demand will be equal. But at lower prices, existing demand will exceed existing supply. This excess demand will compete with the new or migrant demand at these low prices: effectively, the demand for new land will have increased. At higher prices, existing residents will demand less land than now exists, so some of the current stock of land would become available for newcomers. This has the effect of reducing demand in the new-land market.

To account for the amount of new residential land coming on stream in any year, and for its price, it is necessary to bring this 'true' or effective demand into the analysis and not to rely solely on the demand for land created by potential net migrants. Because of the large population in an existing urban area, the effective demand will be much more responsive to price changes than will the migrant demand. This means that changes in the rate at which new land is being made available for development may have very little initial effect on the price of land. Small price changes create incentives for the existing residents and landowners to adjust their uses of land. Since the stock of already-urbanized land is overwhelmingly larger than the annual amount of new land developed, these adjustments in the use of the existing land can dramatically augment or reduce the effective supply of new land, and in this way keep the price relatively stable, at least in the short run.

The upshot of this argument, which is analyzed in more detail in the appendix, is that the price and quantity supplied of new land are influenced both by migrant or new demand and by demand among existing residents in an urban area. Some writers argue that residential property prices are determined entirely by the economics of fringe land development. Others contend that the new-land market is irrelevant, and that prices are determined by existing supply and demand. The truth seems to be that neither part of the market can be ignored, but that the rate at which new land is being made available is less important in the short run, although more important over the long run.

VII. SHIFTS IN SUPPLY AND DEMAND

The basic conceptual framework used in the last section and explained in more detail in the appendix may be used to analyze the effects of any influence on or changes in the conditions of competitive demand and supply. For example, if suddenly more people wanted to move each year to some urban area, land prices in the area would rise, but the rate of price increase would be moderated by the market. Existing residential land within the city would tend to be used more intensively, thus releasing some existing residential land for the newcomers.

The effect of government

In the face of an increase in demand, the upward shift in land prices may, however, be worsened by government regulations that keep the supply of land from increasing as rapidly as it otherwise would. Suppose that new, serviced land has been developed at a relatively constant rate before the increase in demand. Such land will have gone through a series of approval processes, and will probably have required the installation by the government of trunk-line service facilities (sewers, water lines and roads), before being developed. As we have seen, with demand and land price increases, the market will normally respond by releasing more land for current development. But the government has no similar price-responsive, value-maximizing mechanism that will lead it to increase its approval rate or to increase the rate at which service facilities are installed. (In fact, within any jurisdiction, property-owning voters, politicians and administrators may all have an interest in encouraging higher property prices. One way of achieving higher prices is to slow down the rate at which new properties are permitted to be developed. This could be an important element in the politics of land administration during the coming years, as the inflation-adjusted price of land in many urban areas falls away from its peak of a year or two ago.) Because of sluggish government responses, higher land prices may not easily lead to the more rapid development of new land. This forces prices even higher than otherwise, at least in the short run.

Capital gains taxation

However, the rapid increase in the price of urban, residential land in recent years has been not simply the result of inadequate government responses to the pressures of population growth. The general public has become more interested than before in owning residential property, partly as a way of protecting personal wealth against inflation and partly to avoid the capital gains tax levied on other forms of assets. For homeowners, the magnitude of the future net benefit stream has risen, so its capitalized value has increased.

Both newcomers and existing residents are willing to pay more than before for any given property. At the same time, the expectation of higher revenues from land in the future means that suppliers want more money for each parcel of land. With a higher demand and a lower supply at old prices, equilibrium land prices had to rise. Since this increase represents a re-valuation of land, it has not speeded up the land development process, as price rises normally would be expected to do.

VIII. MONOPOLY

No attention has been paid in the preceding sections to the effect of monopoly power on prices and uses in the land market. Neither have the most common ways in which the market allocation of land might depart from some best allocation, received more than passing comment. Although it seems appropriate to end with a word or two about these matters, they stand a little aside from the main point of this essay which is not to analyze and weigh the strengths and weaknesses of the land market, but simply to display the basic ways in which it allocates land to various uses.

Unlike a competitive developer or landowner, a monopolist can exert some influence over market price by controlling the availability of land. In order to have this kind of market power, it is not sufficient simply to own a lot of land. What is necessary, in addition, is that demand for such land be somewhat unresponsive to price changes, so that higher prices do not completely drive people away from purchasing the monopolist's land. If, for example, the price of new suburban land is effectively fixed by the price of existing residential properties in the urban area, then any large scale landowner operating on the suburban fringe is unable to sell land at more than this fixed price, and so has no monopoly power, at least in the short run.†

Over time, a large scale landowner, by adjusting the amount of land developed in any one year, might be able to influence the rate at which prices changed and in this way capture some monopoly profit, although even this kind of monopoly power is somewhat limited. If, for example, there is a fixed supply of developable land around some growing urban area, the future price of residential property after all this land has been developed will be the same whether the initial supply is owned by one person or by many. However, a single owner might develop less of this land in the early years of development than would competing owners, thus driving up the price more rapidly towards the final, post-development level.

There are limits on the extent to which it is profitable to adopt a monopolist tactic of delaying development: a dollar of delayed profit is simply not worth as much as a dollar of profit today, so indefinite delay is not profitable. Moreover, it is hard to imagine circumstances in which developable land is literally fixed in supply. Any competition with other locations, even if those other locations are not as desirable, reduces a large scale landowner's ability to manipulate prices. These conceptual limits on the exercise of monopoly

†Editors' Note: For further discussion of monopoly power in land markets the reader is referred to the papers by Markusen & Scheffman and Carr & Smith in this volume.

power, taken together with what empirical evidence exists, provide on balance little reason to believe that such power is a very important feature of Canadian urban land markets, although elements of it may exist in some places—as much, perhaps, in already developed parts of urban areas as around their fringes.

IX. MARKET FAILURE

Even if the private land market is by and large competitive, there remains the important question of whether or not it serves to allocate land in the best way. The answer to this depends fundamentally on whether the revenue streams generated by various alternative uses for any parcel of land are reasonably good measures of the social benefits of those alternative uses. Generally, the market does seem to choose land uses that maximize the present value of expected net revenues, but if the revenues are not good proxies for social benefits, then this may not lead to the best land use. For example, some particular use of land may generate a value-maximizing revenue stream, but only by imposing costs on other nearby users of land. The revenue stream in this case has overstated the social benefit of that particular land use.

In other cases, the opposite may occur: some particular development on a parcel of land may benefit adjacent land owners, but these benefits may not be reflected in the commercial value of the development. The private market may, therefore, be led away from a socially desirable alternative.

If, in the face of these outside costs or benefits, appropriate taxes and subsidies could be applied by the government to different uses of different parcels of land, so that the revenues and expenses facing private owners reflected all of the benefits and costs of development, then the market could produce better land uses without the need of any further government intervention. But government policy is generally much more blunt than this. Complicated taxing and subsidy schemes are administratively difficult to develop and generally unacceptable to the community. Instead, direct government regulation over land use is a more common way of handling market problems. Zoning laws are used, for example, to prohibit land in residential areas from being developed for commercial purposes, on the ground that commercial uses are detrimental to the residents of the area; other laws limit the height and bulk of buildings so as to reduce or eliminate any negative effect big buildings might have on surrounding properties.

Although it is not difficult to appreciate the broad goals that underlie the use of zoning regulations, it is not always easy to establish that their application has furthered the public interest. Planning officials and the public generally are increasingly skeptical that segregated, homogeneous-use areas, of the sort that zoning regulations tend to produce, are socially beneficial. A heightened awareness of the advantages of mixed-use areas has led many analysts to suggest that homogeneous-use zoning be replaced by performance criteria. These criteria would serve to regulate more directly those particular aspects of land use that clearly harmed, without compensation, neighbouring landowners. This would leave the market free to produce a mixture of land uses within any one area.

On a broader geographic scale, the regulation of private markets so as to achieve greater public benefit is much more difficult. It is frequently beneficial, for example, to have development decisions made jointly by a large number of contiguous landowners, in order to have an integrated development, or to take advantage of any 'economies of scale' that might exist if a whole area were developed beyond some minimum threshold size. Because joint decision-making is not a feature of competitive market decision-making, some public advantage from integrated development may be lost if the market is left to its own devices.

On the other side of the coin, the private market can easily over-concentrate development, simply because many of the external costs of congestion in heavily built-up areas are not borne by the landowning developers. In summary, the market can be slow to develop new spatial centres of activity, and not sensitive enough to the social costs of expanding existing centres.

These matters of broad geographic design are hard to handle simply through the use of zoning regulations. They require a more sophisticated set of policy instruments.[10] To create new towns or to develop commercial subcentres within existing urban areas, public landownership may be the only feasible policy instrument. Paradoxically, in situations such as these, monopolistic land markets may be socially more efficient in allocating land uses than competitive markets.

Notice that these issues, and others throughout the paper, have been dealt with solely from the perspective of land use. The distribution among members of society of the earnings from land has not been part of the discussion. While distributional and land use questions are sometimes closely linked, it is generally possible, and almost always helpful, to handle them separately.[11] Many putative critics of private-market land use allocations are really critics of the existing distribution of wealth, and have little if any concept of society's continuing need for mechanisms by which land uses and development timing will be determined, nor much idea of the way in which the market copes with these problems. If both market critics and market supporters can come to at least a rudimentary understanding of these matters, the land debate may be better focused, and policy better informed.

APPENDIX ON DEMAND AND SUPPLY

Section VI of the text was devoted to a discussion of competitive land markets along the residential fringe of some large urban area. This appendix deals more formally with the same topic. In particular, it describes how the market determines land price and quantity developed in both the short and the long run.

In Figure 1, the demand curve D, on the right-hand side of the diagram, relates the number of acres per year demanded by urban area newcomers (net of out-migrants) to the price of land. The supply of new land for residential development is plotted as line S in the same half of the diagram.

Supply, S, and demand, D, intersect at point 1 on Figure 1. Normally this intersection would establish the price and quantity per year of new residential land coming into use in this urban area. But there are additional influences on this price and quantity that must be taken into account: the urban area will have a huge stock of land already in residential use, and a price-related demand for land on the part of existing residents. At lower land prices, the existing population will tend to want more land, to spread out a bit more and live less densely. Conversely, existing residents will tend to conserve land as land prices rise, by converting dwellings from single-family to multiple-family use or by tearing down low-density dwellings and replacing them with higher-density townhouses or apartments.

In addition, therefore, to the new demand and new supply, there is a given supply of existing land and a price-responsive existing demand, both of which are plotted on the left-hand side of the figure. The existing supply of land is constant at S′, while the demand, D′, slopes down to the left—at lower prices more is demanded.

Existing demand and supply will be in equilibrium at price A, shown in Figure 1. At prices below this equilibrium, existing demand will exceed existing supply. This excess demand will compete with new demand in the flow market, and push outward the demand for new land. At prices above

Figure 1

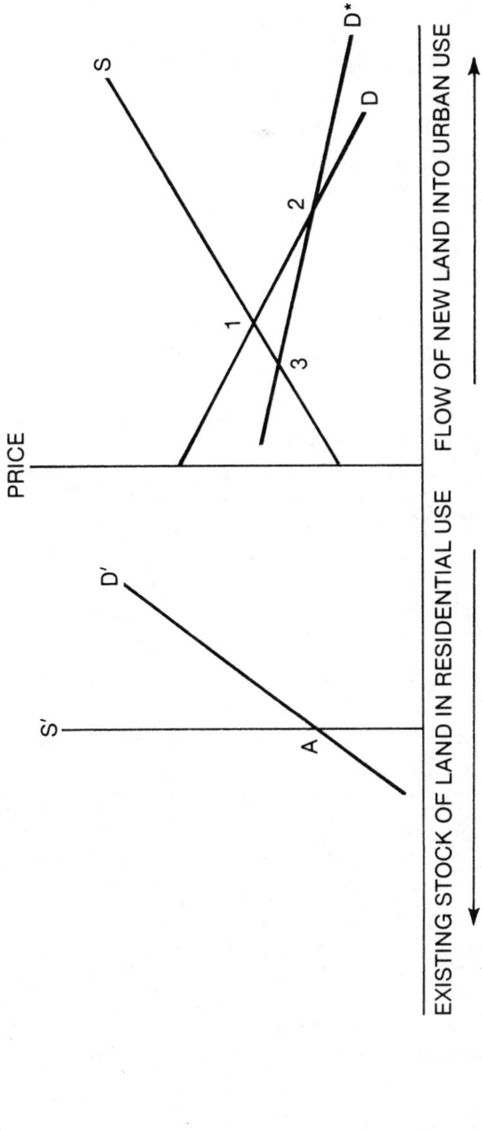
PRICE
S
D*
D
1
2
3
D'
S'
A
FLOW OF NEW LAND INTO URBAN USE
EXISTING STOCK OF LAND IN RESIDENTIAL USE

A, existing residents will demand less land than now exists, so some of the current stock of land will become available to newcomers—the use of existing urban residential land will become more intense. This has the effect of reducing demand in the new-land market, at prices above A, to below the amount shown by the demand curve D.

The line showing the existing demand, D′, is drawn in such a way that we can add or subtract the excess or shortage of existing demand (at prices below or above point A) to the new-land demand curve D, which is denominated in acres per year. At a price of A, the new land demand is unchanged. This is shown as point 2, on demand curve D. Adding excess existing demand at prices lower than 2 (or A), and subtracting deficient existing demand (which is the same as excess existing supply) at prices above 2, gives us the effective demand for new land, shown as D* on the right-hand side.

The effective demand curve for new land intersects the supply curve, S, at point 3. The current price and quantity of new land flowing into residential use are established by the market at this intersection of D* with S.

Notice that this equilibrium price and this quantity are influenced both by the new demand and supply and by the existing demand and supply, and not by either one or the other taken alone, as is sometimes claimed. However, the effect of the existing demand for and supply of land is always to flatten out the true demand curve in the new-land market (i.e. D* will always be flatter than D), and this may keep the market price for new land from moving very far away from price A. If, for example, the magnitude of excess and deficient demand for existing land, at prices below and above A, is overwhelmingly larger than the new demand, D, then the line D* may become almost horizontal. Under these circumstances, a higher or a lower new-supply curve, S, will have almost no effect on the market price, although the equilibrium quantity of new land supplied through the market may vary enormously.

This potentially overwhelming influence of existing land prices on new land prices is, however, only a short-run phenomenon. In the long run—which may be a very long

Figure 2

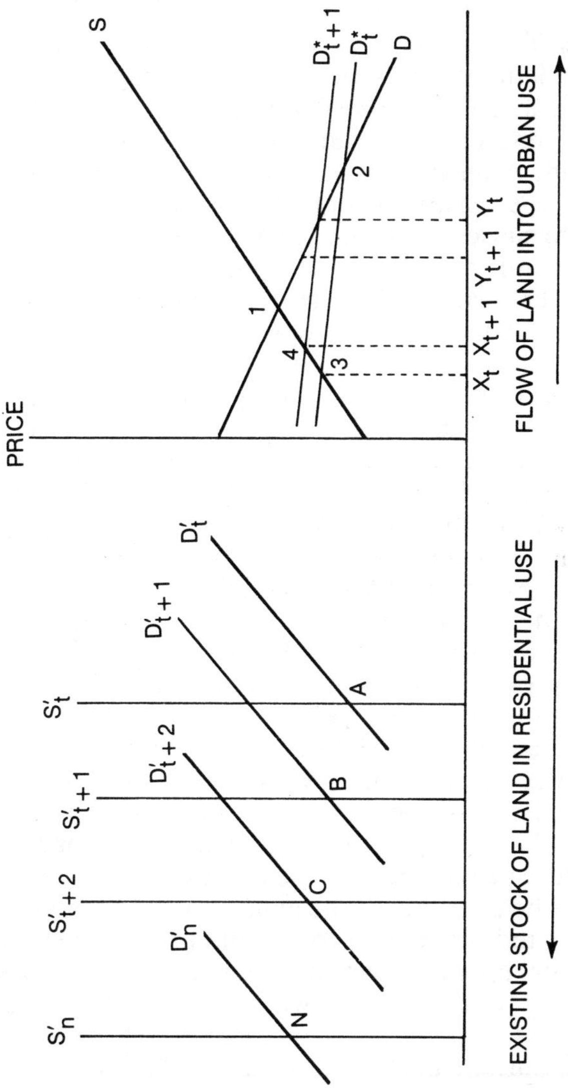
PRICE
S
D*t+1
D*t
D
1
2
3
4
Xt Xt+1 Yt+1 Yt
FLOW OF LAND INTO URBAN USE
S′t
S′t+1
S′t+2
S′n
D′t
D′t+1
D′t+2
D′n
A
B
C
N
EXISTING STOCK OF LAND IN RESIDENTIAL USE

period indeed—the market will tend to come into equilibrium at a price such as that given by point 1 in Figure 1, where new demand and new supply are equated. The way in which this occurs is shown in Figure 2.

The situation shown in this second diagram begins with the demand and supply curves in roughly the same relationship as in Figure 1. Points 1, 2, and 3 on the right side of Figure 2 have the same meaning that they had in Figure 1. Point A on the left side is the same as point A in Figure 1, but the existing supply and demand curves now have the time subscript "t" attached to them. The effective new-land demand curve, D*, also has a time subscript attached. Market price during the first period is established, as before, at point 3, where D^*_t intersects S.

During this first period, an amount X_t of new residential land is developed. This means that the total amount of residential land at the beginning of the new period is equal to the original amount, S'_t, plus the newly developed land, X_t. The sum of these is shown as S'_{t+1} on the left side of Figure 2.

Existing residential demand will have shifted over by more than the increase in supply. At the period-t price represented by point 3, the new addition to demand is the amount Y_t, the amount demanded by incoming residents, at point 3 prices, as shown by the demand curve D. Thus, at the beginning of period t+1, the demand for land by existing residents has shifted over by more than the supply of existing residential land. The new equilibrium price on the left side of the diagram will have moved from A to B.

If we asume that the new-land demand curve D and the new-land supply curve S remain unchanged over time (it would be unusual if these curves remained stable over time, but the principle of the analysis would not be altered even if they did move, and to assume them unchanged saves cluttering up the diagram), then the rising stock-equilibrium price, from A to B, will result in the effective demand curve's shifting up from D^*_t to D^*_{t+1}. The new, market-equilibrium point will shift up and over, from point 3 to point 4. A new amount of land, X_{t+1}, will be added to existing supply, while a larger amount, Y_{t+1}, will be added to total residential demand in the urban area. This gain will push up the stock equilibrium price to point C, on the left side of the diagram.

This process continues until at some time in the future, existing demand and supply are cleared at market price N, which is just the price represented by point 1, where new-land supply-curve S and demand-curve D intersect. At that point, new additions to demand and supply are exactly equal, and this price will therefore be maintained in the residential land market (as long as the demand and supply curves do not shift).

Notes

[1]Shoukry T. Roweis, *et al., The Land Market and the Core of Toronto* (City of Toronto Planning Board, June 1975), p. 8.

[2]R.W.G. Bryant, *Land: Private Property, Public Control* (Montreal: Harvest House, 1972), p. 150.

[3]For a fuller discussion of current restrictions on private rights in land in Ontario, see A.H. Osterhoff, W.B. Rayner and P.E. Vivian, *Restrictions on the Property Right in Ontario* (Toronto: Ontario Real Estate Association, 1974).

[4]If future net income is denominated in terms of today's prices — if inflation, in other words, is not being included — then the annual interest or discount rate must be the actual or nominal rate adjusted to remove the effect of inflation. If government bonds earn 10 per cent annually but the general price level is expected to rise by 7 per cent a year, then the adjusted or "real" rate of interest on the bonds is only 3 per cent. This adjusted rate should be used as the basis for discount factors applied to constant-price income streams. Alternatively, if expected net income takes account of expected inflation, i.e., if actual money earnings in future years are being used in the calculation, then the discount factor should be based on actual, market interest rates, or profit-rate expectations, unadjusted for inflation.

[5] We could also permit the interest rate used in the discount factor to vary from year-to-year, with r_1 the appropriate rate for the first year, r_2 for the second year, and so on. Then,

$$V_1 = \frac{R_1}{1+r_1} + \frac{R_2}{(1+r_1)(1+r_2)} + \frac{R_3}{(1+r_1)(1+r_2)(1+r_3)} + \ldots$$

[6] There is also a relationship between the discount rate and the best development if only use and not timing is being considered as in the example of the last section.

[7] The properties referred to are 2171 commercial lots in the large central core of Toronto lying south of Bloor Street between University Avenue and Jarvis Street. As a percentage of allowable coverage under the old zoning by-law (which was in force up until the end of 1973), these properties were distributed as follows:

	% of Allowable Coverage									
	0-10	10-20	20-30	30-40	40-50	50-60	60-70	70-80	80-90	above-90
# of properties	761	379	277	136	151	82	43	58	24	260

These data are from my report "Property Development in Downtown Toronto", published by the City of Toronto Planning Board in December, 1976. The process of downtown property development is further analyzed in that report.

[8] To see just how the value-maximizing market mechanism works to achieve some balance between the resource cost (the capital cost) and the benefit of a new development, consider the following example:

Suppose only one size and type of development is being considered for a given parcel of land, but that the timing of that development has not been established. For simplicity, let us say that the cost of development will be the same whenever it is undertaken, but that the market value will rise over time. Thus, we have a known capital cost, K, and a known stream of revenue $R_1, R_2, R_3, \ldots, R_n, \ldots$ that can begin whenever the development occurs.

If development were to occur at the beginning of year t, which is sometime now or in the future, the present value of the parcel of land, labelled V_1^t, is given by

$$V_1^t = \frac{K}{(1+r)^{t-1}} + \frac{R_t}{(1+r)^t} + \frac{R_{t+1}}{(1+r)^{t+1}} + \frac{R_{t+2}}{(1+r)^{t+2}} + \ldots$$

If, instead, development were to occur a year later, at the beginning of year t+1, the present value of the land, V_1^{t+1}, would be given by

$$V_1^{t+1} = \frac{K}{(1+r)^t} + \frac{R_{t+1}}{(1+r)^{t+1}} + \frac{R_{t+2}}{(1+r)^{t+2}} + \ldots$$

If contemplated development were delayed from year t to year t+1, the present value of the land would change from V_1^t to V_1^{t+1}. Using the above two equations, we can calculate *change* in the value of land, $V_1^{t+1} - V_1^t$:

$$V_1^{t+1} - V_1^t = \frac{K}{(1+r)^t} - \frac{K}{(1+r)^{t-1}} - \frac{R_t}{(1+r)^t}$$

$$= \frac{rK}{(1+r)^t} - \frac{R_t}{(1+r)^t}$$

Suppose that, up to a point, the development yields a higher and higher present value as we consider later and later development dates. For early years, in other words, V_1^{t+1} is greater than V_1^t. But at some point, the present value reaches a maximum, and later developments begin to yield lower present values. Suppose further, that the present value does not change much for development within a year or two of the best time. This means that if t is the value-maximizing year for development, then development in t+1 or t−1 yields about the same result. Then, as close as it matters anyway, V_1^t equals V_1^{t+1}, and their difference is zero. Going back to the immediate past equation, we get the result that, for the best development time,

$$V_1^{t+1} - V_1^t = 0 = \frac{r\,K}{(1+r)^t} - \frac{R_t}{(1+r)^t} .$$

Re-arranging terms, this implies that when we are at the best time for development,

$$\frac{R_t}{K} = r \text{ , or } R_t = r\,K$$

This result looks quite reasonable, from society's point of view. It says that the best time to develop is just when the current return to capital spending, $\frac{R_t}{K}$, is equal to the appropriate rate of interest. Looked at another way, it says that the value-maximizing time to develop is just when the annual net revenue R_t (which measures in some sense the net annual benefit to society of the development) is equal to the annual value of resources used in the development, r K.

This relationship between the net return on capital spending and the cost of capital becomes slightly more complicated if some of the simplifying assumptions used in this footnote are dropped, but the principle of the argument remains the same.

[9]For land, there is in general no single market price. Every parcel of land is different. Different locations will have different natural features, different surroundings, different accessibility to jobs and shopping, and so on. These differences will cause differences in the net benefit stream expected from each property, and differences therefore in the capital value. The market "price" must be some index of prices. In using the concept of a market-price index, we will generally want to think of the prices of all parcels of land going up when the index goes up, and all going down when the index goes down.

[10]This broader problem is discussed in more detail in my paper "Development Control: Its Purpose and Economic Implications" (Toronto: City of Toronto Planning Board, 1976).

[11]For a discussion of distributional and related policy matters see my "Value and Use of Land," *Urban Forum*, vol. 2, no. 3 (Autumn, 1976).

The Impact of Government Policies on the Supply and Price of Land for Urban Development

LARRY R. G. MARTIN

Associate Professor
School of Urban and Regional Planning
University of Waterloo

THE AUTHOR

Larry R.G. Martin was born in Kingston, Ontario in 1937. He received his Bachelor of Arts degree in geography from Queen's University in 1962. He has received three postgraduate degrees from Syracuse University in New York: the Master of Arts degree in geography in 1965, Master's degree in regional planning in 1966, and his Ph.D. in urban studies and planning in 1970. He joined the faculty of the University of Waterloo in 1969, and now holds the rank of Associate Professor in the School of Urban and Regional Planning. Before entering academic life, Dr. Martin was a private planning consultant and also a planner with municipal government.

Professor Martin is author of *Land Use Dynamics on the Toronto Urban Fringe*, published by Environment Canada in 1975.

The Impact of Government Policies on the Supply and Price of Land for Urban Development*

LARRY R. G. MARTIN
Associate Professor
School of Urban and Regional Planning
University of Waterloo

I. INTRODUCTION

Canada is a nation rich in land resources and yet for urban purposes it is land poor. This fundamental dichotomy remains unappreciated by many Canadians who, in their daily commute between home and work, pass through extensive areas of urban fringe open space. However, of necessity, land available for urban uses must be *serviced* land and it is our chronic failure to make available a plentiful supply of reasonably priced serviced land in the proper location and at the appropriate time that constitutes a basis of the urban land price problem today. Because of its important role in the supply of serviced land for urban use, government must share in the responsibility for land shortages and high prices. This paper examines and comments upon the impact of government policies on the supply and price of land for urban development.

*This chapter is developed from a paper presented to the Canadian Council on Urban and Regional Research, Ontario Forum on Urban Land Management, in Toronto, 2 October 1976. The author would like to thank Chris Bastin and John Edwards for their helpful reading of this material.

Statement of problem

In and of itself, the price and availability of serviced land on the fringe of Canadian cities is not perceived as an issue of fundamental concern for most Canadians. However, serviced land is a major cost input to residential housing and the price and availability of housing in Canada is a problem of seemingly intractable proportions that continues to bedevil and frustrate the public and private sectors alike in every province.

A review of the current literature on housing, for the purpose of identifying a cause or a culprit with respect to high priced housing, no doubt would identify several sources related to supply and to demand. Those related to supply might include the increase in price of the factors of housing production including land, labour, materials, and capital, as a result of general inflation; and distortions in the housing market caused by unscrupulous participants from the private sector and inappropriate government intervention. Those related to demand might include the unrealistic expectations of families desiring to improve their socio-economic status. While each of these sources, singly and in combination, contributes to the price of housing, we are concerned here only with government involvement in the supply and price of land as an important component of housing price.

The high price of housing is in no small part a result of the high price of the land component.† In 1971 the land component represented between 18 and 38 per cent of the cost of a new home in the twelve largest urban centres in Ontario with labour and materials accounting for the remainder of the cost.[1] However, for each urban centre the cost of land component accounted for the greatest relative price increase during the previous decade.[2]

A recent study by Derkowski (1975) reinforces these conclusions. For example, in 1974 the average lot price com-

†Editors' Note: For a discussion of the mechanics of land pricing and why land prices have been rising recently, see the paper in this volume by Professor David Nowlan.

prised more than 30 per cent of the total new house price in six of ten major metropolitan areas—Calgary, Edmonton, Ottawa, Toronto, Vancouver and Winnipeg (Derkowski, 1975, 148). However, two very dissimilar metropolitan areas—Montreal and Saskatoon—displayed the smallest lot prices as a percentage of total new house price in 1974 and revealed no percentage increase in this relationship during the previous decade. Thus, we cannot assume there is a constant relationship in all markets between the price of land and the price of houses, although land costs are important in all markets.

Objectives

The importance of both the demand for and the supply of land in establishing price in the urban land market is axiomatic. However, this chapter is concerned solely with normal supply factors and particular market restrictions influencing the supply of urban land. Emphasis is placed on the impact of government policies in restricting the supply of serviced land. Not only is this approach viewed as useful due to the often overlooked importance of supply in determining land price but also because of recent public and private policies and actions that have directly and indirectly curtailed land supply on the urban fringe of Canadian cities.

Three major objectives are established for this chapter.

They are to:

1. describe the operation of the urban fringe land market,
2. discuss land market distortions in the form of public restrictions on land supply, and
3. describe and recommend public policies for increasing land supply and reducing land prices.

Emphasis in this paper is placed upon practice rather than theory and upon Canadian rather than foreign experience. Given that supply problems have not been uniformly experienced across Canada, it is understandable that some provinces (Alberta and Ontario) will merit special attention.

Because Canadians have been cautious in recognizing and responding to land supply problems we wish to draw attention to the experience of other countries with various policy responses to the problem.

Organization of the chapter follows from the stated objectives. Section II describes a somewhat generalized operation of the land market on the urban fringe of a typical Canadian city. We review the activities of the various primary and secondary decision agents engaged in the land conversion process. We also discuss particular characteristics of land markets as viewed by primary decision agents. In Section III we discuss land market distortions in the form of restrictions on land supply. Actions of both the public and private sectors that lead to supply restrictions are treated here. Public policies for increasing land supply and reducing land prices are discussed in Section IV.

II. THE URBAN FRINGE LAND MARKET

In spite of our society's continuing concern for an adequate supply of housing and more generally for the optimal allocation of land to urban uses, we still possess a very limited understanding of the urban land market. This limited understanding holds particularly true for the land market on the urban fringe. Empirical studies have not kept pace with theoretical statements, with the result that a good deal of our 'understanding' of such topics as land speculation, land banking, profits and market structure are based either on untested assumptions from the academic literature or on often misleading commentaries in the popular press. It is perhaps fair to suggest that the urban fringe is a *terra incognita* in which government and private sector activities flounder for want of adequate understanding.

In this section we will attempt to provide a simplified, descriptive view of the operation of the urban fringe land market. This view will include:

1. examination of the rationale for public intervention (particularly via public planning) in this land market,

2. discussion of the land conversion process, focusing on decision agents and decisions, and

3. examination of the workings of supply of and demand for raw land and serviced lots in determining price.

Our brief reference, in this section, to a hypothetical, perfectly competitive land market and to the real world imperfections of this market will assist us in highlighting one set of market distortions in the form of public and publicly-induced private supply restrictions in Section III.[3]

Public intervention in the land market

For purposes of convenience and simplicity the operation of the urban fringe land market is often described at the outset, as if it was perfectly competitive. The limiting assumptions of any perfectly competitive market are well known and, in the case of the urban fringe land market, the following conditions would have to be realized:

1. such homogeneity of land parcels that a buyer would have no reason to prefer one parcel over another,

2. a large number of buyers and sellers so that one or several buyers or sellers could not influence the price of land,

3. no artificial restraints on the land or on the buyers or sellers of land,

4. a mobility of resources with free entry of firms and individuals into the land development industry,

5. complete knowledge of the market by all economic units, and

6. an absence of external effects.

In theory, if the urban fringe land market were perfectly competitive, it could be argued that a scarce land resource would be allocated efficiently and that there would be no need for government intervention and public planning.

Clearly, the urban fringe land market is quite imperfect. Homogeneous products, a multitude of buyers and sellers, free entry and exit to markets, and complete knowledge are seldom obtained in the real world. Other arguments justifying public intervention in markets are widely appreciated but none are of more appropriate concern to persons involved in the urban fringe land market than those generally identified as externalities.[4]

The presence of externalities associated with the alternative uses of land is a principal justification for government intervention via public planning on the urban fringe. Among other objectives, public planning seeks to minimize incompatible land uses that would otherwise impose social costs in terms of pollution, congestion and loss of amenity.

The preservation of open space and the provision of roads—both quasi-public goods—are additional justifications for public planning on the urban fringe.

Government may attempt to deal with the problems of externalities and the provision of public goods through the application of land use, fiscal and proprietary (landownership) policies. However, when externalities remain uncompensated (non-internalized) or when government policies prove to be inappropriate, the urban fringe market can be said to be distorted.

The land conversion process

The extremely complex manner whereby a city expands at its periphery into the countryside is known as the rural-to-urban land conversion process. An understanding of this process is an essential prerequisite to the deeper appreciation of land supply problems and their possible resolution.

Basically, the process can be viewed as a set of linked sale/purchase decisions involving an array of primary decision agents (farmers, land dealers, developers, builders, and families) and secondary decision agents (financiers, lawyers, realtors, elected officials and planners).[5] Together these primary and secondary decision agents are largely responsible for the spatial and temporal characteristics of development on the urban fringe. Figure 1 depicts the process as consisting of six stages beginning with land in non-urban use and

FIGURE 1
Land Conversion Process
Stages of Development

	Non-Urban Use	Non-Urban Use: in Urban Fringe	Urban Interest	Active Purchase of Raw Land	Active Development	Active Purchase of Developed Land
Description of Stage	In agricultural or other non-urban use	Change in use or degree of intensity of use	Decision agent recognizes development potential	Decision agents negotiate land sales transactions	Physical development of land	Land purchased by property user
Decisions	No decision to sell in present or future	Consideration of future sale	Present use viewed as transitional	Purchase land	Develop land	Purchase home
Primary Decision Agents	Farmer	Farmer Land dealer	Farmer Land dealer Developer	Developer	Developer Builder	Builder Family
Secondary Decision Agents	—	Financier	Financier	Financier Lawyer Realtor Planner	Financier Lawyer Planner	Financier Lawyer Realtor
Financial Support	Unchanged	Farm credit	Negotiation with lender	Vendor mortgage	Development mortgage	Residential mortgage

Source: Martin (1975).

ending with a family's purchase of a home. Specific decisions attached to each stage punctuate the shift from one stage to the next. While the number and sequence of stages and decisions are common to much conversion activity, decision agent involvement may vary considerably. For instance, few decision agents are involved when a farmer severs a lot from his farm for his son who will build his own home and commute to the nearby city for employment. On the other hand, a large integrated development project might involve hundreds of decision agents participating in many complex and even recursive decisions.

The importance of financial support for land conversion is underlined by the almost pervasive involvement of one secondary decision agent—the financier. The capital requirements for physical conversion and the risks entailed are both high relative to the incomes of the primary decision agents involved. Early in the process the farmer, himself, often becomes the financier when he takes back a vendor mortgage from the land dealer or developer. Later, banks and other lending institutions become the source of investment capital.

Three sets of factors, including those of context, site and person, influence the behaviour of decision agents. Contextual (or situational) factors include most importantly operative public policies toward land development and the supporting social and economic 'climate' of the region. Site factors include those of parcel size, shape and surface characteristics. Personal factors include those that involve land use intentions and financial resources of primary decision agents. In this chapter we are mainly concerned with the contextual factors of decision agent behaviour.

The role of public policies

One set of contextual factors—operative public policies—has a profound influence on the land conversion process. Public planners, as overseers of these policies, exercise considerable power for modifying and shaping the practical operation of the process. Planners exercise their powers to regulate the quantity, pace and location of land conversion on the urban fringe of Canadian cities via three public documents—the official plan, the zoning by-law and the subdivision agreement.[6] Although the language of these three public documents varies from province to province the essential purposes of the documents are similar.

The official plan is a statement of public expectation, intentions and wishes with respect to the future physical growth of the municipality. For the edge of the built city, the plan may indicate permitted future land uses including the density of residential uses and the location of service corridors. All land development must be in conformance with the official plan.

Apart from its use within the developed portion of the urban area the zoning by-law is used as a form of development control on the urban fringe in instances where the municipality wishes to encourage particular qualitative development. Employed in conjunction with the official plan, the zoning by-law has become a powerful tool for formalizing and controlling the land conversion process.

Subdivision control impinges most directly on urban fringe land conversion. Delegated to the local municipality but reviewed at the provincial level in some provinces, subdivision control regulates the partitioning of land parcels for urban development purposes. Before subdivision approval is granted, the developer must obtain approval of his plan. It is customary for negotiations between the developer and municipal planners to include various concessions concerning the layout of streets and lots and provision of community services. The potential for extended delays in this process has resulted in widespread criticism directed to government by primary decision agents. The nature of the delays and the substance of the resulting criticism will be discussed in Section III.

Supply, demand and price

The price of housing, serviced lots and raw land on the urban fringe is determined by the interaction of supply and demand. Families demand housing, builders demand serviced lots and developers and speculators demand raw land. The supply of housing, serviced lots and raw land is provided by builders, developers and speculators, and farmers, respectively.

The quantity of housing, serviced lots and raw land demanded is relatively insensitive to price changes and, as a consequence, the ultimate level of housing construction is influenced more by demographic, credit and income conditions in the community than by price changes. Because the quantity of raw land demanded for urban purposes is a derived demand—dependent on the demand for housing and serviced lots—we can speculate that it is least sensitive to price changes. The demand schedules representing the relationship between price and quantity of land demanded can be ordered (in terms of inelasticity of curves) for housing, serviced lots and raw land.[7]

In theory the stock supply of land within a specified area is assumed to be fixed and, therefore, very insensitive to changes in price. However, even if this is true the flow supply of agricultural land for conversion is elastic and will increase relative to its present price for agricultural use. When the price of land exceeds farmers' reservation price they will supply land for urban use.

However, empirical evidence taken from the urban fringe of growing cities indicates that asking prices for land are often in excess of their current production costs for urban use. This suggests that supply is somehow limited relative to demand. First, only agricultural land close enough to urban services can be brought into production. Second, certain public and private controls serve to restrict the supply of land that might otherwise be available for urban use.

In reality the price of converted land is derived from a set of aggregated costs including the price of raw land, public and private improvements, carrying charges and profit. Unlike the cost of improvements which are relatively fixed and are determined outside the land market, profits and raw land costs are variable, being determined by the urban fringe land market. The two latter cost components can be treated as a residual that depends ultimately upon supply of, demand for and resultant price of the final product—in this case, new housing. Total development costs represent the sum of costs realized as a land parcel moves through the several stages from its original agricultural value to its ultimate cost as a house on a serviced lot.

Having taken a somewhat simplified look at the urban fringe land market, we now turn, in Section III, to an examination of land supply restrictions.

III. DISTORTIONS IN THE LAND MARKET: SUPPLY RESTRICTIONS

In Section III we will examine one particular set of market distortions—public land supply restrictions. Most public land supply restrictions *directly* influence supply and are given prominence in this paper. Several public land supply restrictions *indirectly* influence supply by creating or exacerbating existing or perceived privately-induced supply restrictions. The first group of restrictions involve public policies directed to the land. The second group of restrictions are those directed to decision agents involved in land conversion. We will examine these two groups of restrictions in separate sections.

Direct public land supply restrictions

We noted in Section II that the supply of land for urban development is relatively inelastic with respect to changes in price. This results from the absolute limit in total usable supply available to expanding cities in the short run, and due to the time and resources required to actually convert non-urban land. Direct public land supply restrictions play a major role in increasing this expenditure of time and resources.[8] For our purposes, we have identified four general classes of direct public supply restrictions on the urban fringe:

1. land planning policies

2. urban services policies

3. fiscal policies, and

4. intergovernmental coordination policies.

Land planning policies

There are a variety of public land planning policies that restrict the supply of non-urban land for conversion. For convenience we may separate these policies into two groups. One group of policies is usually viewed as single purpose and substantive in nature. Policies for preserving agricultural land or carrying out public land assembly are appropriate examples. The other group of policies is procedural in nature, providing a means by which substantive, general policy objectives can be achieved. Land use controls, such as zoning by-laws and subdivision regulations, for guiding growth on the urban fringe are illustrative of this type.

Substantive policies

Policies that support non-urban land uses on the urban fringe will contribute to land supply restrictions. Policies to preserve agricultural land and open space are examples. Goodall (1970, 15-17) has pointed out the effect of English green belt legislation on land supply and prices. Spurr (1974, 88-97) has described the effect of the Ottawa green belt on land supply, land prices and increased concentration of ownership of land adjacent to the green belt. Although there is limited information available, it is presumed that both the B.C. Land Commission Act and the Newfoundland Land Development Act will have restricted supply and thus contributed to higher prices for urban land.

The Ontario Parkway Belt Planning and Development Act and the subsequent Parkway Belt West Draft Plan (1976) are further restricting land supply in a sector of the Toronto urban fringe that has, in the past, accommodated much of Toronto's suburban growth. A survey by the Urban Development Institute, Ontario (1973) determined that its membership held 6,393 acres of developable land that was frozen by this Act.

It is suggested that legislated restrictions (provided they are viewed as being permanent) on land supply, be they green belts or other forms of permanent open space, create market conditions not unlike those created by the natural restrictions of a large water body in the Toronto region or mountains in the Vancouver region.

Measures designed to prevent 'leap frog' and low-density forms of urban sprawl have also contributed to restrictions in land supply.[9] Derkowski (1972, 6) has indicated that residential land in the major American metropolitan areas is, on the average, less costly than residential land in major Canadian metropolitan areas. Can this be attributed, in part, to American local governments' unwillingness or inability to control urban sprawl?

Some foreign governments have limited urban expansion in larger urban centres in order to encourage the decentralization of population to smaller urban centres and to new towns (Rodwin, 1970; Bourne, 1975). The value of this policy has been discussed widely in Canada. Indeed, the federal government and the provinces of Alberta and Ontario have, at times, indicated interests in this direction. Ontario's difficulties in integrating the Toronto Centred Region Plan's intention of shifting urban growth east of the metropolitan area, with the federal government's wish to locate a major international airport within the region, illustrates an important weakness of decentralization policy within a federal system of government. Nevertheless, no more than an announcement by government of intentions to restrict growth can have a restrictive influence on land supply.

Public land assembly has been widely promoted in Canada for many purposes, including its potential for increasing land supply and reducing land prices. Given Canada's limited experience with this mechanism it can be concluded that the more extensive European experience with public land assembly has served as the source of this recent interest. By acting as a major land developer since the beginning of this century many municipalities in Sweden and the Netherlands have been able to maintain a level of land supply equal to demand. However, moderate land prices may be attributed as much to associated taxation and land valuation practices as to the public land assembly per se.[10]

Although the more recent Canadian experience with public land assembly for urban development has generated a great deal of domestic support (Report of the Federal Task

Force, 1969; Dennis and Fish, 1972; Canadian National Committee, 1976), this experience by no means demonstrates conclusively that increased supply and lower prices necessarily result. Not only have the supply and price objectives of public land assembly been disputed on theoretical grounds (Carr and Smith, 1975 and Chapter 4 in this book), but the achievements of some of the best-known land assembly programmes have been questioned. The widely cited Saskatoon public land assembly has been criticized for its failure to make known the true cost of its operation (Derkowski, 1975). Critics also have pointed to the fallacy in logic of attempting to transfer the results of a programme in a relatively small, slow-growth metropolitan area to others of much larger absolute size and rate of growth (Piper, 1974). Other public land assembly programmes have been criticized for their inordinate delays in moving from land acquisition through to housing construction.[11]

Procedural policy

Land use controls may be the single most important group of public restrictions on land supply for urban development. By their very nature they are negative. Government intervention in the land conversion process can be expected to contribute to its delay, thus reducing land supply and increasing land prices.

The nature of the three most important land use controls (the zoning by-law, official plan, and subdivision regulations) influencing land supply was reviewed briefly in Section II. Here we will examine the delays in land conversion caused by these controls.

Development delays resulting from land use controls have been experienced in all market economies where government has introduced land use planning. Australia and the United Kingdom provide instructive examples.

Bromilow and Meaton (1973) in a study of land conversion on the urban fringe of Melbourne concluded that unnecessary inefficiencies in subdivision and re-zoning procedures increased time requirements by 25 per cent and increased land prices by 10 per cent. On average the conversion of raw land to serviced lots required two years. During this period they noted that:

> "One could not help being struck by the large number of independent planning and servicing authorities which are independent, yet on whose coordination the effectiveness, efficiency and timing of the operations depend."

Coordination among these authorities has proved to be a considerable problem resulting in costly delays.

In a major study of urban development, Drewett (Hall *et. al.*, 1974, Vol. II) observed that local municipal reluctance to release land for development was the major cause of the artificial scarcity of land supply and was a major factor in explaining rapid price increases in the U.K. during the 1960s. Delays in obtaining development permission were noted to have increased dramatically over the decade. In the 1950s a developer was able to begin construction one month after land acquisition. During the 1960s a developer could expect, after land acquisition, to wait between six and eighteen months for development permission. This increased delay (together with national taxation measures) is estimated to have resulted in an additional cost of £600 to £1,000 over the 10-year period to every home buyer.

Reduction in land supply and increases in land price as a result of delays in development permission have received widespread attention in Canada.[12] Conflicts and delays associated with gaining planning permission have been noted in three provinces experiencing rapid urban growth—Alberta, British Columbia and Ontario. Derkowski (1975) estimates that the average delay in conversion resulting from the subdivision approval process ranges from two months in Hull, Montreal and Saskatoon, six months in Edmonton, nine months in Vancouver to eighteen months in Ottawa and Toronto. In Derkowski's opinion the delay in land conversion in Ontario, resulting from the application of a highly complex and restrictive system of development controls, leads inevitably to more costly housing.

Flowers (1976) has determined that plans of subdivision, approved in the City of Mississauga west of Toronto in

1973 and 1974, required an average of 22 months from receipt to registration. He has suggested that these excessive delays have resulted from:

1. the complexity of the process,

2. the shortage of competent municipal staff,

3. the intentional stalling by public bodies in order to exact favourable concessions from developers, and

4. the complete absence of sweet reason as might be expected if a disinterested arbitrator were involved.[13]

Urban services policies

Many observers of the land conversion process have expressed the view that a persistent shortage of serviced residential land is the key to land supply restrictions and increased lot prices.[14] Three limitations have been noted. First, primary and secondary services have not been supplied in the appropriate location in advance of need. Second, servicing has been limited by inadequate financial resources. Third, servicing standards in excess of real need have contributed to a more costly product and delays in servicing.

In most provinces, trunk sewerage and water supply lines, as well as treatment facilities, are required as a prerequisite to urban residential development. Failure to provide these services creates land shortages and increased lot prices in the face of continuing demand for additional housing. Spatial and temporal coordination of services with development is essential. Often the provision of services is not correlated with the degree of demand, so that some municipalities with lower growth rates have excess capacity while other municipalities lack any capacity. The timing of trunk services in anticipation of residential demand is especially important because of the long construction lead time required.

The financing of services across Canada presents two problems. Clearly, servicing is extremely expensive, representing from 35 to 80 per cent of the total price of a finished lot. Also financing policy is highly inconsistent, varying from province to province and from municipality to municipality within any province. Most often the cost of providing services to a lot has been shifted from the municipality to the developer, and thus to the new home buyer, as opposed to all homeowners when the municipality pays. Moreover,

> "there is no consistency of policy from municipality to municipality on whether or not the developer pays, how much he pays, what he pays for, whether he pays directly or through a levy, and why a particular sum is chosen" (Report of the Advisory Task Force, 1973, 44).

A recent report (Proctor & Redfern Ltd., 1976) surveying the fees and levies collected by eighteen Ontario municipalities, with respect to land development, reveals a bewildering variation in amounts assessed and an uncomfortable absence of consistent, philosophical justification. With such variability of financing practice it is extremely difficult, if not impossible, to precisely evaluate servicing practice on a comparative basis.

Even though they were originally introduced to reduce municipal maintenance costs, high (in some instances unjustifiably so) provincial and municipal servicing standards today contribute to the high cost of finished lots and to delays in lot supply. Because the only moderating influence on land servicing costs—the future consumer of housing—is absent, developers continue to comply with the accelerating demands of municipalities by 'gold plating' more and more services. These services are not required, nor can they be afforded, by many current home buyers. In some metropolitan areas, excessive municipal servicing demands can only be regarded as exclusionary in intent.

Fiscal policies

It is difficult to adequately discuss the problem of land supply without returning to the all-pervasive issue of public finances.

The municipality, invested by the province with the responsibility for land use planning, is severely constrained in its activities by its weak tax base. An increase in financial participation by the provinces as well as a greater rationalization of local jurisdictional boundaries, with the shift of responsibilities to higher levels of government, has not improved, to any extent, the adequacy of the real property tax. Indeed, the tendency of senior governments' policies to emphasize housing demand subsidies in preference to land and housing supply subsidies has contributed to a relative increase in housing demand and has ignored the concomitant adverse fiscal impact upon local government.

Being a tax on land and its improvements, the real property tax discourages development and encourages delay as long as land value appreciation continues. Considering its inadequacy for generating municipal revenues and its encouragement of hoarding by owners of raw land the property tax on improvements and improved land is indeed an impediment to increasing land supply on the urban fringe. Fiscal measures including preferential property assessment and deferred property taxation may contribute to the support of agriculture and the preservation of agricultural land. Nevertheless, they also increase the reservation price of farmers and speculators, thus limiting the supply of urban land.

There is a direct relationship between the level of property tax revenues generated and the type and quality of land use developed. Due to its lower level of assessment, residential property is encouraged by municipalities only as a fixed proportion of more valuable commercial and industrial assessment. Among all residential development, as a result of a widespread concern for municipal costs and revenues, higher quality residential housing is favoured by municipalities for its superior contribution to the tax base of the community. The Advisory Task Force on Housing Policy (1973) noted that ". . . the cost of housing to the municipality is often felt to be far more important than cost of housing to the consumer." Thus, even when the quantity of land supplied for urban development is sufficient in gross terms it may still be inadequate for moderate income housing in particular.

Because of continuing fiscal stress, Ontario municipalities have been induced to deploy fees and levies, obtained from processing and implementing proposed plans of subdivision, to defray expenses not directly related to the original purpose of the impost.

Concern of municipalities for their weak tax base is often the underlying justification for a pursuit of policies that restrict land supply. Large lot zoning, development freezes and strict environmental restrictions, while justified for certain plausible reasons, in fact are frequently proposed solely for the purpose of preserving or improving the tax base. Until the present sources of municipal funding are strengthened we can expect land use planning for fiscal objectives to persist.

Intergovernmental coordination policies

Restrictions in land supply have resulted from conflicts among government agencies with divergent interests and objectives. Conflicts may occur horizontally between agencies at the same level or vertically between agencies at different levels. In Ontario, provincial agencies concerned with environmental protection and regional development have worked at cross-purposes with other agencies fostering housing production. The potential conflict of actions under Ontario's Planning Act and the Environmental Assessment Act have been noted elsewhere (Proctor & Redfern Ltd., 1976). Vertical conflicts of interest are widespread and have been noted earlier in this paper. Provincial and federal actions to increase land supply often have been viewed with alarm by municipalities who fear the impact of continuing growth on tax base. The 'no-growth' policies of suburban municipalities strongly supported by citizen groups present senior governments with difficult moral dilemmas.

Even when the objectives of governments are compatible, the complexity of subject matter and administration often lead to conflicts that result in land supply restrictions. Often, horizontal and vertical conflicts are based on differing priorities toward, rather than fundamental disagreement with, land supply objectives. A works department may delay its approval of a subdivision application because it is preoccupied with snow removal. But the results of benign neglect are no less significant than outright opposition.

The inadequacy of the British North America Act to clearly distinguish responsibilities in the field of land development and housing lies at the heart of this problem. However, the resolution of this difficulty is not likely close at hand.

Indirect public land supply restrictions

In this chapter we do *not* discuss a potential set of privately-induced distortions in the land market that, if realized, would result in land supply restrictions. Most important would be the attempt of owners to withhold land from a normally functioning market.† However, government, in its efforts to reduce these privately-induced distortions, has sometimes exacerbated the very problem it intended to remedy. Much research is needed in this subject area. Here we will examine two examples of government attempts to reduce landowner resistance to land conversion.

Many observers of the land conversion process believe that shortages of land for urban development can be related directly to the reluctance of pre-development landowners to sell their land. A land speculator theory of land supply restriction is widely accepted.[15]

As a result of this view of land speculation, Ontario enacted the Land Speculation Tax on April 9, 1974, and several other provincial governments have considered following this example. With reference to the concern of this paper the Act imposes a 20 per cent tax on gains realized on the disposition of raw land. The tax is not imposed if the land is improved before disposition. Experience in the Toronto area indicates that pure speculation in raw land has declined, as has the rate of increase in land prices (Martin, 1976b). However, the tax has encouraged greater concentration of landownership with land speculators avoiding the tax

†Editors' Note: The possibility of monopoly control over supply is discussed by Professors Markusen and Scheffman in their essay in this volume. Their conclusion is that monopoly has not been a source of price rise in recent Canadian experience.

by also developing their land. Smith (1976) has suggested that the short-run and long-run effects of the tax may be quite different. In the short run the reduced acquisition price of raw land should increase developer-speculator profits and lower the price of land to the final user. There is a danger, however, that in the long run increased market concentration and oligopolistic behaviour may offset reduced land-prices, thus contributing to a more inefficient land market.

A widespread belief that foreign ownership of urban fringe land in Ontario was contributing to land speculation led to the enactment of the Land Transfer Tax on April 9, 1974. The Act imposed a 20 per cent tax on land purchased by non-residents of Canada. This tax has resulted in a dramatic decline in foreign equity investment in land development. Spokesmen for the private development industry have claimed that competition among developers, and land and housing production have declined as a result.

Section III has examined a number of direct and indirect publicly-induced restrictions on land supply. In Section IV we will examine remedial policies for increasing the supply and reducing the price of urban fringe land.

IV. GOVERNMENT MEASURES TO INCREASE LAND SUPPLY

In previous sections we reviewed government policies that unintentionally reduced the supply of land for urban development. There was no attempt on the writer's part to weigh the merits of these policies for attaining their intended objectives against the disadvantages created by their impact on land supply. Such an evaluation would only be practical if applied to isolated policies under a very limiting set of assumptions. It would not seem realistic to attempt to generalize the findings of such an evaluation.

In Section III we examined a number of government policies, intended to redress imperfections in the urban fringe land market, that actually distorted this market with respect to land supply. Section IV will seek to modify these policies to minimize their land supply effects and will suggest new policies that serve the land supply objective. Recommendations are discussed under four categories:

1. land planning policies,
2. urban services policies,
3. fiscal policies, and
4. intergovernmental coordination policies.

Land planning policies

Public land planning and the efficient operation of the urban fringe land market need not be contradictory activities. Public intervention in the land market through the exercise of planning can be justified, particularly for the achievement of efficiency objectives related to externalities, and for equity objectives. The writer shares the widely held view that public planning is essential for the proper coordination of development decisions, the prevention of land use conflict, and the achievement of society's land and housing goals.

Despite the benefits associated with public planning we have seen, in Section III, that planning does create diseconomies with respect to land supply. Some recommendations are offered here to minimize these diseconomies.

It is self-defeating to plan for the increased quantity of land supplied while ignoring changes in demand. Attempts to relocate the demand for land by freezing urban fringe development in rapidly growing metropolitan areas simply exacerbates the land supply problem. Demand must be attracted to slower-growth regions while land supply is being increased in the growth centre. The coordination required to manipulate the land market in this fashion can only be achieved at the provincial and federal levels. Therefore, it is recommended that regional development policy receive added support and that land and housing supply policy at the centre and the periphery be treated explicitly as an element of regional development policy.

Public planning has attained a good deal of recent support as a result of its focus upon highly visible and popular issues. Its promotion of development freezes on the urban fringe, to preserve farmland and open space, to promote new satellite towns, and to allow the plan-making function to catch up with events, may be justifiable in the light of a limited set of objectives. But these objectives should also be accompanied by land supply and housing objectives. In order that they understand policy outcomes, citizens should participate in the establishment of priorities, the determination of trade-offs and the making of difficult choices in the face of disparate objectives.

Procedural policies for land use planning have been identified as an important source of delay and as a contributor to the cost of land for urban development.[16] Procedures should either be made more efficient or should be eliminated where the housing priority is high and the procedures are not operating smoothly.

We have very little accurate comparative information concerning the operation of the planning approval process. It is not possible to compare the process in one municipality against an acceptable norm for the province and in so doing identify inefficiencies translated into land costs. It would be extremely useful if each province attempted to monitor the planning approval process within its jurisdiction. The information generated would provide the basis for procedural reforms and incentive programmes.

In some instances the formal planning approval process employed by provinces is, at best, an imprecise guideline for the decision process actually followed by landowners and municipal planners. The real process may be much more unclear and discretionary, resulting in confusion or even subterfuge and dishonesty. For this reason the process must be clearly enunciated and understood by all participants. Time limits should be established with penalties applied where deadlines are passed.

The cost of land conversion is not unrelated to the scale of development. Small scale decision making is inefficient and results in high-cost land. The land development industry has responded to this market imperative by undergoing increased concentration of firms and by increasing project size (for example, by joint ventures) in order to achieve economies of scale.[17] The public is justified in its concern that a more highly concentrated industry might lead to oligopoly and the exercise of market power. Nevertheless, this trend toward concentration has a powerful momentum that can only be restrained at great expense to all parties in land conversion. In recognition of the efficiencies associated with concentration, it would seem practical for government not to discourage it while at the same time exercise whatever controls are required to ensure that an acceptable level of competition is preserved.

The provinces and the federal government will play key roles in efforts to increase land supply for urban development. The provincial governments' roles are assured by their constitutional primacy in land use matters. The federal government's role is assured by its fiscal strength. Edwards (1975) has proposed a Land Availability Planning Assistance Programme that could be initiated by either level of senior government. The programme would provide grants to municipal and regional governments to encourage their participation in land availability planning and implementation. Planning activities would involve:

1. the forecasting of demand for land,

2. the measurement of anticipated supply, and

3. employment of this information when making decisions related to the management of growth.

The programme also would provide low-interest loans to municipalities in exchange for their commitment to provide sufficient serviced land. Together, these two sources of linked assistance should contribute a great deal to the rationalization of the land conversion programme.

In Section III public land assembly was criticized as a means of increasing land supply and reducing land prices. The writer does not recommend any land market control strategy that is based on massive government intervention and acquisition. Such efforts would be extremely expensive, inefficient and, ultimately, unsuccessful. Foreign experience indicates that government can play a significant role in influencing the land market through land price monitoring and limited strategic intervention. Bryant and Martin (1977) have described the French government's use of the zone of deferred development (ZAD) as a means of increasing land supply and moderating price changes. Governments in Canada could explore this and similar less disruptive techniques in order to determine their potential for sustaining a more measured flow of raw land through the conversion process.

Urban services policies

As noted in Section III both the supply of raw land and its cost for development are directly influenced by the provision of primary and secondary services. Martin (1974) has noted that:

> "the rate at which services are provided, the manner in which they are financed, and the quality of these services will each contribute to the cost for an improved lot. If these services are not provided at a rate equal to demand, if they are provided at less than full cost, or if they meet inordinately high standards, then the serviced land will be very expensive, perhaps well in excess of production costs."

In Ontario, inadequate servicing continues to be a problem despite the availability of provincial and federal financial assistance to municipalities. Therefore, we must look elsewhere for an explanation. The lack of regional long-range planning for urban development would appear to be responsible. Neither municipalities nor the province have put sufficient sewer and water services in the ground well in advance of anticipated need. In Ontario there has been a tendency to hold up regional servicing schemes until regional plans have been prepared. This cannot be justified when demand for land greatly exceeds supply and when prices, as a result, are increasing. In these instances it would seem appropriate to employ interim services, even if relaxed standards are necessitated.

Servicing standards in the rapid-growth provinces are often excessive and transparently exclusionary. The provinces should provide to municipalities financial assistance that relates to minimal standards. Municipalities should be solely responsible for the cost of services that exceed these minima. This action would also contribute to greater consistency of municipal servicing policy.

Fiscal policies

The weakness of the real property tax as the financial basis for municipal decision making in urban development has been noted. Nevertheless, there is no reason to expect that other important sources of revenue will be made available to municipalities in the future. However, it is reasonable to assume that the federal government and the provinces will continue to provide intergovernmental transfers to municipalities and that some of these transfers will more closely reflect the land supply and housing goals of the provinces.

Fiscal measures to induce pre-development landowners to bring their land on the market deserve some comment here. The Land Speculation Tax and the Land Transfer Tax should be abolished. The Land Speculation Tax does not appear to be accomplishing its objectives that are, in practice, incompatible with the increased land supply objective. The use of a hoarding tax or highest use tax or a government preemptive right might be more suitable means for bringing raw land on the market.

Intergovernmental coordination policies

The complexity of government involvement in land supply merely reflects the intractability of land supply problems. With problems of this type it is never clear 'who should do what?' It is suspected that an improvement of intergovernmental coordination will not produce benefits for land supply equivalent to those realized from other remedial policies noted above. However, several recommendations are proposed.

The Ontario Economic Council (1975, 38) has noted that 'the locus of final responsibility for housing policy is not clear.' This observation is equally applicable to land supply.

While the Canadian Constitution allocates the regulatory powers for land use to the provinces and the financial resources to the federal government, this assignment has not prevailed in practice. When responsibility is unclear there is a tendency for programme duplication and the shifting of blame for failure. A more distinct allocation of land supply responsibilities in keeping with formal constitutional powers would seem appropriate. A land availability planning assistance programme as suggested earlier is an appropriate vehicle for utilizing these respective powers.

Horizontal conflict among government departments is natural because each department seeks to achieve its own objectives and some of these objectives may be in conflict. Conflict between planning, environmental and housing agencies has occurred in several provinces. Although it is not possible to provide hard and fast guidelines to adjudicate resulting conflicts it is important to illuminate them.

V. CONCLUSION

This completes the examination of proposed policies for increasing land supply and reducing land prices. It is appropriate to note that the goals of government and the private land development industry are not incompatible. Government continues to rely heavily upon the financial resources and the innovative energies of the private sector in order to achieve its objectives in housing and urban development. Because of ever-present imperfections in the urban fringe land market, the private development industry is compelled to acknowledge the need for government involvement. However, government activities that lead to further distortions in the urban fringe land market not only reduce the viability of the private land development industry but also jeopardize those very objectives that government seeks to achieve. Clearly, government's continuing contribution to land supply restrictions and increasing land prices is unjustified and is in conflict with the public interest.

Notes

[1]See Peter Barnard and Associates (1973).

[2]In Sudbury, where there are severe physical limitations to underground construction the land component of new housing cost increased by 341 per cent while labour increased by 95 per cent and materials by 45 per cent between 1961 and 1971. In Windsor, where strong labour unions bring considerable pressure to bear on wage settlements, the land component of new housing cost increased by 227 per cent while the labour component increased by 158 per cent and material by 45 per cent. Data is abstracted from Exhibit 10, Peter Barnard and Associates (1973).

[3]It is appropriate to note here that the urban fringe land market falls far short of being perfectly competitive. While a concept of market failure is useful for explaining the forces at work, it is not necessary in general that government successfully correct these imperfections in order to achieve a society's housing and land price goals.

[4]Other contributions to market failure include: 1) the problem of attaining equilibrium in order to achieve optimality, 2) problems of perfect competition related to increasing and decreasing cost industries, 3) the inability of the market to allocate public goods, 4) the excessive costs associated with the operation of certain markets, and 5) the equity aspect of the price system. These points are discussed in more detail in Oxley (1975).

[5]Widespread usage of the terms 'land dealer' and 'speculator' has been accompanied by some confusion. Employed in this paper a land dealer is a primary decision agent who is engaged in buying underpriced land in one market and selling it at or above the full information price in another market. The ensuing profit results from providing knowledge and increasing the land's liquidity in a financial sense. A speculator, on the other hand, purchases land at its true or full information price and withholds it from the market with the expectation that its price will rise. According to this definition all primary decision agents may engage in land speculation from time to time.

[6]The Alberta Land Use Forum (1974) and Ontario Economic Council (1973) have provided excellent critical reviews of these documents for their respective provinces.

[7]Clawson (1971) has deduced the form and elasticity of the curves in Figure 2. See his Figure 10, p. 118.

[8]There is no agreement among concerned parties as to the degree of supply restriction caused by government nor has there been sufficient rigorous investigation to lend conclusive support to one particular view. Nevertheless, the vast majority of sources examined by the writer indicates that direct public supply restrictions are significant determinants of land supply.

[9]Government may attempt to control urban sprawl for a variety of reasons: to increase urban densities and thus reduce public service costs, to slow down the rate of growth, or to encourage decentralization.

[10]For a discussion of these practices see Neutze (1973).

[11]The public land assembly programme of the Ontario Housing Corporation can be criticized for actually reducing the supply of developable land on the urban fringes of some Ontario cities and, as a result, contributing to the price increase of adjacent land (Ferguson, 1975).

[12]The following references provide a sample of this attention: Advisory Task Force on Housing Policy (1973a), Alberta Land Use Forum (1974), Derkowski (1972, 1975), Edwards (1975), ICO Real Estate Management Ltd., (1974), Ontario Economic Council (1973, 1976), Ontario Welfare Council (1973), Spurr (1974) and Underwood McLellan & Associates (1976).

[13]It should be noted that intentional stalling by public officials can under certain conditions benefit the planning consultants retained by the developer and may even benefit the developer if the value of his land appreciates rapidly. In this instance the future home buyer bears the burden of such shortsighted actions.

[14]Provincial and federal governments have supported this view unequivocally. See C.M.H.C. (1973), Alberta Land Use Forum (1976) and Advisory Task Force on Housing Policy (1973). Among the many references to this subject examined, only Spurr (1974) denies existence of a shortage of serviced land.

[15]Most Canadian studies of land and housing costs have directly or indirectly charged 'speculators' with being important contributors to the problem. Several recent, impartial studies have questioned this view. See Advisory Task Force (1973b), Martin (1976a), and Markusen and Scheffman (1976).

[16]Bromilow and Meaton (1973) concluded that efforts to reduce the time of subdivision approval would produce greater benefits in terms of reduced lots prices than would efforts to reduce the price of raw land.

[17]It would be untrue to imply that this trend to concentration is solely a response to private market forces. Government fiscal and monetary policies that have exacerbated chronic cash flow problems of the development industry have been important influences also.

References

Advisory Task Force on Housing Policy, *Land for Housing, Working Paper C*, Toronto: Queen's Printer, 1973b.

Alberta Land Use Forum, *Housing and Residential Land Demand in Selected Centres*, Technical Report 4C, Edmonton: A.L.U.F., 1975.

Alberta Land Use Forum, *Report*, Edmonton: A.L.U.F., 1976.

Alberta Land Use Forum, *Urban Residential Land Development*, Technical Report 4, Edmonton: A.L.U.F., 1974.

Bourne, L.S., *Urban Systems: Strategies for Regulation*, London: Oxford University Press, 1975.

Bromilow, F.J. and Meaton, M.L., *The Land Conversion Process - A Case Study*, Report OR-73-73. Melbourne: Commonwealth Scientific and Industrial Research Organization, Division of Building Research, July, 1973.

Bryant, C.R. and Martin, L.R.G., "Public Land Assembly and Land Price Monitoring: The Case of the ZAD in the Paris Region," *Plan Canada*, Vol. 16 (Sept.-Dec. 1976), 177-189.

Carr, J. and Smith, L.B., "Public Land Banking and the Price of Land", *Land Economics*, Vol. 51 (November 1975), 316-330.

Central Mortgage and Housing Corporation, "Housing and Land Strategy", Federal Position Paper prepared for the Second National Tri-Level Conference on Urban Affairs, Edmonton, October, 1973.

Clawson, M., *Suburban Land Conversion in the United States*, Baltimore: Johns Hopkins for Resources for the Future, Inc., 1971.

Dennis, M. and Fish, A., *Programs in Search of a Policy: Low Income Housing in Canada*, Toronto: Hakkert, 1972.

Derkowski, A., *Costs in the Land Development Process*, Report prepared for the HUDAC Economic Research Committee, December, 1975, Toronto: Housing and Urban Development Association of Canada, December, 1975.

Derkowski, A., *Residential Land Development in Ontario*, Report prepared for the Urban Development Institute, Ontario, November, 1972.

Edwards, J.D., *Proposal for a Land Availability Planning Assistance Program*, Discussion Paper B.75.7, Ottawa: Ministry of State for Urban Affairs, May, 1975.

Flowers, D., "The Cost of Housing in Ontario", Unpublished paper, University of Waterloo, 1976 (mimeographed).

Goodall, B., "Some Effects of Legislation on Land Values," *Regional Studies*, Vol. 4 (1970), 11-23.

Hall, P., Gracey, H., Drewett, R., and Thomas, R., *The Containment of Urban England*, Vol. I: *Urban and Metropolitan Growth Processes, or Megalopolis Denied*, Vol. II: *The Planning System: Objectives, Operations, and Impacts*, London: Allen and Unwin, 1973.

Hamilton, S.W., *Public Land Banking: Real or Illusionary Benefits?*, Toronto: Urban Development Institute, January, 1974.

I.C.O. Real Estate Management Ltd., *The Land Development Process as it Affects the Supply of New Housing within the Greater Vancouver Regional District*, Report prepared for The Real Estate Board of Greater Vancouver, May, 1974.

Markusen, J.R. and Scheffman, D.T., *Urban Land Development: Speculation and Market Structure*, Report prepared for the Ontario Economic Council, Toronto, October, 1976.

Martin, L.R.G., *An Examination of Land Dealer and Land Developer Behaviour on the Toronto Urban Fringe*, Report submitted to the Lands Directorate, Environment Canada, 1976b.

Martin, L.R.G., "Land Dealer Behaviour on the Toronto Urban Fringe," Paper presented at the Annual Meeting of the Canadian Association of Geographers, Laval University, Quebec, May 25, 1976a.

Martin, L.R.G., *Land Use Dynamics on the Toronto Urban Fringe*, Ottawa: Information Canada for Environment Canada, 1975.

Martin, L.R.G., "Problems and Policies Associated with High Land Costs on the Urban Fringe." *The Management of Land for Urban Development*, Ottawa: Canadian Council on Urban and Regional Research, 1974c.

Ministry of Treasury, Economics and Intergovernmental Affairs, *Parkway Belt West, Draft Plan*, Toronto: Ontario Government Publications Centre, January, 1976.

Neutze, G.M., *The Price of Land and Land Use Planning: Policy Instruments in the Urban Land Market*, Paris: Organization for Economic Co-operation and Development, 1973.

Ontario Economic Council, *Housing Issues and Alternatives*, Toronto: O.E.C., 1976.

Ontario Economic Council, *Subject to Approval: A Review of Municipal Planning in Ontario*, Toronto: O.E.C., 1973.

Ontario Welfare Council, *A Study of Housing Policies in Ontario: General Report*, Toronto: O.W.C., October, 1973.

Oxley, M.J., "Economic Theory and Urban Planning," *Environment and Planning A*, Vol. 7 (1975), 497-508.

Peter Barnard and Associates, *Developments in the Cost Supply and Need for Housing in Ontario*, Report prepared for The Advisory Task Force on Housing Policy, Toronto: April, 1973.

Piper, J., "Saskatoon Robs the Bank," *City Magazine*, Vol. 1 (October 1974), 16-20.

Proctor & Redfern Ltd., *The Review of the Planning Act*, A Submission to the Planning Act Review Committee of the Province of Ontario by the Urban Development Institute (Ontario) and the Canadian Institute of Public Real Estate Companies, Toronto, April, 1976.

Report of the Advisory Task Force on Housing Policy, E. Comay, Chairman, Toronto: Queen's Printer, 1973.

Report of the Canadian National Committee, Habitat and Canadians, Submitted to the Minister of State for Urban Affairs, January, 1976.

Report of the Federal Task Force on Housing and Urban Development, Paul T. Hellyer, Chairman, Ottawa: Queen's Printer, 1968.

Rodwin, L., *Nations and Cities: A Comparison of Strategies for Urban Growth*, Boston: Houghton Mifflin Co., 1970.

Smith, L.B., "The Ontario Land Speculation Tax: An Analysis of an Unearned Increment Land Tax," *Land Economics*, Vol. 52 (February 1976), 1-12.

Spurr, P., *The Land Problem's Problem*, Report submitted to C.M.H.C., Ottawa, August 1, 1974.

Swan, H.M., *Land Market Control Strategy in France: The Case of the ZAD*, Discussion Paper B.75.4, Ottawa: Ministry of State for Urban Affairs, March, 1975.

Underwood McLellan & Associates Ltd., *Building Sites: A Prime Component of Housing*, Report prepared for the Housing and Urban Development Association of Manitoba, Winnipeg, March, 1976.

Government Ownership and the Price of Land

STANLEY W. HAMILTON
Associate Professor of Urban Land Economics
Acting Dean, Faculty of Commerce
and Business Administration
University of British Columbia

and

DAVID E. BAXTER
Assistant Professor
Faculty of Commerce and Business Administration
University of British Columbia

THE AUTHORS

Stanley Hamilton was born in Saskatchewan in 1939. He received his Bachelor of Commerce degree from the University of Saskatchewan in 1960, his M.B.A. from the University of British Columbia in 1965, and his Ph.D. from the University of California (Berkeley) in 1970. He joined the Faculty of Commerce and Business Administration at the University of British Columbia in 1964, where he is currently Associate Professor of Urban Land Economics. In addition he is Acting Dean of the Faculty of Commerce. Dr. Hamilton has advised the federal government in matters concerning urban problems, and has served on the Vancouver City Planning Commission. In 1975 he was appointed to the Province of British Columbia Commission of Inquiry on Property Taxation and Assessment.

Among many books and journal articles, Professor Hamilton has published: *The Real Property Tax in British Columbia: An Analysis* (with Philip H. White), prepared for the B.C. School Trustees Association, 1972; *Public Land Banking: Real or Illusionary Benefits*, published by the Urban Development Institute, 1973; *Housing: It's Your Move*, Vol. I (with F. Pennance and D.E. Baxter), published by the Urban Land Economics Division of the University of British Columbia, 1976.

David E. Baxter is an Assistant Professor in the Urban Land Economics Division of the Faculty of Commerce and Business Administration at the University of British Columbia. For the past five years he has taught courses in Land Economics, Real Estate Finance, and Public Land Policy. Born in 1945, he carried out his undergraduate studies at the University of Alberta and his graduate studies at the University of British Columbia. He has served as a consultant in the fields of housing, land use and land development policy, analysis of regional economic structure, regional employment and land use forecasting, and evaluation of community planning documents.

Among his publications, Mr. Baxter includes: *Landlords and Tenants in Danger - Rent Control in Canada* (with S.W. Hamilton), published by the Appraisal Institute of Canada in 1975; *Capital Taxes Pertaining to Real Property* (with S.W. Hamilton), published by the Real Estate Institute of British Columbia in 1975; and "Market Effects of Legislation Controlling Foreign Investment," in P. Horwood (ed.) *Foreign Investment in Land - Alternative Controls*, published by the University of British Columbia in 1976.

Government Ownership and the Price of Land

STANLEY W. HAMILTON
Associate Professor of Urban Land Economics
Acting Dean, Faculty of Commerce
and Business Administration
University of British Columbia
and
DAVID E. BAXTER
Assistant Professor
Faculty of Commerce and Business Administration
University of British Columbia

I. INTRODUCTION

One sees, with increasing regularity, expansion of government involvement in the process by which land uses and prices are determined. There are several factors which have contributed to the increased intervention in land markets. First, the recent rapid change in real property prices, particularly those for owner-occupied housing and for urban fringe land, has attracted attention to these markets. Second, the size and density of most urban areas have changed rapidly and significantly with the rapid urbanization which has characterized Canadian society since the end of the Second World War. Many people have voiced concern over both the removal of older uses and the quality of the new developments that has accompanied this urbanization. Third, there has been an increase in concern over the quality of both urban and rural environments. Compounding these factors is a rather widely held opinion that somehow land is unique, and that its price and use should not be determined solely through the operation of markets, but rather through some more 'socially' oriented and centralized process.

II. PUBLIC OWNERSHIP

One of the strategies that is often suggested to solve the perceived problems in land markets is greater centralized control through government ownership of all land—the concept of public landownership. This concept has persisted in other countries for many years, and the claimed benefits of the experience in these countries have formed the basis of many proposals for public landownership in Canada. Municipalities in Sweden, in particular Stockholm, have made considerable use of the public landownership concept, combining ownership and control through a system of building leases. Their stated intention has been:

> "to retain title and control by the municipalities, while freeing the land for use by citizens. The increment in land values, was thus, to benefit the city and not merely the private developer or owner. A major advantage was that the leases helped the city to regulate growth and design. . ."[1]

The Australian federal government follows a similar pattern in the national capital of Canberra, where all urban land, and most of the federal territory, is owned by the government. All private development is conducted on publicly-owned land through a system of building leases:

> "There is no statutory planning control system of the planning scheme or zoning ordinance and subdivision regulation type in operation in the federal territory. The National Capital Development Commission's planning control of development and land use is achieved partly through its own development activities and partly through the site leasehold system. . . By its control over the release of sites for private building and the development covenant in the lease it is able to attain a high degree of control over the timing of private develop-

> ment. The Commission is able to control the siting, size and appearance of private buildings through the development covenant. . ."[2]

Public ownership of land is also widespread in Israel, accounting for approximately 90 per cent of all the (pre-1967) lands.[3] Land is made available for private development through leasehold tenure. Similar arrangements are used in the states of Maryland and Hawaii.[4] Hong Kong and Singapore provide two further examples of widespread public landownership.[5] In Hong Kong (and Kowloon) all lands are owned by the Crown and leased for private development. In Singapore, almost all new development occurs on publicly-owned lands through leasehold arrangements.

In each of the aforementioned countries, the concept of public landownership is an integral part of land use controls. It should also be noted that the public landownership programme is, in each case, combined with a leasehold system of land tenure, a point which will be dealt with in more detail later in this paper. Canada stands in contrast with these illustrations of the use of public landownership.

Canadian context

Several factors tend to discourage serious consideration of full public ownership in Canada. *First*, the large proportion of owner-occupiers, both urban and rural, represent a major voting group which would seem to make it politically difficult to turn to public ownership now. *Second*, the majority of Canadians are strongly oriented towards the notion of private ownership of one's 'home and castle'. *Third*, the current priorities in public spending would seem to suggest that the funds would not be available to acquire such extensive land holdings. *Finally*, even if such a programme would have a positive impact, the current Canadian standard of living, including both housing and general environmental conditions, is sufficiently high that there is no widespread belief that the current problems in urban areas are severe enough to justify a major programme of public landownership.

While full public landownership is not actively pursued in Canada, a considerable portion of the lands throughout

Canada are presently publicly owned. Table 1 indicates that more than 90 per cent of Canada's land mass is government owned. Even when the sparsely settled Territories are excluded, the extent of government landownership is a significant 84 per cent of the land mass within the ten provinces.

The data on the extent of public landownership in Canada, however, do not relate directly to the critical issues concerning public landownership. The lands presently held by the private sector represent the majority of lands currently in demand—high value, intensively used lands in and around urban areas (where the majority of Canadians reside) and fertile farmlands. Conversely, the least desirable lands—those in the more remote areas—are generally publicly owned. It seems likely that the major portion of land, measured by value rather than acreage, is privately owned. It is this latter context that gives rise to the proposals for public landownership in Canada.

III. ADVOCATES OF PUBLIC LANDOWNERSHIP

> "The land shall not be sold forever; for the land is Mine; for ye are strangers and sojourners with Me."
>
> *Leviticus XXV*

It is useful to review briefly the position of some well-known advocates of public landownership to gain some insight into the motivation for such a programme. One of the persistent themes amongst the advocates of public landownership is that private landowners should not obtain 'unearned increases' in land values. In the 1870s, J.S. Mill suggested:

> "The ordinary progress of a society which increases in wealth is at all times to augment the income of landlords; to give them both a greater amount and a greater proportion of the wealth of the community, independently of any trouble or outlay incurred by themselves. They grow richer, as it were, in their sleep, without working, risking or economizing. What claim have they, on the general principle of social justice, to this accession of riches?"[6]

TABLE 1
Total Land Area by Tenure, Canada, Provinces and Territories, 1974*

Tenure	Nfld.	PEI	NS	NB	Que.	Ont.	Man.	Sask.	Alta.	BC	YT	NWT	Canada
Federal Crown lands other than national parks, Indian reserves and forest experiment stations	168	6	70	575	476[1]	447	99	2,105	1,177	349	198,159	1,287,251	1,490,882
National parks	903	7	514	167	303	742	1,149	1,496	20,692[3]	1,811	8,500	16,450[4]	52,734
Indian reserves	—	3	44	65	300	2,588	827	2,196	2,549	1,309	2	52	9,935
Federal forest experiment stations	—	—	—	35	7	40	—	—	23	—	—	—	105
Privately owned land or land in process of alienation from the Crown	6,847	1,995	14,645	15,339	43,500	45,955	55,875	95,586	77,801	21,039	65	28	378,675
Provincial or territorial lands other than provincial parks and provincial forests	148,043	112	1,023	11,012	468,796	344,496	184,241[2]	13,937	—	208,684	350	1,122	1,381,816
Provincial parks	107	6	31	83	75,000	18,314	3,390	1,857	2,399	14,740	—	—	115,927
Provincial forests	117	55	5,098	1,078	6,478	—	5,419	134,523	150,644[5]	118,323	—	—	421,735
Total area	156,185	2,184	21,425	28,354	594,860	412,582	251,000	251,700	255,285	366,255	207,076	1,304,903	3,851,809
Percent of total area that is privately owned	4.4%	91.4%	68.4%	54.1%	7.3%	11.2%	22.3%	38.0%	30.5%	5.7%	0.03%	0.002%	9.8%

[1]Includes Gatineau Park (137.5 sq. miles) and Quebec Battlefields Park (0.36 sq. miles) which are under federal jursidiction but are not technically National Parks.

[2]Includes 2,220 sq. miles under lease.

[3]Includes that part of Wood Buffalo Park in Alberta (13,840 sq. miles).

[4]Includes that part of Wood Buffalo Park in Northwest Territories (3,460 sq. miles).

[5]Includes some privately owned land and other provincial lands.

Source: Statistics Canada, ***The Canada Yearbook — 1975,*** (Ottawa, Statistics Canada, 1975), p. 33 — Table 1.8.

Mr. Beer, in the early 1920s, provided an encompassing doctrine in respect of landownership:

> "according to which the earth and the fullness thereof, were, in the original state of society, or the state of nature, the common property of mankind, so that every child born into the world had *ipso facto* an inalienable right to an equal share in the common inheritance."[7]

Statements of this kind, while appealing to emotion, provide no rationale for public ownership, nor do they provide any guidelines for the realization of the goals.

More recent advocates of public ownership have tended to expand on the simple notion of 'equality' as stated above.

> "This sort of arrangement (public ownership) would at one stroke obviate numerous difficulties, all too obvious in existing haphazard ways of doing things. It would eliminate distortions due to speculation, and difficulties connected with dedication of land for public purposes in subdivisions. It would ensure a constant supply of land for the housebuilding industry... It would facilitate rehousing of people displaced by urban renewal."[8]

The central questions

In the foregoing quotation, as elsewhere, the 'need' for public ownership is taken as self-evident, without any attempt to answer any of the following basic questions:

1. What are the actual problems with the current system?

2. Will public landownership resolve these problems?

3. Do more efficient and less costly alternatives exist?

4. Is it valid to assume that the apparently uncoordinated operation of a market in the context of a system of private landownership is the root of the inequities and distortions that are so 'obvious' to the advocates of public ownership?

5. Will the continued centralization of control and ownership in the government sector result in more equity at lower costs? and,

6. What are the fundamental goals that the proponents of full public ownership hope to attain using the strategy?

The central purpose of this paper is to examine these questions in the context of an evaluation of the possible effects on the price and use of land of government monopolistic ownership of land. In order to reach conclusions about the effects of both implementing such a scheme and the pattern of uses and prices of land once public landownership is achieved, it is necessary to first consider the nature of ownership under the current system of land tenure in Canada. Once this basis has been established, it will be possible to turn to the meaning and effects of public ownership. Having considered this monopolist or centralized ownership, less extensive forms of ownership, such as land banking, and means of acquisition of ownership, such as expropriation, will also be briefly considered.

IV. LANDOWNERSHIP: WHAT DOES IT MEAN?

In order to evaluate the proposals for public landownership properly, some understanding of the object (land) and the nature of ownership is essential. The words 'ownership' and 'possession' are frequently used to describe holdings in land, but these two terms have quite different meanings in law. At one time possession was considered equivalent to ownership, providing one possessed the physical might to enforce the retention of the ownership. Today, however, ownership and possession are quite separable, and one can seek legal remedies to protect ownership. This separation of possession and ownership occurs in many areas. Commonplace examples are: lending your fishing gear to a neighbour while retaining ownership or renting your house to a tenant while retaining ownership. In the context of this paper, the concept of 'ownership of land' is of central importance.

While it is a convention to speak of the ownership of land (or alternatively the ownership of real property), this represents an oversimplification which tends to confuse the discussion relating to public landownership. Ownership in this conventional sense applies to the thing itself, whether it be a fishing rod, an automobile or a parcel of land. A second, and lesser known, meaning of ownership refers not to the thing itself but to the legal interest in the thing—the rights in the thing which the law will recognize and protect. It is this latter concept of ownership which is of importance in land and real property.

The two major forms of interest which could be owned under medieval laws were: a) those which granted the holder the right to exclusive use of land for some period of time (estates in time)[9] and, b) those which related to private restrictions on the use of land (interests less than estates).[10] In the context of a contemporary discussion of public and private ownership of interests in land in Canada, the two major estates in time, the estate in fee simple and the leasehold estate, are of critical importance.

Fee simple rights—ownership

The estate in fee simple is the greatest interest in that which can be privately owned. Whenever people speak about owning a parcel of land or a house, the strict interpretation is that they own an estate in fee simple. This interest may endure for an infinite period (through inheritance),[11] and the holder may grant all or a portion of the interest away, subject to the limitations discussed below.

Governments' rights—expropriation

In Common law, and hence in Canada, the estate in fee simple (hereafter referred to as 'ownership' for convenience) is basically the same as the interest granted by the King to his Lords in feudal times — *the private citizen may hold the land subject to certain restrictions and the right of the Crown to reclaim the land.* This right to reclaim is presently embodied in the laws governing expropriation: at the present time the Crown has the right, in Common law, to expropriate any privately-owned land *without compensation.* Compensation is paid only by choice of the governments through their own statutory provisions, just as the limitations placed on expropriation are created by statute.[12] The Canadian courts assume that if the legislature does not expressly provide for confiscation (no compensation), compensation is to be paid.

Other restrictions

The owner of land is encumbered not only by the Crown's right of expropriation, but also by the statutory rights of various governments and agencies. The right to use land is constrained by the various regulations generally referred to as land use controls. Thus, zoning specifies the range of uses to which a parcel of land may be put (although it does not require that the land be used). Hence the use and enjoyment of land is also subject to the powers of the Crown, further encumbering the rights of owners of fee simple interests.

It should be noted that, in Canada, because all land is still essentially part of the 'regal estate', the government is not required (or more correctly, does not require itself) to pay compensation to an owner whose use and enjoyment of a property is reduced as the result of a change in permitted use. While traditionally this treatment has been matched with a decision not to charge the owner when an increase in value results from a change in zoning, the widespread use of impost fees may be viewed as a form of tax on increased land values.

The landowner finds ownership further limited by the requirement that property taxes be paid in order to retain ownership. For example, if a landowner in British Columbia is more than three years in arrears in real property taxes, the local taxing authority may take ownership of the land as compensation for the arrears in taxes.[13] Thus the tax liability attaches itself to the land rather than to the party who is in arrears in payment. Again this reduces the rights of owners of fee simple estates, as the holder of the interest in these circumstances does not have control over the dispositions of the interest.

The general use and benefit of ownership of land is further limited by other statutory controls. For example, the relationship between landlord and tenant, while being technically a matter of contract between parties, is subject to regulation by various landlord and tenant laws. In all provinces, the rent paid for residential premises is subject to the regulation of provincial governments rather than strictly by the negotiation between parties.[14] Each of the other similar statutory regulations of the use and enjoyment of real property affects the rights of the owner, and, consequently, the ownership of property. As a general statement, and one which has significant importance in considering the operation of property markets, one may generalize to state that the greater the restrictions placed on an owner's (feeholder's) rights, through either public or private controls of rights, the lower the relative value of the interest.

These comments outline the restrictions and duties which accompany the feeholder's right to exclusive possession subject to the Crown's right of full ownership of land which may be implemented by expropriation. Before examining the rights and duties of holders of a leasehold estate, private restrictions on feeholders should also be briefly considered.

The first class of restrictions on ownership are those privately-held interests less than estates which limit the use of land. These are easements, rights of way, restrictive covenants, and mineral leases. To the extent that such interests in a parcel of land exist and are held by persons other than the feeholder, the rights of the feeholder will be reduced. The second form of private restriction of a feeholder's rights lies with the Common law concept of the 'tort of nuisance', that is where activity on one parcel of land causes harm to, or interferes with, the use and enjoyment of other parcels of land in the neighbourhood. If such a situation arises, the offender may be liable for monetary compensation to the injured parties and to be compelled to restrain from carrying out the offending activity. Recourse to the use of the law of nuisance as a land use control has been almost eliminated by the use of statutory public land use controls.

The final restriction on the constrained exclusive possession enjoyed by feeholders stems from voluntary granting away of certain rights by feeholders. The most common rights which are granted away include leaseholds, mortgages, and agreements for sale. The rights granted away cannot exceed the rights of the feeholder, and hence are regarded as lesser interests in land: nevertheless to the extent that rights have been granted away, the rights, and hence the value, of the freehold has been reduced. The most important type of estate, in the context of this paper, is the leasehold, as it is a granting away of all or a portion of the feeholder's right to exclusive possession.

The landowner as tenant

From the preceding comments, it is apparent that the private 'owner' of a parcel of land is functionally more akin to a long term tenant than an owner in the general sense of the word. The 'landlord' (the Crown) may evict the tenant (the owner) even if the owner has done no wrong (through expropriation), or if the tenant has not paid the 'rent' (taxes). Further, the 'owner' can only put the land to approved uses and develop it in accordance with the Crown's preferences (as expressed in land use and planning controls). About the only major difference is that the 'owner' has not been traditionally restricted in the right to sell the bundle of rights and restrictions represented by the fee simple interest to other parties whereas tenants' rights to sub-let or assign leases have been traditionally restricted by the landlord. However, recent restrictions and proposed restrictions on foreign ownership of land (such as the federal Foreign Investment Review Act) indicate a movement to restrict the right of fee simple owners to sell their interests in land.

The similarity between the freehold (fee simple) and leasehold estates becomes even more apparent when the leasehold estate is examined in detail. A leasehold estate[15] represents the holder's right to exclusive possession to all or a portion of a parcel of land for a definite and specified period of time subject to the leaseholder's (tenant) honouring the terms of the lease (as modified by government statutes and administrative rulings in the areas of landlord and tenant relations and land use controls) and the rights retained by the feeholder (landlord). Again, generally speaking, the greater the rights granted to the tenant (in terms of the length of the lease or the rights of exclusive possession, including the right to sub-lease all or a portion of leasehold subject to the restrictions in the lease agreement) the greater the value of the leasehold and the lower the value of the freehold. The major difference between freehold and leasehold estates is the requirement that a leasehold must be for a definite period of time.

Lease value versus value of ownership

The leaseholder is constrained by: a) all of the restrictions on the fee estate (including both public and private restrictions) and b) the terms of the lease. Thus the feeholder may, by contract, restrict the use of the land to a greater extent than public land use controls do, but cannot grant the right to use the land in violation of the public controls. Thus if a feeholder grants all of the rights embodied in the fee simple, the difference in the value of the leasehold and an unencumbered freehold would be essentially determined by the length of time for which the lease was valid. In the case of very long term leases where all the rights and duties which the feeholder possesses are granted to the tenant, the value of the leasehold is not significantly different from the value of freehold if the leasehold had not been granted away: this relationship is of critical importance in examining the possible land use patterns and prices which would exist in the context of public landownership.

Consider an example of a fee simple interest on a property which is zoned for commercial use and where a new commercial building has just been erected. Assume this building represents the optimal economic use of the land (highest and best use). This property can be rented at a net income (gross revenue less operating expenses) of $12,000 per annum. Using normal appraisal practices, the market value of this property would be found by evaluating the net annual income at a market 'discount' rate which reflects general interest rates and the risks involved in the management of the property. Assume the appropriate market rate is found to be 9 per cent. The market value is then:

Market Value = Present Value of $12,000 per annum at 9 per cent for perpetuity† = $133,333

†Editors' Note: For a discussion of valuation of property, see the essay in this volume by Professor David Nowlan.

Now assume the fee simple owner needs money and, hence, must decide to either sell the property or to grant a 50-year lease at $12,000 per annum. If it is sold, the owner will realize $133,333. If, however, he chooses to lease, he creates two separate interests in the land—and two separate valuation problems. If net rents are assumed to remain constant over time and no change in expected investment yields is anticipated, then clearly the market value of the fee simple interest in 50 years (when the leasehold expires) is expected to be $133,333 (calculated as above). Then the market value of the fee simple today is composed of two elements:

1. Market Value of rents for 50 years = Present Value of $12,000 per annum for 50 years at 9 per cent = $131,540.

2. Present Market Value of fee simple when no longer subject to lease = Present Value of $133,333 to be received in 50 years at 9 per cent = $1,793.

1. + 2. = $133,333

However, if rents are expected to increase, then clearly the tenant will benefit during the first 50 years. Conversely, the tenant assumes the risk of a decline in rents. Normally one would expect some market adjustment such that the sum of the fee simple subject to the lease plus the value of the reversionary interest (i.e. the interest in the property that reverts to the owner at the expiry date of the lease) will be less than the value of the fee simple without the lease.

It is obvious from this simple illustration that the value of the leasehold estate will generally be less than the value of the fee simple estate, at least by the present value of the reversionary interest. At the same time, this illustration serves to point out the similarity in the process of determining value; in each case, the market value is derived from the future benefits to be enjoyed from the interest in land. It follows that a policy authority wishing to effect the price of a leasehold interest could take action to influence rental values, the lease term or the risk associated with the leasehold estate.

From the preceding comments, it is readily apparent that landowners (i.e. freeholders) are greatly constrained in both the extent and the nature of their ownership by both public and private rights. The owners of land are, functionally as well as legally, more akin to longer-term tenants than absolute owners. Thus, when the suggestion that all land should be publicly owned is presented, it is essential to observe that the public ownership would simply represent the reclaiming of a specific and limited bundle of rights relating to the use of land. Presumably in place of this bundle of rights, known as an estate in fee simple, the private sector would be granted a lesser bundle resembling the contemporary leasehold. As the preceding example indicates, the fall in value of the fee simple may well be matched by an increase in value of the leasehold interest.

V. PUBLIC OWNERSHIP: WHAT DOES IT MEAN?

In order to appreciate the nature of the public ownership debate, it is desirable to agree on some definitions. In the first instance, public landownership appears to be simple and straightforward—the ownership of all lands by the public. More careful examination begins to reveal some practical problems with this simplistic definition. Initially, one must agree on the meaning of 'public'. In Canada, three levels of government, each with diverse attitudes and powers, may lay claim as the appropriate 'public' authority. The appropriate level of government is not necessarily obvious but a review of the objectives of public landownership may suggest which level of government is most suitable for the task.

The second definitional problem centres on the confusion between land as a physical product and land as a legal interest. In the previous section the distinction between possession of the physical product and ownership of a legal interest in the physical product relative to the rights of use and possession was discussed. Obviously the public will not use (possess) all of the land—individuals will continue to use it. Therefore, public landownership must logically refer to the ownership of a specific legal interest in land, the right to determine for an infinite period of time exclusive possession of the physical property, rather than the right of exclusive possession for a definite period of time. In reference to the present situation in Canada, this must imply public ownership of all fee simple interests in land. But, since the 'public' will not use (all of) the land, it would then be necessary to give individuals some bundle of property rights in place of the current fee simple to facilitate private use of property.

The question is, exactly what rights should be given? This will depend to a certain degree on the objectives of the public landownership programme. The new bundle of rights may include:

1. Right to use and possession (for some specific term);

2. Right to develop (subject to certain conditions); and

3. Right to dispose (subject to certain conditions).

All or any part of the granting of these rights can be achieved by way of a land lease (sometimes known as a building lease). The lease can specify the term, it can contain both positive and negative covenants respecting development and it can specify conditions under which the tenant can dispose of all or a portion of the leasehold interest. In practice, as was discussed in section II, long-term land leases are the most common replacement for fee simple interests in land. It follows, therefore, that a programme of public landownership would probably mean the ownership of all fee simple interests, coupled with the granting of leasehold interests in land to the private sector.

VI. THE OBJECTIVES OF PUBLIC LANDOWNERSHIP

Advocates of public landownership have concerned themselves almost exclusively with the necessity of finding acceptable schemes to achieve public landownership. Seldom does one hear any discussion concerning the objectives of, or for that matter the 'need' for, further public involvement in property markets. Judging from current discussions, the objectives of and need for public landownership are taken as self-evident. Yet a quick review of the literature produces a multitude of objectives, many mutually exclusive and most assigned quite different priorities by the various advocates of the programme. One of the most extensive summaries is provided by Professor Denman:

1. easier access to land;
2. better distribution of private wealth;
3. reduction of privilege and power;
4. security of tenure;
5. increased efficiency of land management;
6. control of land values;
7. solution to the compensation-betterment problem; and
8. better planning of land use.[16]

This list might be conveniently grouped into three general objectives:

1. to increase equity;
2. to improve land planning; and
3. to control or manage land prices

Each of these objectives will be examined here in the context of complete public landownership.

VII. EQUITY OBJECTIVE OF PUBLIC OWNERSHIP

The Uthwatt Report (1942), the final report of an expert committee of the British government, dealing in the first instance with an examination of the question of compensation-betterment (how to pay or charge private landowners for decreases or increases in land values created by public decisions and investments), concluded that the ideal solution to the issue would be public ownership of all lands.[17] The compensation-betterment or equity issue is based on the premise that much of the increase in land values is due to public decisions and public expenditures relating to the land and, therefore, the public ought to reap the benefits. One might observe that most public expenditures and policies create secondary benefits and costs beyond their original purpose and there is no unique reason to single out land values for special attention. It should be further noted that only a portion of the increase in land values is due to public decisions, the remainder is due to the multitude of private activities and decisions which influence land values.

Since the Uthwatt Report was published, numerous schemes have been advanced to cope with this equity issue. However, in the process, three points have been ignored or forgotten. *First*, the equity issue is basically a measurement problem. No one can seriously deny that the public have a right to a share, but not all, of increments and losses in land value. The basic problem is to find a suitable measurement tool to determine how much of the change in value arises from public and private activities respectively to properly allocate these changes between the public and the private sectors. *Second*, over the years the broader issue of compensation appears to have been forgotten. We continue to pay compensation if land as a legal interest is expropriated, but no compensation is paid if land values are destroyed or decreased through public decisions or actions. Certainly if betterment is to be collected, the natural and fair corollary is to pay compensation. *Third*, betterment is already collected in part in the form of taxes. Landowners pay income tax on profits, property taxes and direct taxes for services rendered by the public, at a much higher level than was the case in

1942 when the Uthwatt Committee examined the problem. Further, the widespread use of impost fees, development levies, and real property transfer taxes[18] has increased the tax liability of landowners who realize an increase in land value through sale or development.

An example

These three points can be illustrated with a simple example. Consider a public programme to widen a street fronted by retail stores. A 15-foot strip of land is expropriated from all retail outlets on the north side of the street. Since land is taken, compensation will be paid to each owner, (creating a set of interesting appraisal problems). Properties on the south side of the street are not directly affected. In the process of planning the expanded street, a by-pass created on the west corner significantly reduces access to the gas station but since no land is taken, no compensation is paid. At the same time, a vacant property is re-zoned to a lower density to preserve the 'character of the neighbourhood'. Again, since no land is taken, no compensation is paid. The street widening and beautification projects are paid in part from general revenue, from increased property taxes and from a frontage tax charged to property owners fronting the street. Hence all taxes for properties fronting the street are increased. At the same time, retailers have agreed to improve their store fronts to create a common 'theme'.

One year later, property values along the improved street are found to be 20 per cent higher while property values on the next street over have increased only 5 per cent. Assuming a betterment tax or levy is to be assessed, someone must decide:

1. what portion of the 20 per cent increase is due to general inflation, to retailers' capital expenditure to improve their stores, to improved marketing, and to the improved street (public expenditure)?

2. should the owner of the gas station receive compensation since the market value of his property declined due to the (public) by-pass?

3. should the owner of the vacant site receive compensation for the effects of the re-zoning and, if so, how much? and

4. are property owners on adjacent streets entitled to compensation because their property values have not increased at the 'average' rate for the community (the two streets), in part because some retail traffic was attracted away from them to the improved street?

This example makes it clear that while the overall objective may be evident, the allocation of compensation and betterment creates impossible measurement problems.

A programme of public ownership coupled with a system of well-designed leases has often been advanced as an ideal method of recouping increments in land value. It is argued that the leasehold system would provide for a reversion (or recovery of the fee simple estate) to the public sector at a point in time broadly coinciding with the end of the building's economic life. This would enable the public to review the rents and reap the gains arising from redevelopment. Secondly, the leasehold system would theoretically afford the public an opportunity to review rents during the lease term, thereby ensuring the public received full benefit from any increased market values.

Capturing the betterment

In practice, neither of these conditions is apt to work as well as the advocates suggest. In establishing rents, the landlord and tenant must agree upon an equitable level, considering the value of the property and lease covenants and public land use restrictions which will influence its rental value at any time. This is not an easy task since the composite of expenditures and policies from both the private and public sector must be considered. Hence, the measurement problem (to determine a fair rent) is just as difficult under a scheme of public ownership as it is under the present system. In fact, the measurement problems are so great that most public leasehold schemes in existence in other countries make no attempt to recoup increments in land value during the term of the lease but rather emphasize the recovery at the end of the lease and the subsequent re-letting.

The recapture of gains at the time the lease expires, however, is not likely to be realized for a number of reasons. When a system of public landownership and leasehold estates becomes widespread, the frequency of complaints and the force with which complaints are drawn to the attention of politicians generally increase. Moreover, tenants, particularly long-standing tenants, develop a sense of propriety concerning their leasehold estate. While everyone is aware that at the end of a lease the real property reverts to the landlord, a sense of injustice is bound to arise—injustice in that the landlord (in this case the public), without any action on his part, recovers the "tenants' building". The fact that the initial leasehold contract gave full consideration to the recovery of the improved property is often forgotten in the passage of time.

Capture and injustice

The strong sense of social injustice that a system of leasehold tenure tends to create is apt to negate any benefits at the time of reversion. The British White Paper which preceded the Leasehold Reform Act of 1967 reflected this sense of social injustice very clearly:

> "Not unnaturally, an occupying leaseholder who at the end of the term has lived in it for a period of years regards it as his family home. It is in such cases quite indefensible, if justice is to be done as between freeholder and occupying leaseholder, that at the end of the term the law should allow the ownership of the house to revert to the freeholder without his paying for it so that he gets not only the land but also the house, the improvements and everything the leaseholder and his predecessors have added to it . . . In the Government's view the basic principle of a reform that will do justice between the parties should be that the freeholder owns the land and the occupying leaseholder is morally entitled to the ownership of the building which has been put on and maintained on the land."[19]

One might question the sense of 'justice' incorporated in the above quote. An examination of the initial lease contract would reveal that the landlord (public), in establishing rent levels, had considered the worth of the reversionary interest. Tenants, not necessarily current tenants, enjoyed the benefits of the initial contract, and justice, were it to be achieved as between landlord and tenant, would permit the landlord to recover the real property, land and improvements combined. Essentially the British action can be defended only to the extent that tenants were not aware of the eventual outcome, a weak argument at best. The long-run effect of the British action is to cast serious doubt on the viability of building leases—a classic example of 'good politics' and 'poor economics'.

Conclusion on equity

The use of public landownership to achieve equity does not, from a practical point of view, appear likely to succeed. If one considers that equity relates to the distribution of purchasing power amongst individuals in a society, then public landownership shares the general flaws of indirect and selective methods to achieve a redistribution of income: it is expensive to operate and administer, it provides no guarantee that the incidence of costs and benefits conform to the goal of equity, and it distorts the efficiency of the property market in satisfying society's demands. It would appear that if the goal is to move towards greater equity in the distribution of income or purchasing power in a society, unconditional transfer of dollars would be a more appropriate strategy. The administrative cost would be much lower than public landownership, the programme can be directly structured according to the definition of equity, and scarce resources will not be wasted as the result of policy-induced distortions in land markets.

VIII. PLANNING OBJECTIVES OF PUBLIC OWNERSHIP

The second objective of the programme of public landownership is to improve land planning. Of all the arguments advanced in favour of public landownership, this *appears* to be the most cogent. Improved land planning will occur, it is often argued, because:

1. The unification of the landownership, planning and subdivision functions results in economies of scale and organization;

2. It offers the maximum opportunity for positive as well as negative controls on land use via the use of leasehold covenants; and

3. The problems of land re-assembly for redevelopment purposes are minimized by the use of leasehold tenure.

Clearly a case can be made for the unification of ownership, planning control and the subdivision function. There appears to be no question that, from a physical land planning point of view, in certain circumstances advantages can be gained from integration. However, this does not mean that one must accept public ownership as a logical extension. Obviously the same economies of scale and operation could be enjoyed in a (fee simple) private market. Moreover, one must be careful not to confuse technical efficiency and economic efficiency. The technical efficiency is only important if consumer (i.e. citizen) preferences are regarded as irrelevant.

Current difficulties

At the present time and under the present system, private developers exhibit considerable success in assembling large tracts of land for development. In fact, some authorities are presently arguing that large private landowners are obtaining oligopoly control in certain market areas.[20] While no evidence exists to suggest that these private landowners are exercising oligopoly control, the fact that they have assembled such major holdings is clear evidence of their ability to realize economies of scale.†

One might also usefully look at the source of this land assembly problem. There is a tendency on the part of planning officials to permit piecemeal subdivision of large tracts of land in and around major urban areas. This piecemeal approach to subdivision, often permitting and encouraging subdivision to small holdings of five to ten acres serves to increase the profits of land holders while at the same time making it more difficult to organize efficient land subdivisions. If the pre-development parcels of land are too small for efficient development, the fault lies with poor subdivision controls, not private ownership. If parcels of land are too small for redevelopment, necessitating assembly, it is a problem that results from changing preferences and technology for improvements to land, not to planning or private ownership.

Positive planning

The second planning-oriented advantage claimed for the public ownership and leasehold system is the ability to introduce positive as well as negative controls. The argument is advanced that current zoning and building by-laws are essentially negative whereas a lease contract could include positive covenants. (One might argue that these 'positive covenants' are, in fact, negative and that all planning is negative. Presumably these 'positive covenants' will appear to be accepted by the participants in the market only if planning authorities prohibit development on competing sites which do not have such positive covenants.)

Obviously the landlord (public) is at liberty to incorporate any type of controls deemed desirable—providing, of course, that a tenant can be found. One would anticipate that extensive covenants, both positive and negative, would be

†Editors' Note: The issue of concentration of ownership is discussed at length in the paper by Markusen and Scheffman in this volume. Their work does not support the notion that, by assembling large tracts of land, developers have been able to behave as oligopolists.

reflected in the rent payable by a tenant. Planning, in the context of the lease contract, will not be a 'free good'. While the use of a leasehold system would appear to afford the opportunity for improved planning, it is more illusionary than real. The very same leasehold covenants which afford us improved planning today may become major impediments to good planning in the future. A carefully designed leasehold system may become more inflexible than the current system of (private) fee simple, as illustrated in the Australian Task Force Report:

> "It was generally felt that the disadvantage of the leasehold system is that the conditions of the lease as originally set may be unnecessarily restrictive at a future time. It was also contended by some members of the Division that the leasehold system results in a severe running down of the improvements and the land itself over the latter years of the lease period, and the lessee generally has little chance of recouping any expense on the land." [21]

The human element

It appears the leasehold system, whether public or private, affords no guarantee that high standards will be maintained in the face of fundamental market changes. This realization that (public) planners have no more predictive power than any other individual ought to cause their programmes to be viewed with more caution and humility. Planners are, after all, simply individuals attempting to judge the desires of society. While the planner may be in a position to consider non-economic factors (since planning is taken as a 'free good'), they also suffer in that they do not have a capital commitment nor are they necessarily guided by the desires of the citizens as expressed through the price system.

Land use without zoning

Control by lease covenant is thus *not apt to work* in those circumstances where the advocates feel it is *most needed* (in the face of adverse market trends) and is *most apt to work when it is unnecessary* as when the market is in harmony with the covenant. Furthermore, it should be noted that the use of covenants can be applied to a fee simple system through the use of building schemes with restrictive covenants. Perhaps the best example of this is contained in B.H. Siegan's study of land use without zoning. Dr. Siegan found in Houston the public sector had very little cause to interfere with the (private) building covenants.

> ". . . the land-use experience of Houston . . . shows that communities can function reasonably well and the values of homes and other real estate can be maintained and enhanced without the need to give homeowners much more protection than they are accorded by restrictive covenants. The land use powers of the homeowners, usually the most exclusionary group in the community, are limited to what seems reasonably essential to maintaining and maximizing the value of their homes. Specific ordinances concerning land use can and should be adopted only when needed to regulate specific problems of land use. (A parking ordinance would be an example of this)." [22]

Dr. Siegan's research was directed to examining the necessity of zoning control: his conclusions, however, appear to be applicable and worthy of consideration for leasehold systems.

Theory versus practice

In summary, it would appear that the leasehold contract in theory affords some opportunities to implement stronger and tighter land use controls. In practice, however, there seems to be inadequate enforcement of these covenants. Frequently, the political process becomes involved in the enforcement of these planning covenants, particularly as the instrument becomes more widely used, further frustrating attempts to implement 'good planning'. The enforcement of leasehold covenants will, as they become widespread, create at least the same problem as we face today in approving a rezoning or building permit and it appears the problems may even be greater as the individual leases afford less flexibility.

Leases and redevelopment ease

The final suggested planning advantage of the leasehold system is that it affords an opportunity for easy land assembly and redevelopment. An implicit assumption underlying this point is that the end of the lease will coincide with the end of the building's economic life, so redevelopment can occur with minimum inconveniences. Generally, however, this would be the exception, not the rule. The more normal case is that the lease and economic life will not coincide, thus causing some of the most serious problems associated with the enforcement of leasehold covenants; namely that a lease of this type is often viewed as:

> ". . . being inherently unfair to the tenant, inasmuch as the whole of his expenditure ultimately goes to enrich the landlord to whom the premises in their then state, buildings, improvements and all, revert for nothing at the expiration of the term."[23]

Whether this injustice is real or apparent becomes secondary as planner and politician alike move to pacify the tenants. The economic merits of the position appear lost in the ensuing political scramble.[24]

Moreover, whatever planning advantages, if any, which might be found in favour of public ownership accompanied by a leasehold system, ought to be critically examined in light of recent British reforms:

> "In conclusion, it is necessary to recognize and consider the decline of the leasehold system in Britain. This decline would seem to provide a strong criticism of the system.
>
> The Leasehold Reform Act 1967 does in fact indicate the main disadvantage of the leasehold system. It is very vulnerable to political interference. When there are many lessees and a small number of landowner organizations, public or private, then politicians will be susceptible to pressures from lessee groups for concessions such as the preferential allocation of sites, reduced land rents, the automatic renewal of leases and/or en-

> franchisement. Such concessions provide an immediate political advantage while the real social cost is a long term one, and is not immediately apparent."[25]

The ensuing changes contained in the Leasehold Act, while perhaps showing good common sense (not to mention political sense) in pacifying a large proportion of the population *completely ignored all issues of economics, injustice and planning.* The final touch of irony was that publicly-owned properties were exempted.

An expensive redundancy

A further comment on the use of public ownership as a planning tool relates to the incidence of planning on the use of land. The general nature of the use of a site for long periods of time is determined at the time the improvements to the land occur. Thus planning has its greatest impact during the development stage: full public ownership of land in order to control a process which occurs in a relatively brief period of time is a very expensive way to achieve planning goals. It is also difficult to accept that a building lease would give any greater control over the development and use of land than is currently possible through the use of existing planning controls, which regulate the servicing, use, design, construction, access and environmental character of developments. The public ownership of land to achieve planning goals would, at best, be an expensive redundancy in the context of current planning restrictions.

IX. PRICE OBJECTIVE OF PUBLIC OWNERSHIP

The two preceding sections demonstrate that the goals of equity and improved planning do not necessitate public landownership and that attaining these goals may, in fact, be hindered by a public land monopoly. Throughout the preceding discussions, the relationship between landownership and land values has been mentioned. In this section, the third major objective of public landownership—the control or management of land prices—is examined.

The argument is often advanced that public landownership can and will result in lower land prices for the occupier, an assertion which is subject to considerable differences of opinion. Before we can undertake a meaningful consideration of the content of this argument, we must deal with a basic confusion that surrounds discussions of the role of public landownership and its likely effect on 'cost', 'price' and 'market values'. The confusion arises from a failure to discriminate between these various value notions. In this context, 'cost' implies the historical cost of acquiring real property plus the actual holding costs and any improvements made to the property; 'price' is simply the figure at which a property exchanges hands (as in sales price) and 'market value' is the value which the market places on a property at any given point in time. Having established these simple definitions of worth, we can unambiguously ask what effect, if any, will public landownership have on 'cost', 'price' and 'market value'?

Ownership and the market

Before examining the likely impact of public landownership on these three measures of worth, it is useful to consider the nature of the land market under such a programme. Initially the programme of public landownership will involve the acquisition of a fee simple rights, either by expropriation or confiscation, and the creation of leasehold estates. As a matter of convenience, one can assume the fee simple interests are replaced with long-term building leases. How the (private) market responds to the leasehold estates will depend, in part, on the extent and nature of the leasehold covenants and restrictions. This is basically an empirical question: the available evidence suggests the (private) market will be prepared to pay relatively less for a leasehold estate than for a fee simple interest. Logic suggests that if a fee simple interest is the highest private rights offered in the market, then any lesser interest in land, such as a leasehold estate, would have a lower market value.

Consider the potential market reaction to the choice between long-term building leases and fee simple interests in land. Assume the market is presently prepared to pay

\$100,000 for a fee simple interest in a parcel of land. This market value represents the present value of all future net incomes discounted at an appropriate market discount rate, where the net incomes represent the gross rental revenues less operating costs. As an alternative, how might the market assess the value of a prepared 99-year building lease providing the lease contains no restrictive or limiting covenants (e.g. the tenant becomes a 99-year 'fee simple' owner for practical purposes)? The market value of the leasehold will represent the present value of all future net incomes over the next 99 years calculated at an appropriate discount rate. The *minimum* difference between the market values of the fee simple and leasehold interest will be the present value of the property in the hundredth year. In practice, the differences are apt to be greater. The leasehold estate is not so readily accepted as security for a mortgage and, as a result, the discount rate applied on the leasehold will be higher, giving a lower market value.

The difference between the market values of the fee simple and leasehold interests is apt to be even larger as a public authority attempts to add positive and negative covenants to a lease contract. For example, the leasehold contract may provide for periodic rent reviews (to provide equity) in which case the tenant's risks are increased. Similarly, the landlord may wish to place limits on the rights to sub-let or assign the property and these restrictions will further increase the risk for the tenant, thereby reducing the market value.

It follows, therefore, that public landownership combined with long-term building leases will result in lower market values for the *available interests* in land. This, however, is irrelevant from a policy point of view since long-term leases available from private landlords are also worth less than fee simple ownership. The comparison is between 'apples and oranges' and has no significance.

If public landownership is to have any meaning in terms of its effect on 'cost', 'price' or 'market value', it must result in decreases for *any* given interest in land, not simply a creation of a different interest in land. The more meaningful question is whether a public landowner in a monopoly position can provide land by way of building leases at a lower cost than a private landlord.

Government monopoly and land values

The argument is advanced that public landownership will result in lower land values because:

1. public authorities can purchase land well in advance of needs, thereby reducing acquisition charges;

2. public authorities have lower holding costs;

3. land can be re-leased for use in an orderly fashion as required; and

4. land speculation will be eliminated.

Each of these arguments will be examined in detail.

The first argument is one advanced more in favour of land banking than for public landownership since, by definition, all lands would be owned in fee simple at all times. Under a programme of public landownership, public authorities would own all lands in advance of needs and providing they granted flexible interim leases, reacquisition for development purposes would not be an issue. While it is true that the public authorities would, at any point in time, hold an inventory of lands which had lower acquisition costs, the average time that the land is held and hence, the holding costs, would be increased drastically. Hence, if public landownership is to effect a reduction in land values, public holding costs on any given parcel of land must be lower than those in the private markets.

The second reason why public landownership is thought to reduce land values is that *the holding costs for the public sector are lower.* In reality, this is an extension of the first reason given above. Holding costs in the public sector are thought to be lower for two reasons: (i) the interest rate to the public sector is lower and (ii) the public sector knows in advance where land development will occur, therefore land can be released in an orderly fashion. Looking first at the question of lower interest (holding) charges, it is questionable if the public costs are less than the private costs. This proposition arises out of the notion that governments can raise capital at lower apparent interest rates than the private sector. However, this is not true for all junior governments, and would become even less true if governments were to enter into large scale land banking, since their larger borrowing needs would reduce their creditability and increase their cost of capital.

Opportunities foregone

The notion of 'true' versus 'apparent' costs can be extended. A point which is almost always overlooked by advocates of public landownership is that to use actual costs as the criteria is always likely to mislead. What counts is the costs measured in terms of the alternatives foregone in favour of public land assembly. Already municipalities, and to a lesser extent provinces, are complaining of the severe shortages of capital for public projects. If this limited capital is then used for land acquisition purposes, the constraints on other activities would become even more severe.

Viewed in another way, the question of public ownership ought to be put as a choice between more and better public amenities now and the supposed longer-run benefits of public landownership. This is clearly a different proposition than one based solely on the 'cost reductions' accruing from public ownership. Government, for its part, would do more to reduce land values if it was to use its limited funds to open up new areas with servicing. This would, of course, increase some land values immediately because landowners would shift their attention to the newly opened areas, but it would at the same time ensure an adequate supply of land available for development and use.

A second aspect of the lower holding costs for the public sector is the prior knowledge of where development will occur. The insight to predict where development will occur enables the landowner to reduce his holding and servicing costs in areas not about to be developed and hence, lower overall holding costs. Several points mitigate against significant net savings because of this inside knowledge. First of all, the possible directions of future growth are, in general, very limited. Already private developers hold much of the land in the most logical path of development. It is not the direction so much as the timing of development that is in question. Secondly, as the public agency buys fee simple interests in land, the very process of land acquisition will enhance speculation. Any public purchase of land would arouse suspicion and create more speculation. Furthermore, a real conflict will occur between the pricing objective and the planning objective. It is not certain that the best process to achieve the public 'price reduction' objective will result in the best planning. Possibly good planning would be sacrificed to achieve reduced land values.

Costs and subsidies

Finally, and perhaps most important of all, the 'price' arguments advanced for public landownership fail to recognize the differences between *actual costs and opportunity costs* as reflected in the market value. If it is assumed that there will be some economies in acquisition or holding costs for a public agency, will this reduce the price of land? The suggestion is made that these economies could be passed on to developers and consumers by selling at cost or slightly above cost. This completely ignores the opportunity costs of such a move, or viewed another way, this involves a subsidy to some selected beneficiaries. For example, assume the government acquired a property for $100,000 and held it for several years, at which time the actual cost (holding and acquisition costs) totalled $140,000 while the market value was $200,000. If the government elected to sell this land at a price of $140,000 (or lease it at an equivalent rate), they would be ignoring the opportunity costs or true value of the land. In fact, the government would be providing a subsidy of $60,000 or the per annum equivalent.† Yet this is one of the

†Editors' Note: The case of AHOP housing in Ontario and land sold by the Saskatoon land bank cited in the essay by Professor Nowlan illustrates the fact that these subsidies are quickly realized in cash form by original purchasers who re-sell the land or house at its market value.

key arguments put forward by the advocates of public land assembly. For example, an assessment of the Ontario Housing Corporation project of Malvern stated:

> "... Raw land, originally purchased for about $1,000 per acre and now having a 'book value' of about $3,000 an acre, has a current market value of about $32,000 per acre, or more than ten times the original cost. If servicing is added to the raw land costs, the book value of an acre of serviced land is about $36,000 while the market value is about $63,000 to $75,000 per acre. While the market value of the serviced land is only one factor in increased housing costs, the savings possible in this one factor are obviously tremendous."[26]

The 'book value' mentioned is the original cost plus actual holding costs. While it is true that the O.H.C. could sell the land at anything over $36,200 and make a 'profit'; to sell at anything less than $63,000 to $75,000 is to use public funds to subsidize the purchasers of the land. The opportunity cost is $63,000 to $75,000 and the figure of $36,200 is only of historical interest. Consider the alternative case. If these lands had a book value of $36,200 and a market value of $20,000 per acre, then to be consistent, the opportunity cost is $20,000 per acre. The critical point is not whether subsidies should or should not be given, but how these subsidies should be given.

Prices and planners

It is understandable that the advocates of public landownership ignore the subsidy involved in these proposals. It is possible to have considerable sympathy with the long-standing desires of planners to reduce or disguise the costs of planning decisions by reducing the costs of land acquisition for schools, parks, etc. through hidden subsidies. But sympathy is one thing and proper, efficient decision-making is another.

If more and better public amenities can only be achieved by disguising the true cost in terms of foregone alternatives, it is not likely to produce rational decisions for the best use of resources. For example, if planners wish to take land from one use upon which the market places a certain value and put it to a lower use, then, from the viewpoint of society's economic welfare, nothing is gained by allowing them to obtain it cheaply. This merely encourages the wasteful use of land, with less regard for the alternatives foregone.

It must be recognized that any particular planning alternatives, whether positive or restrictive, should be undertaken if they are rational in a cost-benefit sense. If they are not considered desirable on this basis, then nothing is gained by making them worthwhile by hiding some of the costs. Planning decisions in 1977 cost more than they did previously. All decisions relating to land are more expensive, not just public decisions. The high market value of land provides a useful measure of the alternatives foregone through planning decisions. Planners, like politicians, must be accountable for their decisions. If the true costs of planning are hidden, accountability is not possible.

Speculation

It is further argued that the proper use of public lands and a well-drafted lease would eliminate land speculation—however, no case is made to explain why speculation ought to be eliminated, except it may 'ensure a more orderly market'. This presupposes that speculation causes disorder but the opposite is more likely to be the case. In any event, the destabilizing influence of speculation has yet to be demonstrated. In the second instance, it is not clear how a leasehold system would eliminate speculation. Presumably the advocates have in mind a system of lease covenants restricting the rights of tenants to assign or sublet. Restrictions of this type are not apt to provide the necessary flexibility to ensure a smooth operation of the market. Moreover, if rents are reviewed at the time of assignment or transfer of leasehold interests, the problems of isolating land value from improvement (tenant created) values will repeatedly come into focus, necessitating frequent confrontations with the compensation-betterment issue.

Summary of price effects

In summary, the case for public landownership to reduce land values is not convincing. Obviously the public authority could lease land at less than its market value but this represents a granting of a subsidy and not a real or meaningful reduction in price levels. Subsidies tied to the leasing of particular parcels of land will seldom, if ever, represent the optimal allocation of public funds. Since land speculation will only be altered, but not reduced, the only possible source for effecting meaningful price reductions could arise from the orderly release of land for development. However, no significant evidence is available to suggest that a public authority would be any more likely to provide land where and when required, than occurs under the current development process with private ownership. Moreover, any error in judgment in the case of a public monopoly will have more significant implications. In the private and decentralized system operating today, errors in judgment by one landowner are largely offset by the actions of other landowners and, as a consequence, major collective errors are avoided.

X. SYNOPSIS—THE OBJECTIVES AND REALITIES OF PUBLIC OWNERSHIP

To summarize the points raised in this paper, it seems appropriate to review the objectives and determine to what extent they will be achieved or facilitated through public landownership and a leasehold programme.

1. *Compensation-Betterment (Equity Question).* The use of public landownership will not resolve the allocation of increases in property values. It could, however, ensure that the private tenant be placed in a position of having to recover (or maintain a rent level to provide equity) his share from the public, rather than the present system where the public must recover from the private owner. On balance, however, a system of taxation coupled with a more appropriate allocation of direct development costs, would provide the same degree of equity without the administrative burdens of public ownership. Moreover, the

compensation-betterment issue is less relevant today as many local governments have passed forward many direct and indirect costs of development to the private sector.

2. *The Planning Objective.* The introduction of public landownership and the logical extension into a leasehold system will not necessarily result in improved planning. Public ownership, the consolidation of ownership, planning and development functions, may result in technical efficiency but this is hardly a desirable yardstick for action. All of the important planning advantages held in favour of public ownership could be instituted, with less disruption, into our present system. Moreover, with three levels of government and multiple departments at each level, it is not at all certain that technical efficiencies will be realized.

3. *The Price Objective.* Public landownership will not result in a lowering or stabilization of land values unless a steady flow of land, ripe for development where and when required, is made available. Most of the so-called 'price advantages' are really 'cost advantages', the majority of which are debatable. But cost and value or market price are not one and the same. Clearly public landownership would offer no advantages over our present system in terms of monitoring supply.

Contradictory objectives

One final point ought to be observed. The condensed version of three objectives represents a contradictory set of goals. The price objective clearly conflicts with the equity objective. If land is sold at less than market value, the equity objective is defeated. Conversely, if land is sold at market, the price objective is defeated. Similarly, one can cite numerous examples where costs, prices and equity have been placed before 'good planning'. Even if one super organization were to have absolute control over all public lands, it would take the wisdom of Solomon to mediate these conflicts contained within the three objectives.

XI. VARIATIONS ON PUBLIC LANDOWNERSHIP

Advocates of public landownership have come from a wide variety of backgrounds and institutional settings. Variations in the legal and institutional arrangements amongst most Western countries have necessitated a variety of different means to achieve full public landownership. Some countries, because of the early public involvement in land markets find it relatively easy to achieve public landownership while other countries, such as Canada, with their strong bias for private ownership, find it difficult to make serious progress towards full implementation of a programme of public landownership.

The degree of private ownership in a country will create significant problems in respect to implementation of a programme of public landownership. Furthermore, fiscal and political considerations may necessitate some less ambitious programme. Public landownership of all lands, particularly in a country such as Canada with a strong owner-occupied component, would be politically controversial. In addition, the costs would be a significant hurdle. The financial commitment of public funds would necessitate a scale sufficient to interfere with most other social programmes of the day. Finally, the necessary administrative machinery would be more complex and extensive than that envisaged in Great Britain because of our tri-level system of government.

In response to these points a number of 'partial' public ownership schemes have been advanced. These partial measures or systems of land nationalization (the process of gaining public landownership) are advanced as schemes designed to achieve many of the suspected benefits of public ownership without encountering the same degree of financial, political or administrative difficulties. Three main types of 'partial public ownership' schemes have been considered recently.

The first of these three schemes involves either permanent or temporary public ownership of a portion of the lands (those undeveloped at the present time). The second and third schemes involve the creation of new interest in land for the purpose of ultimate full public ownership. While these three programmes overcome some of the controversy surrounding immediate nationalization, they create some distinct problems of their own.

A. Partial and/or temporary fee simple ownership

This concept involves the assembling, under public ownership, of only those lands suitable for development in and around urban areas. This would involve a smaller capital outlay, avoid the political controversy of acquiring owner-occupied and/or currently developed properties, yet encompass most properties within the rural-urban conversion planning in the immediate future. This programme could involve either temporary and limited public ownership (with outright sale at the time of development) or permanent public ownership (under a leasehold scheme). This programme, modelled after the Swedish system, is best demonstrated in the City of Saskatoon in their land banking programme.[27] This programme would give public ownership in the 'active' market areas without the political controversy of acquiring fee simple interests in developed properties. It would, however, still be subject to all the previously raised criticisms of public land banking.

B. Permanent acquisition of development rights

An alternative scheme designed to avoid the problems of immediate public landownership was recommended in the Uthwatt Report. This scheme calls for the acquisition by the public of the *development rights* for all privately owned property. This is equivalent to a restriction on future changes or development. This restriction could only be removed upon payment of a fee to the public authority. This plan could apply to either all privately owned lands or just to privately owned and currently undeveloped lands. The rights of established properties would not be disturbed until such time as development or redevelopment occurred. Such a plan was enacted in Great Britain in 1947 as the Town and Country Planning Act. This plan provides maximum control over development but does not give public landownership. After a brief but disastrous trial, it was abandoned in 1952 but reappeared again in 1967 and 1975 in modified forms. The plan failed largely because private owners delayed development hoping for the removal of the laws with the next change in government.

C. Future acquisition of reversionary (fee simple) interests

Under this scheme, the public authority would acquire a deferred interest in land—the reversionary rights—via a system of statutory leasehold based on the life of existing improvements. This scheme, designed to avoid the political issues and the financial burden involved in immediate acquisition cannot be seriously considered. The essence of the scheme is to implement legislation directed to future generations in the expectation that the government of the day (say eighty years into the future) can then convince the population at that time to agree to a scheme which is politically unacceptable today—a sleight of hand which has no contemporary worth, except to deceive the current population.

XII. CONCLUSIONS

From the preceding discussion, it is obvious that increased public landownership in Canada offers few, if any, benefits, and would involve significant costs. Each of the general goals of such a transfer of fee simple interests could be achieved much more efficiently and cheaply using existing techniques. Further, the claim that more (rather than less) public involvement in land markets is necessary to solve 'problems' in these markets is not substantiated by an analysis of the effects of public landownership on the use and price of land. The proposals for implementation of increased government ownership of land do not clearly indicate the fundamental problems in land markets, nor do they demonstrate that these problems are attributable to private ownership of fee simple interests in land.

Private landowners are not free to either do as they wish with their land or to charge the prices they wish for use of their land or for their interests. Owners are greatly constrained by public and private restrictions through both law and market operation. Further reducing the rights of users of, and of owners of interests in, land is not an efficient or equitable method to achieve social goals of equity and efficient use of scarce resources.

Notes

[1]Passon, S.S., "Land Reserves and Teamwork in Planning Stockholm," *Journal of the American Institute of Planners*, 36:3, pp. 180-181.

[2]Archer, R.W., "The Use of the Site Leasehold System for Planned Urban Development," *Urban Planning and the Property Market*, (London, University College, 1971), p. 5.

[3]*Ibid.*

[4]*Ibid.*; see also du Bois, A.J., "The Long Term Lease as an Instrument of Home Finance," *Appraisal Journal*, XL:3, p. 360; and Shenkel, W.M., "Residential Net Ground Leases," *Journal of Property Management*, 29:4, pp. 180-193.

[5]Government of Hong Kong Press, *Hong Kong 1967*, (Hong Kong, Government Press, 1).

[6]Mill, J.S., *Principles of Political Economy*, Book V:2, para. 5.

[7]Beer, M., *The Pioneers of Land Reform*, (London, 1920), pp. v-vi.

[8]Bryant, R.W., *Land: Private Property - Public Control*, (Montreal, Harvest House, 1972), pp. 221-222.

[9]The two major estates in time are the freehold estate (including the fee simple estate, and the less common life estate, dower, and homestead rights) and the leasehold estate.

[10]Interests less than estates include easements, restrictive covenants and mineral leases.

[11]The holders of the fee simple do so for all time, unless they die intestate and without heirs (in which case it is returned to the Crown), and may grant all or a portion of the interest away to one or more persons: this right is subject only to the rights of the Crown, as are discussed in the text.

[12]For further discussion, see Todd, E.C.E., *The Law of Expropriation and Compensation in Canada*, (Toronto, Carswell, 1976), pp. 32-35.

[13]See *Municipal Act*, R.S.B.C. 1960, Chap. 255, Sec. 370-371, 389-412.

[14]For further discussion, see Hamilton, S.W. and David Baxter, *Landlords and Tenants in Danger - Rent Control in Canada*, (Winnipeg, Appraisal Institute of Canada, 1975); and Hayek, F.A., et. al., *Rent Control: A Popular Paradox*, (Vancouver, Fraser Institute, 1975).

[15]The greatest distinction between freehold and leasehold interests lies in the duration of the interest. The freehold is for an infinite period of time (through inheritance) while leasehold is for a definite period of time. As the tenant (lessee) has the right of exclusive possession—subject to the rights reserved by the landlord in the lease agreement—to all of the property covered in the lease (all or a portion of the property included in the fee simple), the rights of a tenant do not form the basis of the distinction between freehold and leasehold estates.

The concept of 'leasehold' covers a wide variety of interests, differing in duration, character and importance. At one extreme, there might be a tenant holding a property on a term of 999 years—a fee simple owner in all respects save for his liability to pay rent and to respect other lease covenants; at the other extreme are the weekly or monthly tenants renting a cabin or apartment for their own use. The term 'leasehold' is simply an omnibus expression covering the whole spectrum of leases used to make property available for development or occupation. Within this overall expression, it is analytically convenient to distinguish between *occupation* leases and *building* or *ground* leases.

Occupation leases cover a wide variety of tenancies but their distinguishing characteristics are that the rent is usually fixed by reference to the full market value of a developed property. Customarily the terms of these leases tend to be short—rarely longer than 25 years. In contrast, a *building* or *ground* lease typically is for a long term; 99 years was for many years considered typical and indeed, the term '99-year lease' has been used synonymously with building lease. However, the main distinction between occupation leases and building leases relates to the other covenants, not the term. As the expression 'building lease' implies, the tenant covenants to erect the improvements on the site. This explains why the terms building lease, ground lease or site lease are used interchangeably. At the end of the lease, the ownership of the total parcel, land and improvements, reverts to the fee simple owner.

[16]Denman, D.R., "Land Nationalization - A Way Out?", in A.A. Walters, et. al., *Government and the Land*, (London, Institute of Economic Affairs, 1974), Readings no. 13, p. 35.

[17]United Kingdom Ministry of Works and Planning, *Expert Committee on Compensation and Betterment: Final Report* (The Hon. Mr. Justice Uthwatt, Chairman), (London, Cmnd. 6386 H.M.S.O., 1942).

[18]For further discussion, see S.W. Hamilton and David Baxter, *Capital Taxes Pertaining to Real Property*, (Vancouver, Real Estate Institute of British Columbia, 1975).

[19]Government of the United Kingdom, *Leasehold Reform in England and Wales*, (London, Cmnd. 2916 H.M.S.O., 1966), p. 3.

[20]For example, see Spurr, P., *Land and Urban Development*, (Toronto, James Lorimer, 1976), pp. 180-244.

[21]Australian Institute of Urban Studies, *Second Report of the Task Force on the Price of Land*, (Canberra, A.I.U.S., 1972), p. 17.

[22]Siegan, B.H., *Land Use Without Zoning*, (Lexington, Heath, 1972), p. 84.

[23]Government of the United Kingdom, *Leasehold Committee: Final Report*, (Lord Justice Jenkins, Chairman), (London, Cmnd. 792 H.M.S.O., 1950), p. 12.

[24]However, before the apparent advantage of land assembly for redevelopment is dismissed on practical grounds, the supposed weakness in the present system ought to be explored more fully. Essentially land redevelopment under our present system encompasses two problems. The first is the 'hold-out', the individual property owner who either refuses to sell or will only sell at an excessive price which, as a result, will cause the redevelopment to be abandoned or postponed. In effect, the 'hold-out' is hoping to reap a gain arising from the externalities present in the market.

Some caution must be exercised in that one seems to assume the 'hold-out' is always wrong or at least unusually selfish. In many occasions the 'hold-out' may be justified in that his land, taken as a single site, is currently in highest and best use as expressed by the market. If this is the case, society would suffer by forcing the 'hold-out' to sell for redevelopment. The second problem involves the scale of operation in urban renewal and redevelopment—the so-called 'prisoner's dilemma'. 'The prisoner's dilemma' refers to situations where all parties could gain were they to act collectively but it is nevertheless in each single person's own interest to act in a contrary manner. Thus each of several suspects in a criminal investigation may be faced with a choice of confessing (and receiving a light sentence) or remaining silent and risking one of the others' confessing (and receiving a more severe sentence). If each suspect confesses to minimize his own risk, all will suffer more than if none confessed. No individual property owner can justify being the first to redevelop, at least until conditions are so bad that redevelopment by others is obvious or the opportunity cost of not redeveloping is too great. These arguments are not convincing in that most urban renewal and redevelopment is presently carried out without leasehold reversions, power to expropriate or public planning.

The tendency in the past has been to concentrate public renewal and redevelopment in those areas where the political advantages are greatest—the ribbon cutting syndrome. These generally relate to locational considerations (i.e. central city core areas) rather than scale considerations. Historically, however, private urban redevelopment has been the predominant force. Moreover, the private sector has repeatedly demonstrated its ability to adapt to circumvent a 'hold-out' property owner or create a cooperative venture amongst adjoining property owners. Furthermore, it is not abundantly clear that the proposed leasehold system would be superior to our present system with some modification to the expropriation laws to handle the extreme hold-out case. Only in the unlikely event the lease term corresponds to the economic life of the building is one apt to find any advantage to the system of public ownership and leasehold.

[25]Archer, R.W., *The Leasehold System of Urban Development*, (Canberra, Metropolitan Research Trust, 1972), p. 77.

[26]Government of Ontario, *Land Banking: Investment in the Future*, (Toronto, Bureau of Municipal Research, 1973), p. 31.

[27]For further discussion, see Ravis, D., *The Saskatoon Experience*, (Ottawa, C.P.A.C., 1973).

Public Land Banking and the Price of Land

JACK CARR
Associate Professor of Economics,
University of Toronto

and

LAWRENCE B. SMITH
Professor of Economics
Associate Chairman, Department of Political Economy
University of Toronto

THE AUTHORS

Jack Carr was born in Toronto in 1944 and was graduated from the University of Toronto in 1965 before taking his Ph.D. at the University of Chicago in 1971. In 1968 he joined the Department of Political Economy at the University of Toronto and became Associate Professor in 1973. Professor Carr is also a Research Associate of the Institute for Policy Analysis at the University of Toronto. During the 1975-76 academic year he was a Visiting Scholar at the Department of Economics, University of California at Los Angeles.

Professor Carr's publications include: *The Money Supply and the Rate of Inflation*, a study prepared for the Prices and Incomes Commission in 1972; *Cents and Nonsense* (Holt, Rinehart and Winston), a book of popular essays on economic policy, and numerous contributions to scholarly journals. Professor Carr has also contributed to two previous Fraser Institute publications.

Lawrence Berk Smith was born in Toronto, Ontario in 1939. After receiving his B.Com. at the University of Toronto in 1962, he went to Harvard University, where he obtained his Ph.D. in Economics in 1966. Professor Smith has held teaching positions at both Harvard University and the University of Toronto, where he has been a member of the Department of Political Economy since 1966. He is currently a Professor of Economics and Associate Chairman of the Department of Political Economy. In the academic year 1973-74, he was a Visiting Scholar in the Graduate School of Management, University of California at Los Angeles. Professor Smith is a member of the Editorial Advisory Board of the Fraser Institute.

Professor Smith is widely-known as one of Canada's leading specialists in housing and land economics. He is the author of two books on housing, his more recent being *The Postwar Canadian Housing and Residential Mortgage Markets and the Role of Government* (University of Toronto Press, 1974), and is co-editor, with L.H. Officer, of two books on Canadian economics, the more recent being *Issues in Canadian Economics* (McGraw-Hill Ryerson, 1974). Professor Smith is the author of *Anatomy of a Crisis: Canadian Housing Policy in the Seventies*, published by the Fraser Institute in 1977.

Public Land Banking and the Price of Land*

JACK CARR
Associate Professor of Economics, University of Toronto

and

LAWRENCE B. SMITH
Professor of Economics
Associate Chairman, Department of Political Economy
University of Toronto

I. INTRODUCTION

Public land banking is a process in which a government authority assembles land, usually on the periphery of an urban centre, with a view to selling this assembled land for development at some future date.[1] This process has been advocated by a number of economists and public officials in reaction to the sharply rising price of land for new residential construction.[2] They support public land banking on the grounds that it would restrain the rising cost of residential land for new construction, would provide for more orderly urban growth patterns, and would "reserve to the public gains in land values." Because restraint of land prices is crucial to most arguments for public land banks, especially in Canada, and because the process by which public land banks

*This paper is based upon an earlier study "Public Land Banking and the Price of Land" *Land Economics*, 51 (Nov. 1975), pp. 316-330 by the authors.

would restrain land prices has never been clearly stated nor rigorously examined, it is the purpose of this paper to examine the mechanisms by which public land banks might affect residential land values.[3]

Section II of this paper presents a discussion of the arguments usually advanced for the influence of land banks on land prices. Since land banking is generally proposed to eliminate the role of the land speculator, any discussion of the effects of land banking on land prices must include a discussion of the effect of land speculators on land prices. Consequently, Section III discusses the influence of land speculation on land prices under the assumption that the individual speculator cannot affect land prices (i.e. he has no market power). Section IV considers how the arguments of Section III would be modified if participants in the land market had some market power. In this Section, some empirical evidence is presented on the degree of concentration of participants in the land market surrounding Metropolitan Toronto. Section V briefly looks at the case of land banking in Sweden. The conclusions of the paper appear in Section VI.

II. ARGUMENTS FREQUENTLY ADVANCED FOR PUBLIC LAND BANKS

Six reasons are often advanced why the accumulation of large public land holdings will restrain the increase in new residential land values.[4] Of these six reasons the first two require some elaboration. They are listed here and are discussed in Sections III and IV. The remainder are discussed in this section.

1. There is no speculative profit in publicly-owned land prices

A publicly-owned land bank can acquire land in advance of need and sell it for acquisition, servicing and carrying costs with no premium paid for speculators' profits. Because the validity of this argument hinges on the role of speculation, consideration of this point is left for Section III.

2. Large-scale public land holdings can be used to 'flood the market' whenever price increases become 'excessive', moderating the rise in new land prices

Because the accuracy of this argument depends upon the industrial structure in land development, discussion of this point is left to Section IV.

3. Government agencies can acquire land more cheaply than private developers since government agencies possess the power of expropriation

Because government and government agencies are most reluctant to use their expropriation powers in all but extreme cases and because the price in an expropriation is subject to appeal to the courts and to the political arena, governments are likely ultimately to offer a price at the upper end of an uncertain price range to avoid the inconvenience, cost and adverse publicity of an expropriation and/or an expropriation appeal. Moreover, when public agencies fail to offer a fair market price appeals to the courts frequently result in a higher price being awarded. Consequently, the use or threat of expropriation will reduce acquisition costs only against the extreme holdout. However, since extreme holdouts are rare in the case of undeveloped land and since private developers would probably have by-passed them, there is little reason to expect expropriation powers to reduce land acquisition costs, except in isolated cases.[5] Furthermore, there is no reason to expect government agencies to be able to acquire land more cheaply than private developers when expropriation powers are not used. On the contrary, because of the greater possibility of information leaks of a land assembly, government acquisition costs are likely to exceed private costs.[6]

4. Government possesses planning powers that can ensure all of its land is marketed

That is, government agencies will always buy in the right places because government zoning and planning regulations will make their purchases turn out 'right'. Private developers, on the other hand, must charge enough on their correct parcels to cover losses on their incorrect parcels, and hence have a higher cost than government agencies.

Three points can be made about this argument. First, in general, zoning and planning decisions involve uncertainty both for the public and private developer. These decisions are *not* known at the time of land acquisition either to the public or private developer because at that time these decisions have not been made. If such decisions have been made, it is socially optimal for this information to be disclosed to everyone. Second, there is really little reason to anticipate the government agency will be right more often than private developers since the planning and zoning authorities are usually independent and the government agency would have no more information than private developers.[7] Third, if a planning or zoning authority were to make decisions based on the ownership of the land rather than its intrinsic merits, development would proceed in a disorderly and suboptimal fashion. The costs of this for society would be enormous. If planning and zoning decisions are based on the intrinsic merits of a site, private developers are as likely to recognize these merits as are government agencies.

5. Public carrying costs are lower

The true cost of raw land at the time it is to be used is the acquisition cost plus carrying costs, which include interest and property taxes. Because government borrowing costs are generally lower than private borrowing costs, it is often stated that public carrying costs are less. This, however, is uncertain and would depend on the nature and jurisdiction of the government agency. If the agency borrowed without a government guarantee, or with a municipal or even provincial guarantee, it is not clear that its borrowing costs would be lower than a highly rated private corporation. For example, during 1973 the McLeod, Young, Weir average yield on municipal bonds was 8.54 per cent compared to 8.47 per cent for industrial bonds. Moreover, increased government borrowing with a government guarantee would reduce the borrowing and guaranteeing body's credit worthiness and hence increase its borrowing costs. Second, when calculating public carrying costs some increment should be added for the costs of running the government agency created for this purpose.

When these administrative costs are added for the public authority it is doubtful that their carrying costs are less than private costs. Finally, if the higher borrowing costs were a major issue in land prices, a government agency could lend money to development corporations on the security of the land and avoid the ownership issue.

6. Public servicing costs may be lower than private costs because of economies of scale or a reduction in service standards

Although this may be true these points have nothing to do with the question of public land banking or the ownership of land. If government servicing costs were lower, government could provide the services without owning the land. Similarly, it could reduce servicing standards regardless of ownership. However, there is little evidence or presumption that government costs would be lower.

The above discussion indicates that there is no reason to anticipate that public land banking would restrain the rise in the price of land for new residential construction unless such restraint were to be brought about by the reduced speculation or 'flooding the market' mechanisms. The likelihood of these mechanisms restraining land prices is discussed in the next two sections.

III. PUBLIC LAND BANKING AND LAND SPECULATION

The mechanism most often suggested by which public land banking will restrain land price increases is through the elimination of speculative profits. If land banking is to have the effect of lowering prices because it reduces speculation, then two things must occur. First of all, land banking must, in fact, reduce the amount of speculation. Secondly, reduced speculation must lead to reduced upward pressure on land prices. To permit us to focus on the second aspect, we will assume that land banking does, in fact, reduce speculative activity. It is reasonable to assume that land banking would reduce speculative activity because land banking would create additional uncertainty about future land prices as a result of uncertainty as to the location, scale and timing of large land bank acquisitions and sales.[8,9] To the extent that land banking does not increase uncertainty it will not reduce speculation and the postulated mechanism between land banking and price reduction breaks down.

Our purpose in this section is to examine the effect of speculation on land prices. In so doing we must make a distinction between two types of speculation: competitive speculation, where a speculator does not consider himself to have any influence on the market price but believes that the price is going to rise or fall quite independent of his own actions; and monopolistic speculation, where a speculator attempts to buy or control a significant proportion of the existing stock of a commodity with the view of influencing the market price of this commodity.[10] Because monopolistic speculation requires a high concentration of development land under the control of relatively few participants it may be thought of as requiring a structure where land market participants have significant market power, and this is discussed in the next section. This section considers only the case of competitive speculation.

A. Speculation with identical land parcels and independent speculators

To simplify the discussion we make the following assumptions which we later remove:

1. land is a homogeneous commodity, i.e. all land parcels are substitutable one for the other;

2. speculators as a group can be distinguished from non-speculators as a group since the demand of speculators depends on both the current and expected future price while the demand of non-speculators depends only on current prices;[11]

3. the demands of speculators and non-speculators are independent—in particular the activity of speculators does not influence the demand or supply curves of other participants in the market;

4. desired land holdings by speculators at the beginning and the end of the full speculation cycle are zero; and

5. the full effect of speculation is indicated by the change in equilibrium conditions at the end of the full speculation cycle.

Destabilizing speculation

The effect of speculation on land prices can now be determined by introducing some assumptions about speculators' forecasts of prices and comparing the market price of land after the entry of speculators with the price that would have occurred in the absence of speculation. Assume that the real market price of land in the absence of speculation would follow a cyclical pattern with no trend as shown by the solid line in Figure 1.[12] Assume further that speculators correctly forecast the turning points in price movements but that their forecasts overestimate the extent of price fluctuations (both increases and decreases) as shown by the dashed line in Figure 1A. Since speculators expect during period one that the price of land will be higher than the price that would actually have prevailed, they would be net purchasers throughout period one, increasing the net demand and causing the price to rise above the non-speculation price. This 'after speculation price' is indicated by the dotted line in the Figure. During period two, they forecast that the equilibrium price (dashed line) will be lower than the non-speculation price and hence they would be net sellers, causing the market price to be lower than the non-speculative price. Because speculators would be net buyers when the price was high and net sellers when it was low relative to the long-run trend, speculation in this case would be destabilizing and increase price fluctuations compared to the non-speculative case. *This destabilizing speculation would cause speculators to suffer losses.*

FIGURE 1
Price Fluctuations with Destabilizing and Stabilizing Expectations

1A. Destabilizing Expectations

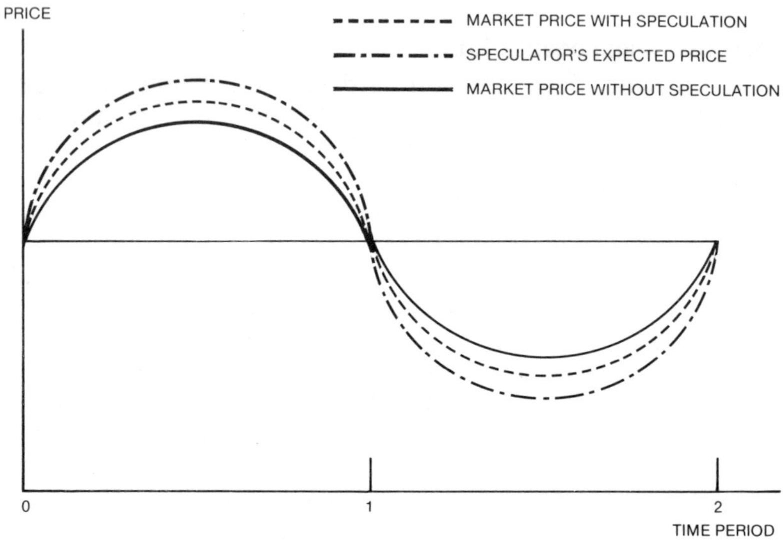

The dashed line represents the speculators' expectations or forecast of the price of land. The speculator expects a higher price in period one than would actually have occurred (the solid line represents what would have happened with no speculators in the market). Accordingly, the speculator will buy land during period one, thus causing the price to be higher than it would otherwise have been. (The dotted line indicates the 'after speculation' price.) In the second period, operating on a forecast of lower prices than would have occurred, the speculator is a net seller. Owing to erroneous forecasts, speculators in this case cause more price fluctuations than would otherwise have occurred – they also lose money.

1 B. Stabilizing Expectations

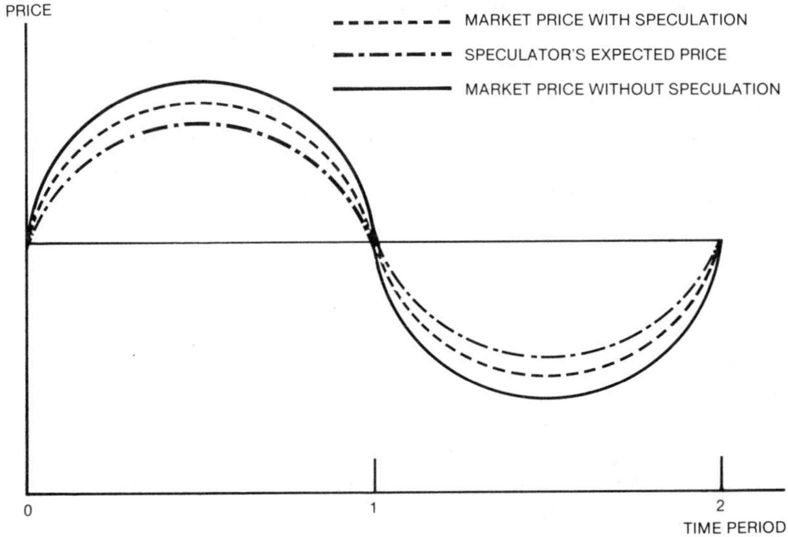

The dashed line represents the speculators' expectations or forecast of the price of land. The speculator expects a lower price in period one than would actually have occurred (the solid line represents what would have happened with no speculators in the market). Accordingly, speculators will sell land during period one, thus causing the price to be lower than it would otherwise have been. (The dotted line indicates the after speculation 'price'.) In the second period, operating on a forecast that prices will be higher than would have occurred, speculators buy land. In this case, speculators will profit from their operations and the market price of land (the dotted line) fluctuates less than it would have in the absence of speculation.

Stabilizing speculation

Assume now that speculators expect smaller price fluctuations than would have occurred, as shown in Figure 1B. In this case, speculators would be net sellers during period one since they expect the price should be lower than the non-speculative market price and hence would mitigate the rise in price during this period. During period two, they would anticipate higher prices than would have occurred and hence they would be net buyers, raising the price of land above the non-speculative level. Because speculators would be net sellers when the price was high and net buyers when it was low, speculation would be stabilizing and reduce price fluctuations. *Speculators would also profit by their activities.*

Thus, it can be seen that:

1. speculation can be stabilizing or destabilizing (i.e. cause the amplitude of price fluctuations to either increase or decrease);

2. if speculation is stabilizing, speculators on average will make profits;[13] if speculation is destabilizing, speculators on average will make losses;[14]

3. speculation increases prices during the purchasing phase of the speculation cycle (i.e. when speculators are net purchasers) and reduces prices during the selling phase of the speculation cycle; and

4. under our assumption that speculator inventories are zero at the beginning and end of the speculation cycle and that non-speculators' actions are independent of speculators' actions, speculation has no effect on the long-run or equilibrium price of land.[15]

B. Speculation with non-identical land parcels

In this section we remove the homogeneity assumption because every land site is unique, if only in location. The primary implication of this non-homogeneity of land is the absence of an organized land exchange, where land is bought and sold and where there exists a daily bid and ask price. This means that costless or low-cost information about land prices is not readily available and land is a relatively illiquid asset whose 'exchange value' is uncertain (i.e. there is a wide discrepancy between the bid and ask price with considerable uncertainty as to what will be the final sales price). Typically, the price at which the land would sell if all buyers and sellers had all of the information is higher than the average price bid, and lower than the average price asked.

These conditions are well suited for the entry of professional arbitragers who attempt to purchase land when it is underpriced, i.e. when the bid price is below that which would prevail with perfect information, and sell it at a price below the original asking price and at or above the full information price. The profit from this arbitrage is not the result of speculation (since the full information price did not change) but rather the result of providing search and information services and for increasing the liquidity of land. Final demanders are willing to pay a price above the full information price or a price slightly above their estimate of this (but above by less than their own search costs), and sellers are prepared to sell below the full information price but above the bid price to effect a quick sale.[16] This process is illustrated in Figure 2. The initial large spread between the bid and ask price allows arbitragers to bid in between but below the full information price. Since the spread declines over time as more information is known, the successful arbitrager can sell at a higher price as the bid price approaches the full information price. Since the bid-ask curves do not shift, the profit is not from speculation but is the return for providing search and information services. A speculative profit would be obtained if the bid and ask curves, and hence the full information price, were to shift up over time.[17]

Although arbitrage (the purchasing of underpriced land in anticipation of a sale at the true or full information price)

FIGURE 2
Bid-Ask Price Adjustments Over Time

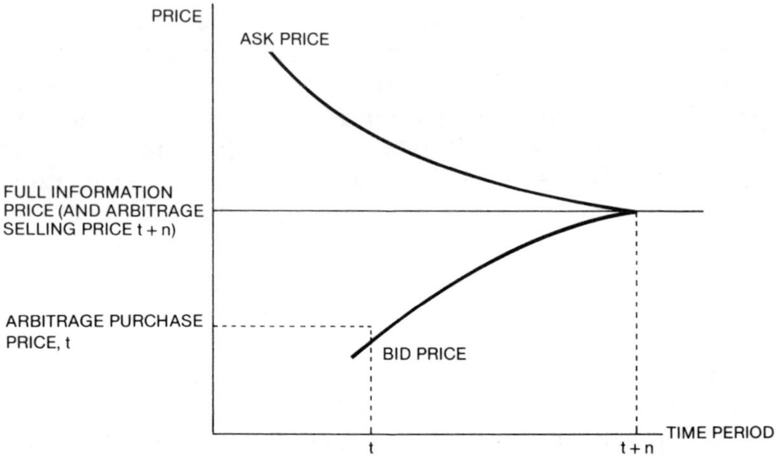

The price that an owner of land asks for the land will usually be much higher than the price that a prospective buyer is willing to bid for the land at the outset. The discrepancy is caused by, among other things, the fact that neither the buyer nor the seller usually know precisely what the land is worth. The 'full information' price line represents the price at which the land would sell if both the buyer and seller knew exactly what the land was worth. Professional arbitragers, who accumulate information about the land market, buy land when bid prices are too low. In this way arbitragers profit from knowing the price at which land should and can be sold. Over time, the bid and ask prices will converge on the full information price as a result of the effects of arbitrage.

is quite different from speculation (the purchasing of land at its full information price in anticipation this will rise) these activities overlap considerably and have many joint costs. These activities are thus often conducted by the same people, and if land banking eliminates some speculative activity it may also reduce arbitrage activity. The reduction of arbitrage will increase search and transactions costs associated with land, and the total cost of buying land (i.e. the price of land plus transactions cost) may therefore increase. Nevertheless, the removal of the homogeneity assumption does not alter our basic conclusions about the role of speculation.

C. Speculation when speculative and non-speculative demand for land are not independent

The assumptions that speculator and non-speculator demand functions are independent and that non-speculator demand depends only on current prices are also inapplicable to the land market. It would be difficult to find a group of pure non-speculators in the land market in the sense of a group whose demands for land did not depend on expectations. Even if we define non-speculators as participants in the land market who primarily need land for their own use,[18] the decision of when rather than if to buy or sell will be affected by the expected price of land, and thus the non-speculator has in a broad sense some speculative motive in the timing of his purchases and sales.

Since the timing of some 'non-speculative' activity depends upon expected future prices, speculators' activity will now affect the demand of non-speculators at a given point in time. The nature of the relationship depends upon the way in which non-speculators' expectations are formulated. If expectations are adaptive, i.e. when actual prices exceed expected prices, expectations for the future are revised upward to incorporate the existing higher than previously expected price, then destabilizing speculation will become more destabilizing. In this case, price changes generate expectations of further price changes in the same direction, and the demand of non-speculators will be higher when speculators expect the price to be above the price level that would have existed in the absence of speculation, i.e. when speculative demands cause prices to rise they generate expectations among 'non-speculators' which increase their demand and hence the price. Similarly, when speculators expect the price to be lower than the price in the absence of speculation, they depress prices and generate expectations of falling future prices. This reduces 'non-speculator' net demand and further depresses prices. On the other hand, when expectations are adaptive and speculation is stabilizing, then stabilizing speculation becomes even more stabilizing. In this case the interdependence of expectations mitigates price fluctuations compared to the independence of behaviour case.

If expectations of non-speculators are regressive, i.e. if price changes generate expectations that prices are 'out of line' and that prices will move in the opposite direction back toward their initial levels, the interdependence of demand causes price fluctuations to be less when speculation is destabilizing and greater when speculation is stabilizing. These modifications, however, do not alter any of our conclusions about the equilibrium effects of speculation since they only affect the amplitude of cyclical fluctuations.

D. Summary of theoretical arguments on land speculation

Our analysis has assumed that speculative holdings at the beginning and end of the speculation cycle are zero. This assumption arises out of the need to define the equilibrium effects of speculation. Pure speculation implies by its very nature that land is bought with the intention of selling it. Speculators do not hold permanent inventories of land. The end of the speculation cycle is defined by two conditions: net purchases of land by speculators is zero (i.e. purchases by some speculators are exactly matched by sales of other speculators) and the total sales of land by speculators over the selling cycle just match the total purchases of land by speculators over the buying cycle. In the real world, equilibrium may never be reached because of shocks which continually alter the expectations formed by speculators. The theoretical 'equilibrium' concept tells us where the system would settle down to, in the absence of further shocks.

The preceding analysis has focused only on the equilibrium effects of speculation and has ignored the temporary or inter-speculation cycle effects. In commodity and security markets this is valid because these markets adjust quickly and the speculation cycle is relatively short. In the land market, however, inter-speculation effects are more important because the speculation cycle can be quite lengthy. This occurs because land markets adjust slowly and because speculative activity is often combined with developmental activity in the sense that speculative purchases are made in advance of future development. The effect of a long speculation cycle is that speculative holdings can be positive for a long period of time and hence exert a considerably longer than temporary upward influence on price. To the extent the public land banks would reduce speculative activity they would reduce this temporary effect. On the other hand, if they create additional uncertainty they could increase the adjustment lag and hence the temporary price effect.

The foregoing analysis suggests that the introduction of public land banking will have little effect on the long-run price of land by altering the level of competitive speculation. Speculation may alter the price of land at any point in time during the speculation cycle, but will not effect the long-run equilibrium level of land prices. Hence, a reduction in this activity will have no permanent effect on prices, although it may affect the temporary price for a long period of time.

IV. LAND BANKING WHERE PRIVATE PARTICIPANTS IN LAND MARKETS HAVE SOME DEGREE OF MARKET POWER

The preceding analysis assumed a competitive industrial structure with a sufficiently large number of market participants that no individual participant feels his actions can have a significant impact upon the price of land. Because of the close substitutability of different land sites this, or a monopolistic competition framework with close substitutes, seems reasonable.[19] However, the amount of competition and degree of substitutability of alternative sites is an empirical question. In the absence of this empirical information for each and every land market, the implications of an alternative market structure, a market structure where the actions of an individual participant can significantly affect land prices, must be considered. In such a market structure a public land bank can exert downward pressure on prices by introducing an element of competition into the market and by thwarting monopolistic speculation.

The theory

Assume a land development industry in which there are a small number of land developers who are the only demanders of land at the full information price, but where there is competition among the initial holders of land in the sale of raw land and among homebuilders and homebuyers in the demand for developed land. Assume further that the presence of arbitragers prevents land developers from exerting any sort of market power in the purchase of raw land, i.e. they only purchase land at the full information price, so that their market power is reflected only in the sale of developed land to homebuilders or homebuyers. In this case, if the developers act in concert by withholding some of the land they have acquired, the selling price of developed land will rise and developers as a group will make monopoly profits. In this situation a public land bank with a large initial land inventory could compete with the cartel in the land development industry and could force land prices down toward the competitive level. The original developers could no longer market their land unless they reduced their price to the competitive level.

However, the above analysis is considerably complicated if the land bank did not start with a large initial inventory, and by the fact that the land bank must replenish its inventory. If the land bank is just beginning it must acquire a considerable stock of raw land. This increases the demand for raw land and if the supply of raw land is not perfectly elastic (an unlikely circumstance) this will increase the price of raw land. In this situation the competitive price of land will rise during the period of land inventory accumulation. Similarly, there will be a temporary upward trend in land prices if the land bank begins to purchase land to maintain its inventory.

A number of implications can be drawn from the above analysis for the introduction of a public land bank in a land market where private participants have market power.

1. The competitive price of raw land will be higher with a land bank than without it because of the increased demand for the land bank inventory.

2. The land in the public land bank can be used, or be threatened to be used, to introduce more competition into the development industry and to force down the price of developed land toward the competitive level.

3. The price of developed land will be reduced if the new competitive price of land is lower than the profit-maximizing price for developers when acting in concert, i.e. if the increase in the competitive price as a result of the introduction of the land bank is less than the spread between the cartelized price and the original competitive price.

4. The increase in the competitive price of land arising from the land bank will be lower:

   a. the smaller the size of the land bank;

   b. the more elastic the developer demand for raw land (i.e. the more sensitive the developer demand for raw land is to price changes);

   c. the more elastic the initial holder supply curve of raw land (i.e. the more sensitive the initial holder supply curve of raw land is to price).

The practical situation

Having looked at the theoretical effects of land banking on land prices where participants in the land market have some degree of market power, it is natural to ask the question, how likely is it that land market participants will have market power? When one thinks about the nature of land markets a strong case can be made for the proposition that under most circumstances land markets will be competitive and hence participants will have no market power. This conclusion arises because of two characteristics of most land markets. Although any parcel of land is unique, if only in location, in most land markets there exists land at different sites that is a close substitute for any given parcel. Having a monopoly of a product for which there are readily available good and close substitutes is having no real monopoly at all. In the second place, the demand for land is a derived demand. Developers do not demand land for its own sake. They need land, in general, as an input in producing residential (or non-residential) structures. In the case of residential accommodations, old houses are a good substitute for new houses. Hence old land is a good substitute for new land. In any metropolitan area, there are a large number of potential suppliers of the finished product housing services (for which land is used as an input). This fact severely limits the market power of participants in the land market.

Although we would expect most land markets to be competitive, one would still like some empirical evidence to confirm this fact. Recently, a number of studies have been done for the market for undeveloped land surrounding Metropolitan Toronto. The most comprehensive of these studies was done by J.R. Markusen and D.T. Scheffman. Their results are reported in this volume. They collected a sample of 71,600 acres of undeveloped land between 30 and 45 minutes commuting distance from the core of Metropolitan Toronto and found that the four largest landholders owned in total only between 17.5 per cent and 22.7 per cent of all land in the sample (the range depending upon which definition of ownership was used). These four-firm concentration ratios are low by industrial organization standards. In surveying this evidence, Markusen and Scheffman conclude that "under all sets of assumptions presented . . . ownership concentration in the entire sample was far too low to suggest market power and resource misallocation under commonly used industrial organization standards."[20] In other studies done for the Ontario Economic Council, using a different data set, R.A. Muller and Coopers and Lybrand arrived at essentially the same conclusions.[21]

Although these results support our conclusion that participants in the land market are unlikely to have any significant degree of market power, it nevertheless does not rule out this possibility. If market power does exist in the land market there is no reason why governments should use land banks to counteract this market power. Governments have at their disposal more traditional anti-trust remedies to counteract market power.

V. ACTUAL EXAMPLES OF LAND BANKING: THE CANADIAN AND SWEDISH CASES

Although there are examples of governments in Canada assembling land on the periphery of urban centres with a view to selling this assembled land for development at some future date,[22] this land assembly by governments has been small relative to private sector assembly of land. In fact, most proponents of government land banks criticize this lack of government involvement. Dennis and Fish place a large part of the blame for the meagre role governments have played in land banking on the role of the federal government, "A large measure of responsibility for the failure of the public sector to act to curtail rapidly increasing land prices must thus be placed on the federal government . . . From 1954 to 1970 CMHC lent $6.5 billion for housing, one third of it for low income housing. During that same period, $90 million was advanced for land assembly. In 1970, $965 million was put into housing and $20 million into the land assembly programs. 44 per cent of the meagre land assembly funds have gone into centers of less than 30,000 in population. They have not been used to deal with the cost problems in the largest cities."[23] Apart from any aversion by governments for land banking, constitutional problems have hampered government involvement. Since problems of land development in Canada are clearly a provincial responsibility, the role of the federal government in land development has been a very limited one.

In 1969, the Federal Task Force on Housing and Development "... concluded that to achieve both cost efficiency and planning effectiveness, municipalities ... should acquire and service all or a substantial proportion of the land required for urban growth within their boundaries. It believes, further, that the Federal government should be prepared to make loans to municipalities for that purpose."[24] No action was taken on these Task Force recommendations. As a consequence of the limited Canadian experience with land banking it is difficult to test the propositions advanced in this paper concerning land banking and land prices using Canadian data. In fact, these are difficult propositions to test, in general. Nevertheless, it is useful to look at a country where government land banking is a significant force in the land market and see what lessons, if any, we can learn from this country.

Sweden

Land banking is much more common in Europe than in North America. Land banking has been carried to its fullest in Sweden.[25] Local governments in Sweden have acted as developers since before 1900, and in the earlier 1970s approximately three-quarters of all new houses were built on land owned by Swedish municipalities. Although land banking policy is carried out in Sweden at the local level, national government loans have been made available since 1968 to municipalities to assist them in financing their land banks.

During the 1960s, Swedish municipalities were faced with increased costs of purchasing new land. To get around this problem, Swedish municipalities, since 1968, have had the right to expropriate land for future development at the price of the land prevailing 10 years prior to the expropriation. Land values cannot even be increased to keep in line with general inflation. Such a policy is tantamount to confiscation of real property by the government and in all probability would not be allowed by the courts in either Canada or the United States. In addition, such a policy makes the life of a private Swedish land developer very precarious. It is not surprising that such an expropriation policy, combined with a policy of selling the developed land at acquisition plus servicing costs, keeps the price of housing low in Sweden. However, such a policy does not keep the price of housing low. As Neutze has noted "various controls keep down the price of land and even the price at which the completed house is sold. But because of under-supply the value on the market is much higher and a windfall gain goes to the first purchaser, or is shared between him and the builder."[26]

Swedish land banking has thus succeeded in keeping the price of developed land low. However, this has been a trivial success since Swedish land banking has not succeeded in significantly influencing the price of houses. What the land banking policy accomplishes is to take away gains of increased land values from the original owners of land and give these gains to builders or first-time homebuyers. How this is a socially desirable policy is hard to see. In addition to this redistributive effect of Swedish land banking there is a misallocative effect. The dominance of Swedish municipalities in the land market artificially keeps the price of raw and developed land too low. This suppresses the normal allocative role that prices play in all markets. Land which is better suited for agricultural purposes may be developed for urban use. When the incentive to economize on land is gone, land for urban use may be developed at too low a density.

Because of the confiscatory nature of Swedish expropriation policy, Swedish land banking is unlikely to be very relevant to the Canadian case. It is, however, very useful in demonstrating the dangers of carrying land banking policy to extremes.

VI. CONCLUSIONS

The preceding theoretical analysis indicates that the introduction of a public land bank is unlikely to reduce the price of developed land. Arguments that it will reduce the price by reducing the level of speculation, allowing cheaper land assembly and enabling lower carrying costs and servicing costs, are all unfounded. Land banks cannot permanently affect land price. The main rationale for public land banks is to counteract market power of land market participants. However, this reduces land prices only if the price increase resulting from market power exceeds the increase in the competitive price arising from the introduction of the land bank. Finally, even in this situation the arguments in favour of land banking are not necessarily persuasive since the government has at its disposal other techniques to introduce more competition in the land development industry. The enforcement of anti-trust legislation plus the elimination of any barriers-to-entry would appear to be a more efficient way of eliminating any monopolistic practices in the land development industry.

Notes

[1]For a general discussion of land banking, see Kamm 1970, pp. 6-7.

[2]Proposals for public land banking in Canada include the Federal Task Force on Housing and Urban Development 1969, pp. 40-43 and M. Dennis and S. Fish 1972, pp. 315-343. Proposals in the United States include National Commission on Urban Problems 1968, p. 250; President's Committee on Urban Housing 1969, p. 228; and Advisory Commission on Intergovernmental Relations 1963, pp. 161-162.

[3]The other objectives of controlling land use patterns and reserving gains for the public are not examined here. It should be noted, however, that governments have a variety of techniques including zoning, taxing and servicing powers to meet these objectives. Since we are concerned only with the price objective, an implicit assumption in our analysis is that land use patterns will be unaffected by the land bank except as a response to price changes, if any, generated by the land bank.

[4]See, for example, M. Dennis and S. Fish 1972, p. 325.

[5]Extreme holdouts are only of significance when they have some monopoly power, e.g. their piece of property is unique and crucial to the development. Only in these cases can the government acquire land at a cheaper price than the private developer. In these cases the government through its coercive power confiscates the monopoly profits.

[6]There is another argument why government may have higher average acquisition costs. There are certain skills at acquiring and assembling land. If a private developer is inefficient in the use of these skills he will lose money and go out of business. With an inefficient government agency there seems to be no equivalent 'law of the jungle' of survival of the fittest.

[7]A classic illustration of this independence is the so-called 'Spadina Expressway' in Toronto. In this case one governmental agency acquired land for an expressway, demolished dwellings, installed sewers and drains and commenced construction, only to have the project halted on appeal by another government body.

[8]It is possible that public land banking will push the speculation back further with respect to the time of development, rather than reduce speculation, i.e. to the stage prior to acquisition by the land bank.

[9]It should be noted that the uncertainty assumed pertains only to price and not zoning or development patterns. This is inconsistent with the use of land banks for land use planning and orderly development, and follows solely from uncertainty as to the timing of government activity within an unknown subset of a planning area.

[10]For a discussion of different forms of speculation see Meade 1950, and Lerner 1946, p. 69. It should be noted it is monopolistic speculation which leads people to condemn speculation and believe that *all* types of speculation are *per se* bad.

[11]One problem with this distinction is that nearly everyone might be put in the speculation class. An alternative approach is to consider the effects of an additional set of transactions made by an additional group of people who shall be called 'speculators'. This avoids the problem of defining speculation. For an illustration see Friedman 1960.

[12]An upward or downward trend can easily be introduced and would not affect the analysis. For a more rigorous analysis see Baumol 1959.

[13]This result ignores transactions and carrying costs.

[14]For evidence on speculation forecasting see Houthakker 1957 and Stein 1962.

[15]See Carr and Smith 1975 for a more rigorous analysis of the effects of speculation in land markets.

[16]In this way the 'arbitrager' in the land market reduces the spread between the bid and ask price in much the same way as arbitragers (called brokers or dealers) reduce the spread between the bid and ask price in the commodity and stock markets.

[17]Arbitrage may also arise because of the different characteristics of each land parcel. Differences in size, shape, location, soil, topography, condition of existing dwellings, etc., may not be reflected consistently in the per acre price of lands providing an opportunity for arbitrage and return for information.

[18]This includes developers whose sole function is to build structures for sale or rent.

[19]See Chamberlain 1933.

[20]See study by J.R. Markusen and D.T. Scheffman prepared for the Ontario Economic Council, Ch. 5, p. 46.

[21]See the studies by R.A. Muller, 1976, and Coopers and Lybrand, 1976 prepared for the Ontario Economic Council.

[22]The two best known examples of land assembly by governments in Canada are the land assembly in the early fifties in Malvern, in the eastern part of what is now Metropolitan Toronto and the land assembly programmes in Saskatchewan (for the cities of Saskatoon and Regina).

[23]M. Dennis and S. Fish 1972, p. 320.

[24]Federal Task Force on Housing and Urban Development 1969, p. 40.

[25]For a discussion of land banking in Sweden see Peter Heimburger 1973 and G. Neutze 1973.

[26]G. Neutze 1973, p. 71.

References

Advisory Commission on Intergovernmental Relations. 1963. *Urban and Rural America: Policies for Future Growth.* Washington, D.C.: U.S. Government Printing Office.

Baumol, W.J. 1959. "Speculation, Profitability and Stability." *Review of Economics and Statistics* (August): pp. 263-271.

Carr, J. and Smith, L.B. "Public Land Banking and the Price of Land" *Land Economics*, 51 (Nov. 1975) pp. 316-330.

Chamberlain, E. 1933. *Monopolistic Competition.* Cambridge, Mass.: Harvard University Press.

Clower, R.W. 1954. "Productivity, Thrift and the Rate of Interest," *Economic Journal* (March): pp. 107-115.

Coopers and Lybrand, *Report to the Ontario Economic Council: Data on Land Available for Housing in Toronto CMA*, Ontario Economic Council, Toronto, 1976.

Dennis, M. and Fish, S. 1972. *Programs in Search of a Policy: Low Income Housing in Canada.* Toronto: Hakkert.

Federal Task Force on Housing and Urban Development. 1966. *Report.* Ottawa: Queen's Printer.

Friedman, M. 1960. "In Defence of Destabilizing Speculation," in *Essays in Economics and Econometrics* ed. R.W. Pfouts. Chapel Hill: University of North Carolina Press.

Friedman, M. 1962. *Price Theory.* Chicago: Aldine.

Heimburger, P. 1973. *The Use of Municipal Land Ownership as an Instrument in Influencing the Structure of Urban Development: Sweden's Experience*, OECD Paper U/EWV/73.8.

Houthakker, H.S. 1957. "Can Speculators Forecast Prices." *Review of Economics and Statistics* (May): pp. 143-151.

Kamm, S. 1970. *Land Banking: Public Policy Alternatives and Dilemmas.* Washington, D.C.: The Urban Institute.

Lerner, A. 1946. *The Economics of Control.* New York: MacMillan.

Markusen, J.R. and Scheffman, D.T. *Urban Land Development: Speculation and Market Structure*, published for the Ontario Economic Council by the University of Toronto Press, Toronto, forthcoming 1977.

Meade, J.E. 1950. "The Degree of Competitive Speculation." *Review of Economic Studies* (August): pp. 159-167.

Muller, R.A. *The Market for New Housing in the Metropolitan Toronto Area*, preliminary report submitted to the Ontario Economic Council, Toronto, 1976.

National Commission on Urban Problems. 1968. *Building the American City* Washington, D.C.: U.S. Government Printing Office.

Neutze, G.M. *The Price of Land and Land Use Planning Policy Instruments in the Urban Land Market*, OECD, Paris, 1973.

President's Committee on Urban Housing. 1969. *A Decent Home.* Washington, D.C.: U.S. Government Printing Office.

Stein, J.L. 1962. *The Nature and Efficiency of the Foreign Exchange Market.* Essays in International Finance: Princeton University.

Ownership Concentration in the Urban Land Market: Analytical Foundations and Empirical Evidence

JAMES R. MARKUSEN
Assistant Professor of Economics
University of Western Ontario

and

DAVID T. SCHEFFMAN
Associate Professor of Economics
University of Western Ontario

THE AUTHORS

James R. Markusen is a native of Minnesota, where he was born in 1948. Now an Assistant Professor of Economics at the University of Western Ontario, he was educated at Boston College where he received his Bachelor of Arts degree in 1970, and his Ph.D. degree in 1973. He has served as a consultant to the Ontario Economic Council, and at the present time is a consultant to the Federal-Provincial Task Force on Supply and Price of Serviced Residential Land.

Professor Markusen's scholarly publications include: "Timing of Residential Land Development: A General Equilibrium Approach" (with D.T. Scheffman), *Journal of Urban Economics*, forthcoming, 1977; and "Ownership Concentration and Market Power in the Urban Land Market" (with D.T. Scheffman), *Review of Economic Studies*, forthcoming, 1977.

David Scheffman is a native of Minnesota, where he was born in 1943. He received his Bachelor of Arts degree in mathematics from the University of Minnesota in 1967, and his Ph.D. in economics from the Massachusetts Institute of Technology in 1971. He was also elected to Phi Beta Kappa. Dr. Scheffman joined the faculty of the University of Western Ontario in 1971, where he now holds the rank of Associate Professor of Economics.

Among his publications, Professor Scheffman has authored a book (with J.R. Markusen) entitled *Urban Land Development: Speculation and Market Structure*, to be published by the University of Toronto Press in 1977.

Ownership Concentration in the Urban Land Market: Analytical Foundations and Empirical Evidence *

JAMES R. MARKUSEN
Assistant Professor of Economics
University of Western Ontario
and
DAVID T. SCHEFFMAN
Associate Professor of Economics
University of Western Ontario

I. INTRODUCTION

The recent boom in land and housing prices in most major Canadian metropolitan areas has generated a growing amount of public controversy. One of the most popular targets to blame for this rapid price inflation has been the asserted existence of 'monopoly' landowners or developers. Works by Dennis and Fish (1972) and Spurr (1976) in particular have left the impression that ownership of undeveloped land in the Toronto area is concentrated in the hands of a small number of large developers who have caused land and house prices to rise above competitive levels. Both works have attracted considerable public attention, as is evidenced in Lewis (1972) and Lorimer (1976).

*The authors would like to thank Thomas J. Courchene for helpful comments and suggestions.

Yet in spite of this interest in the role of large developers in determining land and house prices, there has not been a careful examination of:

1. what is meant by concentration in the ownership of land and how can it be measured;

2. the relationship between ownership concentration and the existence of market power (market power exists if some agents are large enough to affect *market* prices); and

3. the effects of exercised market power on land prices and the rate of land development.

As will be argued below, approaches to these questions that are borrowed from analyses of other markets are often quite inappropriate for the land market. The first purpose of this paper is to address these three questions. The second purpose is to apply the results of this analysis to an empirical investigation of ownership concentration and market power in the Toronto land market. The paper will then conclude with a discussion of the implications for public policy that are provided by the analytical and empirical results.

We would like to point out to the reader that much of what follows is drawn from Markusen and Scheffman *Speculation and Monopoly in Urban Land Development: Analytical Foundations with Evidence for Toronto.* In that book, which is the result of a study funded by the Ontario Economic Council, the interested reader will find a thorough analysis of the issues presented here plus original data on the Toronto land market which cannot be presented in this article. The data presented in Section VI below are drawn from the empirical material, and readers are referred to the full book for data such as the holdings of individual large developers and the linkages among these developers. The reader is also referred to that book for a detailed analysis of land speculation and for empirical evidence on the land assembly process in Toronto.

II. OWNERSHIP CONCENTRATION AND MARKET POWER

The major source of concern by economists about the presence of monopoly elements in any market is that monopoly elements have *market* power, i.e. they are able to distort *market* prices from the levels that would be achieved if the market were competitive. Economists generally agree that there are two conditions necessary for the existence of agents possessing market power in any given market. The first of these conditions requires that there be a small number of agents who are large enough in aggregate for their actions to have a significant effect on total market supply. If this condition exists we say that there is significant *concentration* in the market.

The second condition necessary for the existence of market power in any particular market is that there are significant barriers-to-entry. A barrier-to-entry is any impediment to the entry of new firms into the market. If there are no significant barriers-to-entry in a given market, market power will not exist even if there is significant concentration, since the threat of entry of new firms and hence of potential competition will keep price at competitive levels.

Defining the market

To verify whether these two conditions exist in any market, the first problem is to define the *market.* In any context the market must be defined so that it includes all products whose prices (or alternatively, sales) are jointly determined. For example, sales of new Chevrolets do not constitute a market. This is because Fords, Plymouths, etc., are very good substitutes for Chevrolets, and it is therefore unrealistic to think of the price (or alternatively, the sales) of Chevrolets as being determined independently of the price of other cars. Thus, although General Motors is the only producer of GM cars, it is not a monopolist (i.e. the *only* seller in the market), although it is probably large enough to have market power.

Let us now discuss these general concepts of market power, concentration, barrier-to-entry, and definition of the market, in the context of the land market. For simplicity, let us confine ourselves to *residential land*, i.e. land which can be used for residential purposes. What is the definition of 'the' residential land market in a particular urban area? According to our earlier discussion, the definition should include all types of land for which the prices are jointly determined. The easiest way to go about defining the residential land market is to first determine what land can be *excluded* from the market.

Since among the most important determinants of where people live is where they work, all land which is not within 'reasonable' commuting time of employment centres can be excluded. This exclusion defines the outer boundaries of the market. The second type of land which can be excluded from the market is land which because of topographic features, lack of servicing, zoning, etc., is not suitable for residential use. The last type of land which can be excluded is land which has been developed for industrial or commercial use. This latter type of land can, in principle, be reconverted for use as residential land, but this could not occur to a significant extent except over a considerable period of time.

Developed land included

Now that we have seen what land can be excluded from our definition of the residential land market, let us see what land is left. Included in the land which is left is, of course, developable land within reasonable commuting distance. Notice also that *developed* residential land (within reasonable commuting distance) is included in our definition of the market. This must be the case because a developed residential lot, (e.g. a lot with dwelling), is a very good substitute for vacant land which can be built on for residential use. One consequence of this is that an increase in the price of residential building lots always *occurs simultaneously* with increases in the prices of 'used' houses since the increase in used house prices reflects an increase in the implicit value of their lots.

Concentration yields power

We have now seen that the market for residential land must be defined to include developable and developed residential land within reasonable commuting distance from employment centres. From this we can determine the conditions under which potential market power will exist in this market. The critical difference between the land market and most other markets is the existence of natural absolute entry barriers in the land market. For an agent to 'enter' the land market, he must purchase land from an existing agent in the market. This situation is entirely different from the automobile market, for example, where a new firm could, in principle, go into the automobile manufacturing business by building a new factory and producing its own brand of cars. In the land market, however, 'new' land cannot be created. Therefore, because of the natural absolute barrier-to-entry in the land market, 'significant' concentration of land ownership is, itself, sufficient for the existence of potential market power.†

What determines whether the concentration of ownership of *undeveloped* land is 'significant' or not by this definition? Two key elements are location of the large landowners' holdings, and the growth rate of the urban area. For example, if one large landowner owns *all* the undeveloped land around a city, with static or falling population, he will not have market power, since he owns a commodity for which there is little or no demand. The other key element in the determination of the significance of a given level of concentration is the price elasticity of demand for land (i.e. the responsiveness of the demand for land to changes in the price of land). In the next section we will discuss how these two key elements determine the significance of a given level of concentration.

III. MARKET POWER IN THE LAND MARKET

In the preceding section we showed that the existence of 'significant' concentration in the ownership of land would be sufficient to ensure the existence of potential market power in the land market. We will now discuss how the presence of market power will affect the functioning of the land market.

†Editors' Note: However, the attributes of land can be changed by investment, rezoning, etc. In the short term, this may not be a significant factor, but in the long term, it could reduce the natural barrier-to-entry in the land market.

In any market, the *exercise* of market power requires a distortion of market supply from competitive levels. For example, in the textbook story of the simple monopolist, the monopolist restricts supply to raise price. As we will see in the next section, the exercise of market power in the land market is more complicated than the simple textbook model, because of the inherent intertemporal nature of suppliers' decisions in the land market. However, before adding these complications, let us first see how a distortion in supply in a given year affects market prices in that year.

The maximum increase in prices

To take the simplest possible case, consider a city where one large landowner owns *all* the *undeveloped* land. As we indicated in the previous section, if the population of the city is not growing, the large landowner will not have significant market power. Therefore, to analyze a situation where market power exists, suppose the population growth is such that the demand price for housing (and therefore that of residential land), for the current stock, is growing at x per cent per year. A reasonable estimate of x under normal conditions would be approximately the net growth rate of families of homeowning age in the city plus the rate of increase of per capita income.[1] Under this circumstance, the maximum percentage the price can rise is x per cent, and this occurs only if the large landowner withholds *all* his land from the market (i.e. he does not allow any increase in the housing stock).

Let N be the total number of housing units in the city. Suppose the large landowner supplies enough land to the market to increase the number of housing units by n. Then the percentage change in housing units is 100 × (n/N). Let us denote this percentage change as y per cent. Most measures of the demand for housing in Canada estimate the price elasticity of demand to be about one. This means that a 1 per cent decrease in house prices will lead to about a 1 per cent increase in demand for a constant population. This implies that if the large landowner provides a supply of land which increases the housing stock by y per cent, the rise in house prices will be approximately (x − y) per cent for population increases of x per cent.

Since land costs are a proportion of total housing costs, in the short run the elasticity of demand for *land* is probably less than one. A reasonable lower bound for this elasticity is .25. That is, a 4 per cent change in the price of building lots is associated with a 1 per cent change in demand. Thus while a 1 per cent decrease in new housing caused by a developer withholding building lots will increase the price of housing by about 1 per cent, it is likely to increase the price of building lots by about 4 per cent.

The large landowner will distort prices from competitive levels if he distorts y from its competitive level. However, how much distortion is possible? In most cities capacity in the construction industry will at most permit a 5 per cent increase in supply in one year, i.e. y per cent = 5 per cent at most. This means that the *smallest* the rate of change in house prices could be under competitive conditions would be (x − 5) per cent. Therefore, if the construction industry had a capacity of 5 per cent of the existing stock and the landowner withheld *all* land from the market, he would distort *house* prices by *at most* 5 per cent. If the short-run price elasticity of demand for land was as small as .25, he would distort *land* prices by at most 20 per cent by withholding *all* land.†

Monopoly power can't explain the boom

By distorting land prices by 20 per cent in this manner, however, the monopolist would be selling nothing at all and receiving no revenue—not a very profitable strategy. Instead, he might wish to supply only half his capacity, thus causing price to rise above competitive levels by 10 per cent. In the short run, a 50 per cent reduction in supply in exchange for a 10 per cent rise in price is not profitable. Because these price effects are cumulative over time, however, it may in fact pay the monopolist to restrict supply to a lesser extent over a long period of time. Thus we are not arguing that the effects of exercised market power are too insignificant to worry about.

†Editors' Note: The assumption of a price elasticity of demand of 1.0 is critical to this analysis. In the short run it could be lower and, as a consequence, the distortion would be greater.

Although we have shown that the distorting effects of exercised market power will be small in any given year, if this power is continually exercised over many years, the cumulative effect would certainly be significant. If, for example, a monopoly developer was able to restrict development enough to raise prices 2 per cent per year above the competitive level, for 10 years, prices would be 22 per cent higher at the end of the 10-year period under monopoly than they would have been under competition. However, the reader can, and should, conclude from the argument which we have advanced that exercised market power cannot have been the important cause of the urban real estate boom of the 1970s, since the *yearly* price increases far exceed a monopoly landowner's ability to raise prices.

IV. OWNERSHIP CONCENTRATION: DYNAMIC EFFECTS

The previous two sections provided answers to two of the three questions posed in our introductory remarks, i.e. we have shown how concentration in the land market should be defined and measured, and we have analyzed the relationship between ownership concentration and market power. To deal with the third question (the effects of exercised market power on land prices and the rate of development) we must explicitly recognize the intertemporal nature of the development process.

Two features of the land market require an intertemporal analysis. First, unlike other goods, the supply of land of given characteristics (e.g. commuting time to employment centres) is fixed. Any decision to develop land for residential use, therefore, necessarily reduces the total stock of undeveloped land with these characteristics. The second important feature of the land market is embodied in the demand for land. Consumers receive satisfaction from the total stock of land they own. Because land is among the most durable of goods, increased sales of developed land in the current period will decrease demand for new residential land in future periods.

Development decisions and time

Let us now consider the determinants of the amount of land supplied to the market over time by a small developer. (In this context a developer is small if variations in his supply have no appreciable effect on market price.) The developer must determine how much land to develop in the current period and how much land to hold for future development. There are two necessary conditions which must be met if an individual small developer is willing to develop *any* of his land in the current period. *First*, the price received by the developer must at least equal development costs plus the agricultural value of the land. The relevant price is, of course, the price of a serviced lot or the price of a lot plus house, depending on whether the developer is selling lots to builders or finished houses to consumers. The *second* necessary condition for a developer to be willing to develop and sell land in the current period is that he does not expect market prices to rise sufficiently in the future for it to be profitable to wait to sell. If current prices are much lower than the developer expects future prices to be, he will withhold land in the current period. If all developers are small, these two conditions will together determine the total amount of land developed and the distribution of land development over time.

Now let us consider the determinants of the amount of land supplied to the market over time by a large developer. (In this context a developer is large if variations in his supply can have an appreciable effect on market price). The decision of the large developer on current versus future development involves two extra complications. First, a substantial increase in his supply in the current period will depress current prices. Second, a substantial increase in his supply in the current period will reduce demand for new residential land in future periods.

With these added complications the conditions determining the pattern of the large developer's supply over time are as follows. *First*, the large developer will be willing to develop land in the current period up to the point where the change in sales revenue from the last unit of land sold (which economists call marginal revenue) is at least equal to development costs plus the present value of the stream of agricultural revenue foregone. Assuming that the developer must lower price on all land sold in order to increase sales by one unit (i.e. he cannot charge different prices to different customers) then marginal revenue from that last sale is less than the price received. This is true because some revenue is lost by selling all the rest of the land at a slightly lower price than would have occurred without that last sale. Marginal revenue is, therefore, the price of the last unit sold *minus* the loss of revenue on the rest of the land sold due to the price decrease needed to sell the last unit. The *second* necessary condition for the monopolist to be willing to develop some land in the current period is that the large developer does not expect future demand to rise so fast that he could increase his profits by withholding all land until the second period.

On the average over time, marginal revenue will be less than price. Thus there will be such levels of demand that a competitive industry will develop more land at a lower average price than a concentrated industry. This is the usual result of economic theory for most types of markets. Specifically for the land market, if the growth rate of the city is such that a competitive industry would not develop all of the land in the foreseeable future (demand is relatively low), then it can be demonstrated that concentrated industry would develop even less. On the other hand, a technical analysis will also demonstrate that it does not necessarily follow that a concentrated industry will develop less land in *each* period. Nevertheless, total consumer payments for land over time will be larger under monopoly than under competition.

V. OWNERSHIP CONCENTRATION IN THE TORONTO REGION

The preceding sections of this paper attempted to arrive at a definition of ownership concentration in the land market and to link that definition to the existence of market power. In a dynamic context, the effects of market power on the rate of land development and on the movement of land prices over time were also analyzed. These results have identified a number of interesting empirical questions, the answers to which are critical in assessing the impact of present government policies on, and in recommending new policies for, the land market.

Using Metropolitan Toronto as a case study, we shall now address the question of whether or not there is sufficient concentration in the ownership of undeveloped land to suggest the existence of significant market power. Toronto is of particular interest due to rapid increases in land prices in the early 1970s and the coincident charges of a number of people that there is significant ownership concentration in Toronto. We have found the research on which these charges are based to be highly unsatisfactory.

Errors in the Spurr Report

A few words should be said at this point concerning previous research on the subject of ownership concentration in the Toronto land market. In particular, we should like to comment on the work of Spurr (1974) which has been popularized by Lorimer (1976). We regard a portion of Spurr's work as open to serious misinterpretation because it presents statistics that can be used to demonstrate high concentration no matter what the true market structure happens to be. Spurr presents data (p. 112) that is derived from the Urban Development Institute's Development Corporations Survey. He then added up the total amount of acres reported in this survey and implies (but does not explicitly state) that this total represents the appropriate universe of land for compiling ownership concentration figures. What is essentially reported then, is, for example, the amount of land held by the top four developers as a percentage of land held by the top forty developers. Not surprisingly, one finds that concentration of ownership is high (the top four own 58.65 per cent of the total and the top six own 76.74 per cent).†

This methodology produces meaningless results. The reason is that it grossly underestimates the actual amount of undeveloped land that is available for future development. Our research demonstrates that there are literally hundreds of agents currently holding land in the Toronto area. Many of these agents are private individuals who hold enough land to rank in the top 25 land holders. Such individuals were not, of course, picked up in the UDI survey. Further, well over 100 small development and speculative holding companies that were not surveyed by UDI, hold acreage well in excess of Toronto's development needs for the next ten years. The fact is that the *proper* universe of undeveloped land for estimating ownership concentration is somewhere in the neighbourhood of three times larger than the figure Spurr derived from the UDI survey.

Errors in Dennis and Fish

A similar problem is found in a book by Dennis and Fish (1972). They argue that there is significant concentration of landownership in Toronto on the basis of the fact that the top six developers in Toronto control enough land to satisfy the estimated land requirement for ten years. We must emphasize that the relevant questions are what percentage of the total universe do the top developers hold and what percentage of actual development do the top developers account for? The former question is addressed in this study and the latter is addressed in a study by Muller (1976). Muller's study shows that the ten largest subdividers accounted for 59 per cent of dwelling unit approvals during the period 1971-1973 and that concentration falls off rapidly thereafter, the top 24 accounting for 75.5 per cent. It is most

†Editors' Note: In contrast to Spurr's results, a study by Coopers and Lybrand (1976) surveying approximately the same developers but correctly relating their holdings to the total developable residential land in the metropolitan Toronto area indicated that the six largest land holders and developers control less than 40 per cent of the developable land.

unfortunate that this work by Dennis and Fish seems to be influencing public policy and political debate [see, for example, Lewis (1972)] since policy based on erroneous notions can have potentially disastrous effects.

As we have seen, any attempt to analyze market concentration must immediately confront the issue of defining the market. In the case of Toronto, the amount of undeveloped land in the hinterland depends, of course, on how far one is willing to travel from the metro core. It was precisely this issue that led us to develop the analysis of ownership concentration and market power presented earlier. That analysis argues that with land spatially differentiated by transport costs, 'significant' concentration of ownership within subsets of land at a fixed commuting distance from the urban core is sufficient for the existence of market power, if the amount of land held by large landowners is 'significant' relative to an appropriately defined universe of undeveloped and developed residential land.

Defining the market

On the basis of the theory presented earlier, we decided to examine ownership of undeveloped land within a 30- to 45-minute commuting distance to major metro employment centres. The 30-minute figure is approximately the current boundary of completely built-up areas. Since the ownership of undeveloped land is likely to be more concentrated than the ownership of undeveloped plus developed residential land (which we earlier argued is the correct universe for judging concentration), the decision to sample only undeveloped land results in an upward bias of the concentration figures. A second requirement was that land included in the sample be serviceable with all required utilities within five years. Lack of planned trunk sewers in such areas as Vaughan eliminated significant areas of land on this basis. We were somewhat skeptical, however, about eliminating land from the sample on the basis of current zoning restrictions. Our interviews with planners and developers led us to have little faith in the permanence of these restrictions.

The full sample

The universe of land around metro that satisfied these restrictions on commuting distance and servicing is quite large. (That universe is also characterized by a number of ambiguities, especially in connection with sewer servicing.) Within this universe, we drew a sample of 71,600 acres that satisfied our restrictions on commuting distance and servicing. No area, that planners thought satisfied our sampling criteria, was left out. Second, we were careful to include in the sample all large holdings of land by large developers even if planners doubted that some of that land could be serviced in the next ten years. The purpose of this sampling decision was to bias the sample towards indicating the presence of concentration. Ownership data were then compiled from the assessment rolls of Brampton, Markham, Mississauga, Pickering, Richmond Hill and Vaughan: the six municipalities in the sample.

The restricted sample

One issue that we had to confront was that our sample (henceforth the 'full sample') included far more land than will be developed in the next twenty years. We took this problem into account by forming a second sample which was simply a sub-sample of the full sample. On the basis of our interviews with planners and studies of official plans, we were able to determine what land included in the sample was unlikely to be developed in the next ten years due to the reasons just developed. This land was then eliminated from the sample leaving the second sample which we shall refer to as the 'restricted sample'. As with the full sample, our restricted sample is, if anything, biased towards exhibiting concentration, since all large holdings of large developers were included in the restricted sample.

One point remains to be made in connection with sample design. In collecting the data, all holdings under 2 acres were immediately eliminated unless one firm or individual held several such parcels. Such parcels are unlikely to account for significant housing starts in the next ten years and their elimination cut data collection costs drastically. Second, acreage held as commercial or industrial property was eliminated from the sample. Net acres in the full sample came to 48,313 acres versus 34,272 acres in the restricted sample. The size of these figures relative to future development needs can be judged by Central Mortgage and Housing Corporation figures which estimate residential land requirements for the Toronto region for the period 1971-1980 at 19,600 acres for Toronto Census Metropolitan Area (considerably larger than our sample area).

The data

Sample results for the entire sample area are shown in Table 1 which gives the top 25 owners in the full and restricted samples. Table 2 presents these results for the city of Mississauga, which had the highest ownership concentration of the six municipalities in the sample area. The total number of companies that held land in the sample and were registered in the land development business numbered about 300. Before reporting our analysis of the results, we shall dispense with two potential sources of weakness in our data: farm use and linked ownership.

Although much of this land is actively farmed at present, little is owned by farmers, the overwhelming portion being rented or leased to farmers by the developer or holding company. Ownership of land by private individuals accounted for no more than 25 per cent of the land in the full sample and significantly less in the restricted sample. With very few exceptions, these individuals do not own enough land to generate even moderate ($10,000) levels of income from farming. It is, therefore, fairly reasonable to conclude that most of this land held by individuals is held for speculative reasons and does, in fact, represent a competitive source of raw land to the large developers. As a consequence, we strongly doubt that our net acreage figures, which we use as a base to calculate concentration, overestimate the true universe due to the prevalence of farmers who do not wish to sell their land.

TABLE 1
Concentration of Nominal Ownership in the Toronto Region Sample Area

Ownership Rank	% of Full Sample 48,313 acres	% of Restricted Sample 34,272 acres
Top 4	17.5	24.3
Top 6	21.4	29.3
Top 10	27.7	37.4
Top 15	32.6	43.9
Top 20	36.6	49.1
Top 25	40.1	53.3

TABLE 2
Concentration of Nominal Ownership in the Mississauga Section of the Sample Area

Ownership Rank	% of Full Sample 17,292 acres	% of Restricted Sample 13,127 acres
Top 4	40.2	51.4
Top 6	45.6	58.5
Top 10	52.2	66.0

Linked ownership

The most obvious difficulty with this analysis of nominal ownership is that it overlooks possible linkages among companies. Popular opinion among planners, realtors, and developers themselves is that these linkages are quite common. The problems involved in establishing linkages arc, however, substantial, involving both arriving at a definition of a linkage and then obtaining the data on whether or not a linkage exists. Given that many of the companies involved are privately owned and that several others are owned by foreign companies (e.g. Monarch), we decided to try to establish linkages by overlaps in principal officers and directors rather than by the seemingly impossible task of tracing links in equity ownership. It is interesting to note that this method of linking via officers and directors did show clear linkages in all the cases where we had *a priori* knowledge of links in equity ownership.

TABLE 3
Concentration of Effective Ownership in the Toronto Region Sample Area

Ownership Rank	% of Full Sample 48,313 acres	% of Restricted Sample 34,272 acres
Top 4	22.7	31.0
Top 6	30.5	40.1
Top 10	37.1	49.1
Top 15	41.7	55.3
Top 20	45.5	59.6
Top 25	48.7	63.0

TABLE 4
Concentration of Effective Ownership in the Mississauga Section of the Sample Area

Ownership Rank	% of Full Sample 17,292 acres	% of Restricted Sample 13,127 acres
Top 4	44.7	56.5
Top 6	49.5	61.9
Top 10	56.1	68.4

One individual sitting on the board of directors of each of the two companies need not imply joint decision making between the two companies. It is not uncommon, for example, for a representative of a large bank to be placed on the board of directors of more than one company in the same industry when the bank has large financial commitments to each firm. Such a director may only be interested in the financial solvency of each company and may have no knowledge of the day-to-day business activities which may bring the two firms into competition. Representatives of large law firms often sit on boards of directors for similar reasons. Nevertheless, we decided to form composite companies from companies which share one or more principal officers or directors. The resulting effective ownership concentration figures are shown for the entire region in Table 3 and for the City of Mississauga alone in Table 4.[2]

The results

Having dealt with potential sources of weakness in the data we can proceed with our analysis. Several interesting results were immediately apparent. *First*, the concentration figures for the entire sample area are very much lower than the figures for all of the individual towns, implying that developers tend to stick 'close to home'. This result was true in both the full and the restricted samples and for both nominal and effective ownership. In the effective ownership restricted sample, for example, the top ten firms own 37.4 per cent of the land, while the *lowest* figure for an individual town is 47.9 per cent (Vaughan). Figures of at least 66 per cent are registered for Brampton, Markham, Mississauga and Pickering. There are obvious advantages to a firm concentrating in one town, such as minimizing the number of government units with which the developer must deal. Developers have asserted to us in interviews that a major component of a developer's value added in land development is moving the subdivision application through the various levels of government red tape. A major portion of this process occurs at the municipal and regional government level.

Another result that occurred in the entire sample area and in all of the individual towns was that concentration in the restricted sample was significantly higher than the concentration in the full sample. For example, nominal ownership statistics for the top four developers in the entire sample area jump from 17.5 per cent to 24.3 per cent. Similar statistics for effective ownership increase from 22.7 per cent to 31.0 per cent. On average, the increase in four-firm concentration ratios was about one-third in the individual towns. Not only was concentration low in the land eliminated from the full sample (as described above), but the bigger developers were seldom among the owners of the land. In a static sense, this means that land nearer to development is more likely to be held by the larger developers. In a dynamic sense, it suggests that land is traded up from farmers to speculators and then from speculators to developers as the time for development approaches. This suggests that much, if not most, of the risk bearing on land is done by small developers and speculators. This is particularly true in the unzoned land that was eliminated from the full sample in forming the restricted sample.

Evidence on market power

In order to assess the likelihood of the existence of market power in the Toronto area we must draw on the analysis of Section III above. In that section, we showed that market power would exist if the following two conditions hold:

1. there is a significant concentration of ownership of land near the boundaries of current development; and

2. the growth rate of the urban area and the amount of developable land are sufficient for the amount of this developable land to be significant relative to the totality of developable and developed land in the appropriately defined urban area.

Earlier in this chapter we discussed various estimates of the amount of land necessary for future development needs for the Toronto area. It seems very likely that the Toronto area will grow enough to roughly encompass at least our restricted sample within twenty years, so condition (2) may hold. However, *it is important to note that our concentration figures have a substantial upward bias*, since we used the amount of land in our sample rather than the totality of developable and developed land in the relevant area as the base for our calculations.

With this bias in mind we are now in a position to discuss whether or not sufficient concentration of ownership exists to suggest the existence of market power. Traditional statistics on market concentration have often looked at the holdings of the top four or six firms in the industry as a percentage of the total. Table 3 shows that the top four companies (effective ownership) hold only 22.7 per cent and 31.0 per cent of the full and restricted sample acreage. Concentration of effective ownership in the individual towns ranged from a high of 46.9 per cent and 60.0 per cent for the top four in Brampton to a low of 31.7 per cent and 39.8 per cent for the top four in Vaughan.

The concentration figures for the entire sample area are too low to imply market power by traditional industrial organization standards.[3] While no industrial organization economist can give an exact answer to the question of what level of concentration implies market power and resource misallocation, four-firm concentration ratios of less than 70 per cent have typically not generated accusations of market power on the basis of concentration alone. The individual towns do not approach this figure even in effective ownership in the restricted sample where the figures range from 60.5 per cent in Brampton to 39.8 per cent in Vaughan.

Given the significant difference between the degree of concentration in the entire sample area and in the individual towns, an important question arises as to what geographic domain is appropriate for measuring market power? While it is true that all areas in the sample are in the same commuter shed relative to the metro core, there are a number of reasons why different locations in the sample area may not be good locational substitutes from the consumer's point of view. In other words, it may be that our sample area consists of a group of somewhat differentiated products. In this case the degree of differentiation (measured by cross elasticity of demand) determines how many separate markets there are.

The first reason the sample area may not be perfectly homogeneous from the consumer's point of view follows from the fact that employment is not centralized in the metro core, but spread out to a certain extent over the metro area. Levels of public services also differ among municipalities. Per capita expenditures on schooling, for example, create a form of product differentiation in the eyes of households with school age children. Related to differences in public services are differences in municipal tax rates. Low tax rates are obviously attractive.

All of the above argue for the recognition of the fact that there is a heterogeneity arising from factors other than location within a fixed commuter shed to the central core. It is beyond the scope of this study to assess the extent to which this phenomenon reduces the cross elasticity of demand for land between the different locations. Perhaps the best that we can do is simply argue that the concentration statistics for the entire sample area are an underestimate of the 'ideal' measure of concentration and that the statistics for the individual towns are likely to be an overestimate of this measure. Notice, however, that the use of political boundaries to delineate subsets of land is probably not appropriate. That the results are sensitive to this delineation can be seen by the fact that if we aggregate adjoining townships (e.g. Brampton and Mississauga) the concentration ratios fall dramatically. Whatever the appropriate definition of market area for the short run, we would argue the long-run cross elasticities of demand for land at different locations is very high, since production location decisions (and therefore employment centres) will certainly respond in the long run to land price differentials.

Conclusions on market power

In our opinion, it *cannot* be concluded on the basis of the evidence on concentration that we have presented that exercised market power is an important characteristic of the Toronto land market. We base this opinion on the data and our belief that consumers regard land in adjoining municipalities as reasonably good substitutes. Finally, we also base this belief on the data of Muller (1976) which shows that a further reduction of our sample to land recently approved for subdivision will not show concentration which is large enough by industrial organization standards to imply significant market power.

VI. PRICES AND PROFITS IN THE SHORT RUN

In Sections III and IV of this paper, we have argued that the existence of market power must be based on the concentration of ownership in the potential supply of land. Concentration in the market must not be measured in terms of those agents who, in particular, choose to develop land in a particular period. Section IV argued that if developers have good expectations about the future, then a competitive market will tend to generate a time path of such prices that each developer will be indifferent as to precisely when he will develop his land. Unlike many other markets, therefore, a competitive market structure may be quite consistent with a situation in which only one developer accounts for all sales of serviced lots in a given year.

In each year, of course, the *maximum* supply of lots to the market is constrained by the number of lots which are approved for subdivision and for which trunk servicing facilities are available. It is also well known that there is often a lag of several years between requesting subdivision approval and the granting of that approval. But this matters little if developers have good expectations about the future since in such a situation they are able to make the appropriate decisions in the present regarding development three or five years hence.

The long lags involved in the subdivision approval process, together with unforeseen fluctuations in demand, however, imply that in any particular year, the total number of lots that can actually be supplied to the market may fall far short of demand at what would be competitive prices if there were no lags in subdivision approvals. In such a situation, owners of land may be able to reap substantial profits but this is not, in itself, evidence of market power. It might be interesting to note that developers who find themselves having to develop or sell land (or incur heavy carrying charges) in periods of unexpectedly low demand would not normally be accused of having market power. The point here is that demand uncertainty together with long lags in subdivision approval can be a source of high profits for a few lucky developers even in a competitive market.

One example may be in order. Suppose Developer A had 100 lots approved for subdivision this year and that he was the only developer with approvals. Further assume that 100 new lots was a competitive equilibrium supply if demand turned out as anticipated. But now assume a strong surge in demand that is unanticipated. If our developer attempted to hold, say, half of his lots off the market, could he increase significantly the price of his remaining lots (i.e. would he have market power)? According to the analysis of Section III, he could not. Holding 50 lots off the market has virtually no effect on the total Toronto housing stock, meaning that the demand faced by the developer is virtually perfectly elastic. Therefore, there is no benefit to the developer in withholding lots from the market. Thus, while the increase in demand will prove very profitable for developer A, it must not be confused with a raising of prices through the exercise of market power, since optimal government policy is clearly different in the two cases. The problem of short-run disequilibrium in a competitive land market is best dealt with by ensuring that there is always a healthy stock of lots approved for subdivision with readily available trunk servicing.

VII. CONCLUSIONS AND IMPLICATIONS FOR PUBLIC POLICY

Early sections of this paper presented arguments as to how one should define and measure ownership concentration and determined the relationship between ownership concentration and the existence of market power. It was argued that the appropriate basis of the measure of concentration for a suitably defined urban area is the totality of developed and developable land within the estimated future boundaries of the urban area. It was also argued that concentration is, itself, a barrier-to-entry in the case of the land market so that market power can be assessed on the basis of concentration statistics alone.

Within a static context, exercised market power will have effects on the land market that are similar to the effects of market power in other markets: less land will be supplied to the market and consumers will face higher prices than would prevail in a competitive situation. Land development, however, is a dynamic process and land itself can be thought of as a depletable resource. The combination of these two facts makes the effects of market power in the land market more complex in other markets. Over a long time horizon, a concentrated industry may, for example, develop just as much land as a competitive industry. Even in the case where a concentrated industry does not develop as much land as a competitive industry over time, concentration nevertheless, may result in more development in some particular years.

What can be said is that total consumer payments for newly developed land over a number of years will generally be higher under concentration than under competition but that this difference may be small.

Section V then presented some empirical results on ownership concentration in the Toronto region, taken from Markusen and Scheffman. These empirical results lead us to advance the following conclusions. *First*, even when linkages among companies are taken into consideration, concentration of ownership in the Toronto region was far too low to imply market power. *Second*, concentration of ownership increased as land unlikely to be developed in the next ten years was eliminated from the sample. This suggests that land is traded up from small developers and land speculators to large developers as the time for development is approached. Nevertheless, statistics by Muller (1976) show that even at the actual subdivision stage, the supply of lots is not concentrated enough to imply market power. The *third* conclusion was that concentration in individual municipalities was in all cases significantly higher than concentration in the entire region, indicating that developers wish to restrict the number of governments with which they have to deal. In several of the municipalities, concentration was high enough that an argument for market power could be made, but only if consumers regarded residences in the different municipalities as very poor substitutes. Our judgment is that this is not likely to be the case, especially in the long run.

The finding that ownership concentration in the Toronto region is too low to imply significant market power leaves social critics such as Lewis (1972) and Lorimer (1976) without a factual basis for their explanations of the recent land price boom. An alternate explanation, which is fully developed in our book for the Ontario Economic Council, and which fits the facts, can be outlined as follows.

The early 1970s witnessed a strong boom in the demand for residential land for two reasons: first, this was a period of high inflation and a period in which most financial assets (e.g. common shares) were performing very poorly. Less risky assets such as government bonds were also yielding poor returns because of the unanticipated accelerating rate of inflation. This resulted in a shift in asset demand to non-financial assets such as land, housing, gold and art. Second, enactment of a federal capital gains tax in the early 1970s exempted owner-occupied residences which also acted to shift asset demand from taxable assets to owner-occupied housing on the part of households that had been renting or leasing housing. This shift in asset demand plus demand resulting from population growth resulted in a total growth of demand that far exceeded the expectations of developers and planning authorities.

Coupled with this increase in demand for housing were severe restrictions on the supply of new housing. This occurred for a number of reasons. First, because much of the increase in demand was unanticipated, subdivision applications (which are now taking at least three years to process) were not made at the proper point in time. Second, a number of the municipalities surrounding metro Toronto were moving towards no-growth policies in this period, which resulted in the slowing down or outright killing of many existing subdivision applications. Third, a lack of proper planning left large areas of land without trunk servicing facilities, especially sewers, that were essential for new construction. Thus the red tape of the subdivision approval process and the lack of trunk servicing facilities left the development industry little scope to respond to the surge in demand.

As prices began to take off in response to this situation, it seemed that prices were further stimulated by an upswing in speculative purchases by individuals and companies who expected additional price rises. The main effect of this speculation was on the price of speculative undeveloped land. This 'speculative bubble' was burst in April, 1974 with the enactment of the Ontario Land Speculation Tax.† Evidence now suggests that the real price (price adjusted for the rate of inflation) of housing has fallen in Toronto since that

†Editors' Note: It is interesting to note that according to Smith (1976) the Speculation Tax actually tends to create a long-term problem by increasing the concentration of land holdings by major developers although reversing destabilizing short-term expectations.

time. We predict that *real* prices will fall further towards previous levels in the next few years following the completion of the York-Durham servicing scheme, which will open up large tracts of land for development (provided, of course, that the subdivision approvals are granted, and that there are not drastic changes in government policy, such as making mortgage interest tax deductible).

We wish to emphasize that different theories have radically different implications regarding optimal public policy. If we accept the theories of those that blame concentrated landownership for high land prices, then large developers should be broken up, and perhaps the government should enter the land development business directly. If we accept the alternate theory just put forward, the optimal policy to reduce land prices is to increase trunk servicing capacity far ahead of projected needs, expedite subdivision approvals, and generally streamline government involvement in the land market so that it facilitates rather than hinders development. In conclusion, the housing stock can be increased and prices brought down only if we correctly perceive the true underlying causes of the current problem. Even the most well-meaning social critics are quite capable of making the problem worse if they operate on the basis of incorrect assumptions.

APPENDIX A

A technical analysis of competitive and monopolistic situations indicates the following results.

Proposition 1

> For 'relatively low' levels of demand, a concentrated industry will develop less land than a competitive industry (and, therefore, raise the average price over time) but will not necessarily develop less in any given period.

This result is certainly not surprising. What is of more interest is the situation where the growth rate of the city is high enough that the concentrated industry finds it profitable to *eventually* develop all the land it currently holds. In such a situation, of course, both a competitive and a concentrated industry will develop the same virtual total amount of land in the long run. This possibility arises because total potential supply is fixed. Such a case cannot occur in the production of other types of goods where production can always be expanded by purchasing additional factors of production.

A second interesting fact that arises when large developers find it profitable to eventually develop all their land is that the rate of development in a concentrated industry may be faster than a competitive industry. The reason is quite straightforward. If a large developer attempts to reduce land development in the current period, he will have more land to develop in the future. Higher current prices will be paid for by lower future prices (future prices will be depressed as he sells more land in the future). The optimal decision for a large developer depends upon a number of demand elasticities and technical analysis will demonstrate that it cannot in general be determined whether or not a concentrated industry will develop land faster or slower than a competitive industry.

Proposition 2

> For 'relatively high' levels of demand, both a monopolist and a competitive industry will develop the same virtual total entire stock of land in the long run.

> The concentrated industry may develop the land faster than the competitive industry.

It is also of interest in this high demand situation to note the relationship between the rate of land development and the equilibrium rate of land price increase over time. If the concentrated industry developed land slower than the competitive industry, a technical analysis will also demonstrate that the current price of land for the concentrated industry will exceed the corresponding price under competition but that future prices for the concentrated industry will be lower, on average. This is summarized as follows.

Proposition 3

> For 'relatively high' levels of demand, a concentrated industry cannot lead to both a slower rate of land development and a faster rate of price appreciation than would occur under competitive conditions.

Thus while concentration will generally lead to one or the other of these situations, it cannot lead to both.

What we can say about the concentrated industry is that total payments for land made by consumers over both periods will be greater than under competition (although the difference may be quite small). Even when the large developers eventually develop all their land, a technical analysis will demonstrate that they will generally have a different allocation of land sales between periods relative to a competitive situation. This different allocation of the same total amount of land results in higher profits and higher costs to the consumer.

Proposition 4

> Regardless of whether or not the total development over time of a concentrated industry is equal to or less than that of a competitive industry, total payments over time to the concentrated industry by consumers for land will exceed such payments under competition.

A final point we would like to make concerns capital gains taxation which has been advocated both to speed land development and to redistribute the increases in land values back to society as a whole. While it is fairly easy to show that a capital gains tax *will* speed development in a competitive situation, such a result does not necessarily follow in the case of a concentrated industry. Again the reasoning is fairly straightforward. If a large developer attempts to develop more land in the current period in response to the tax, he is left with less land to develop in the second period. This will raise second period price and increase his total taxable capital gains if the increase in price outweighs the reduction in quantity supplied. Algebraic analysis again can be used to demonstrate that the direction of a large developer's response to a capital gains tax depends on certain demand elasticities.

Proposition 5

> The effect of a capital gains tax on a large developer's timing of land development is indeterminate due to the trade-off between the rate of development and the rate of price appreciation.

In summary, we see that the effects of concentrated ownership of undeveloped land become complicated when the problem is placed in an intertemporal context. On the one hand, if the existing amount of undeveloped land is large enough relative to the growth rate of the city so that a competitive development industry is not likely to develop all the land over a long time horizon, a concentrated industry will tend to restrict land development and raise the average price over time above the competitive level. On the other hand, if the amount of land is significantly restricted relative to the level of demand, both a competitive and a concentrated industry will develop all the land in the long run. In neither case is it possible to compare *a priori* the supply of the concentrated industry vis-a-vis the competitive industry in any one period. In both cases, however, total consumer payments for land over time will be larger for a concentrated industry than under competition.

Notes

[1]This estimate is based on the fact that most estimates of the price and income elasticity for housing are approximately equal to one. For readers not familiar with this term, 'price elasticity' of demand is defined as the percentage change in demand resulting from a 1 per cent change in price. Thus, if a one per cent increase in price decreases demand by 2 per cent, the price elasticity of demand is equal to 2. Income elasticity is defined in a similar fashion.

[2]A justification of this methodology, explicit listings of which companies are linked together in this process, and the exact nature of the linkages are given in *Speculation and Monopoly in Urban Development: Analytical Foundations with Evidence for Toronto.* In that study we also consider third level linkages. Companies A and D are said to be linked at the third level if A shares an officer or director with company B which in turn shares an officer or director with company C who is not shared with A. C in turn shares an officer or director with D who is not shared with either A or B. Only one significant linkage exists at the third level and raises the percentage of land held by the top 10 to 40.6 and 52.7 in the full and restricted samples respectively. Our personal feeling is that these level III figures should not be used for the formulation of public policy and we refer the interested reader to our book for a more complete discussion of the issues involved.

[3]This is true even at level III effective ownership where the top four own only 28.9 per cent and 37.4 per cent of the full and restricted samples respectively.

References

Coopers and Lybrand, *Report to the Ontario Economic Council: Data on Land Available for Housing in Toronto CMA*, Ontario Economic Council, Toronto, 1976.

Dennis, M. and S. Fish, *Low Income Housing: Programs in Search of a Policy*, Central Mortgage and Housing Corporation, Ottawa, 1972.

Lewis, D., *The Corporate Welfare Bums*, James Lewis and Samuel, Toronto, 1972.

Lorimer, J., "Their Land, Your Money," *Weekend Magazine*, May 22, 1976.

Markusen, J. and D. Scheffman, *Speculation and Monopoly in Urban Development: Analytical Foundations with Evidence for Toronto*, University of Toronto Press, forthcoming 1977.

Muller, A., *The Market for New Housing in Metropolitan Toronto*, Ontario Economic Council, Toronto, 1976.

Smith, L.B., "The Ontario Land Speculation Tax: An Anatomy of an Unearned Increment Land Tax," *Land Economics*, February 1976.

Spurr, P., *The Land Problem's Problem*, Central Mortgage and Housing Corporation, Ottawa, 1974.

The Economic Implications of Foreign Ownership of Canadian Land

STUART McFADYEN

Associate Professor
Faculty of Business Administration and Commerce
University of Alberta

and

ROBERT HOBART

Economist
Ministry of State for Urban Affairs

THE AUTHORS

Stuart M. McFadyen was born in Winnipeg in 1938. He received his B.Sc. degree from the University of Manitoba in 1959, majoring in mathematics and statistics. He became a chartered accountant in 1963, and is now a member of the Institute of Chartered Accountants of Alberta. He received his M.A. degree in economics from the University of British Columbia in 1967, and his Ph.D. degree from the University of California (Berkeley) in 1969. Since 1969 he has been a member of the faculty of the University of Alberta, and now holds the rank of Associate Professor, Faculty of Business Administration and Commerce.

Among his publications, Professor McFadyen includes: "Control of Foreign Ownership of Canadian Real Estate," published in *Canadian Public Policy*, Winter 1976.

Robert J. Hobart was born in Lloydminster, Saskatchewan in 1950. He received his B.Comm. degree with distinction from the University of Alberta in 1972, where he held Queen Elizabeth and Francis Reeve fellowships. He received his M.B.A. degree in 1973, also from the University of Alberta. At present he is an economist with the Urban Economy Directorate of the Ministry of State for Urban Affairs.

The Economic Implications of Foreign Ownership of Canadian Land*

STUART McFADYEN
Associate Professor
Faculty of Business Administration and Commerce
University of Alberta
and
ROBERT HOBART
Economist
Ministry of State for Urban Affairs

I. INTRODUCTION

In 1972, foreign-controlled firms owned 34.9 per cent of non-financial business assets in Canada and received 36.5 per cent of sales revenue and 44.2 per cent of profits generated in Canada.[1] Because of these large magnitudes of foreign ownership in the Canadian economy, national concern has been raised as to whether or not Canadians can control their economic environment. For example, in a recent study conducted by the Ontario Economic Council, 50.8 per cent of the respondents considered American ownership of Canadian companies to be detrimental to the Canadian economy while only 31.7 per cent responded in a positive fashion.[2]

More recently, possibly because of the more fundamental nature of the land resource, concern has shifted towards the foreign ownership of Canadian recreational, agricultural and urban real estate. Foreign individuals and firms have

*This paper reflects the opinions of the authors and not necessarily those of the Ministry of State for Urban Affairs.

been criticised for driving up the price of recreational and agricultural land, driving up the price of housing, misusing the land that they own, destroying the shape of Canadian urban centres, forcing Canadian land developers and farmers out of business, destroying small communities, speculating in property markets, and other undesirable activities.[3] Most of these criticisms are not justified and several even conflict. For example, foreign development firms have been accused of not developing their land holdings at the urban fringe thus creating housing shortages and rising prices. On the other hand, foreign development firms have been accused of developing urban fringe land too quickly, thus taking agricultural land prematurely out of production. In order to evaluate the validity of these criticisms properly, the benefits as well as the costs of foreign investment in Canadian land must be considered. Three different categories of land will be examined in turn: recreational properties, agricultural land and urban fringe land.

II. THE ECONOMIC IMPLICATIONS OF FOREIGN OWNERSHIP OF CANADIAN LAND

A. Recreational Land

The basic argument against the foreign ownership of recreational land is that the increased demand created by foreign individuals increases the price of recreational land to such an extent that Canadians are priced out of the market and thus are prohibited access. There is little doubt that increased demand for recreational land will increase its price, given a constant supply, but the question remains, "Are foreigners a significant factor in the market for Canadian recreational land?"

Extent of foreign ownership

Unfortunately, a lack of reliable data does not permit a detailed examination of this question for Canada as a whole. However, data is available for three provinces where there are thought to be large amounts of recreational land held by foreigners. In Prince Edward Island, 38,500 acres or 3.0 per cent of the land in the province is owned by non-Canadians.[4] In Nova Scotia, which in percentage terms has the largest concentration of foreign-owned recreational land in Canada, the actual amount estimated to be owned by non-Canadians is 482,000 acres or 3.7 per cent of the total land area.[5] Finally, in New Brunswick, it was estimated that 4,928 parcels of land were owned by non-residents of Canada in 1972. This represented 2.1 per cent of the total parcels in New Brunswick in that year.[6] The foreign holdings in these three provinces represent accumulations over a long period of time. Thus, the actual acreage demanded by foreigners in any given year and the resultant effect on price tends to be small. In other provinces the case is even weaker.

It is true that every piece of recreational land purchased by a foreigner is one less piece available to Canadian buyers. Accessibility for Canadians may be reduced. But this is a two-way street; every Florida or Washington State vacation property purchased by a Canadian is one less available to American buyers. Accessibility for Americans may be reduced. Measures designed to protect 100 per cent Canadian access to Canadian vacation property may invite retaliatory measures which prohibit Canadians from acquiring the vacation or retirement property of their choice abroad. If this demand were then shifted to Canada, the price of Canadian recreational land might be even higher than in the no-control case.

Gains and losses

While in the general case foreign purchasers of land may be in such a small minority as to have little effect on the market value of recreational land, localized price effects may result if foreigners concentrate their purchases in specific areas. A 1971 study, for example, found that 16.4 per cent of the acreage in the Bras D'Or Lakes Region of Cape Breton Island was owned by American citizens.[7] If the demand for recreational land in a given area is significantly augmented because of foreign interest in the region, both existing Canadian owners and potential Canadian purchasers are affected. The welfare of the existing owner is increased because of the increased price offered for his property. On the other hand, the welfare of the potential Canadian purchaser is decreased because he is forced to outbid foreign purchasers.[8] Unfortunately, it is not possible to aggregate these welfare gains and losses to reach an overall evaluation of the price effect of foreign purchases.

The situation is further complicated where large amounts of land are owned by the public sector. Inverness County in Nova Scotia, which has the largest acreage owned by foreign individuals of any county in Nova Scotia, provides a good case in point. Foreign individuals own 66,000 acres, individual Canadians own 520,000 acres, while 302,000 acres are Crown land.[9] If only a small portion of this Crown land acreage is suitable for recreational uses and the province pursued an active policy of public park provision or cottage lot leases, welfare losses to the Canadian demander of recreational land services would be minimal.

Effect on taxes

The question of property taxes is often raised in conjunction with the price issue. It is argued that by paying high prices for land, foreigners drive up the price of land, which in turn increases assessed values and property taxes for land in the surrounding area. The property tax burden of local residents is thus increased. It is incorrect to use this line of reasoning as an argument against foreign ownership of Canadian land. Increased property values create an increase in the wealth of individuals in the community but have no effect on the amount of government expenditure needed to maintain a constant level of services. Property tax burdens can be maintained at a constant level in the face of increases in the assessment base simply by means of downward adjustments in mill rates.

The claim that absentee ownership of land is detrimental to the local economy also has little basis. Alien landowners pay their property taxes, gasoline taxes and sales taxes. On the other hand, they need no school services, libraries or snow removal. The alien thus pays local taxes, but does not require the full complement of local services.[10] This means that the local government can provide a better level of services to the resident populace. As well, alien owners of land provide a stable tourist trade since their purchase represents a commitment to the area. The fact that the alien owner is absent during the off season would seem irrelevant. All communities that depend on the tourist trade suffer seasonal fluctuations regardless of who owns land in the area.

B. Agricultural land

Three basic criticisms are levied at alien owners of agricultural land. First, it is argued that foreign purchasers pay high prices for agricultural land. This in turn raises the market value of all agricultural lands, prohibiting the entry of new farmers and the expansion of existing farms to a more efficient size. The second criticism is that foreign owners of agricultural land do little to support business in the local community. It is alleged that foreign individuals purchase the majority of their machinery and other materials in the United States. Finally, foreign owners are accused of misusing their land. It is alleged that many foreigners come to Canada to merely 'hobby-farm'.

The price effects

First, consider the impact on the price of agricultural land. Studies regarding the foreign ownership of agricultural land have indicated that the concentration of foreign ownership is relatively small. In Manitoba, for example, a study conducted by the Manitoba Department of Agriculture in 1974 found that less than 1 per cent of Manitoba's agricultural land was owned by foreigners.[11] The Resource Economics Branch of Alberta Agriculture 1973 investigation found that only 1.2 per cent of the acreage studied was held by aliens.[12] Jacob Brown's comprehensive study of American land holdings in Saskatchewan within 55 miles of the American border found that 2.34 per cent of the land was owned by Americans.[13] This figure, of course, overstates the percentage of agricultural land owned by Americans in Saskatchewan inasmuch as areas where foreign ownership of land is less likely were not included in the study. In a questionnaire survey conducted throughout Saskatchewan in 1972, it was estimated that slightly less than 1 per cent of agricultural land in Saskatchewan was owned by non-Canadians.[14]

Foreign demand in any one year appears modest. Figures released by Alberta Agriculture in September of 1976 indicate that, of the 3.1 million acres of land transferred in Alberta between June 1975 and May 1976, only 80,000 acres or 2.5 per cent were transferred to non-Canadians.[15] Because of this modest demand, it would appear that foreign demand has been a relatively minor factor in recent farmland price increases. Increased agricultural productivity and higher prices for farm products have likely played the dominant role.

Benefits

Although the foreign component of the agricultural land market is small, Brown found that it does play a beneficial role in Saskatchewan by facilitating

> ". . . the farm sales of some farmers wishing to retire and of small operators who wanted to quit farming. It was indicated in a few cases that this increased the difficulties of beginning farmers in Saskatchewan, but the net effect likely was beneficial because of the improved, more active land market and benefits to sellers."[16]

One cause of the new farmer's problem in acquiring land was identified by Brown as the slow and restrictive credit practices of the Farm Credit Corporation which served to put Canadian buyers at a competitive disadvantage.

Support of local business

The second criticism levied at foreign landowners is that, by not purchasing supplies locally, they have threatened the viability of small farming communities. Once again, the magnitudes of the situation must be considered. Surely, even if foreign landowners did not purchase locally, it would not make a great deal of difference since they are relatively small in number to begin with. As in the case of recreational land, alien landowners pay their taxes and do not require the full complement of local services. Canadian residents benefit. As far as the support of local business is concerned, Brown found that:

> "Fuel, combines, swathers and some repairs, for example, have been purchased in substantial quantities in Canada by Americans. Also, some have purchased tractors in Saskatchewan, especially in Regina. The larger operators, whether American or Canadian, are tending to purchase such large items in the larger market centres."[17]

Thus, it appears as if both Canadian and American farmers are threatening the viability of the smaller towns in Saskatchewan. This is the result of a better road system, better communications, and the efficiency of large scale implement dealers.

Hobby-farm syndrome

The final criticism of foreign owners of agricultural land is that they misuse their land and simply 'hobby-farm' for recreational purposes. Again, the evidence uncovered by Brown does not support this claim:

> "Almost all of the interviewees indicated that the Americans were good farmers—using recommended farm practices, advanced technological innovations and complying with regulations that affect farming practices."[18]

Rather than a concern over misuse of land, one might view foreign ownership as a beneficial transfer of new technology to Canada.

Also of importance is the fact that 25 per cent of the land purchased by Americans was rented to other farmers. This, of course, gives young farmers an opportunity to begin operations and existing farmers an opportunity to expand operations without making large investments in land.

C. Urban fringe land

Because the foreign ownership of owner-occupied dwellings in Canada is insignificant and land is a relatively minor component in the value of most developed income properties such as apartments, the discussion in this paper will focus on the foreign ownership of urban fringe land held for development purposes. When the necessary government approvals have been obtained and services have been installed, land becomes an important input into the production of commercial properties and both owner-occupied and rental housing.

Extent of ownership

Although there is little reliable information on the foreign ownership of urban fringe land in Canada: Montreal, Toronto, Edmonton, Calgary and Vancouver have been identified as markets where foreign investment in all types of real estate (including developed properties) tends to concentrate. British and German funds have appeared to be predominant and it is interesting to note that funds flowing into Canadian real estate from the OPEC countries are negligible.[19] It is unclear what proportion of foreign funds are used to purchase urban fringe relative to developed properties. In a study conducted by the P.S. Ross Company, it was found that of the $142 million of foreign investment flowing into the Vancouver real estate market in 1973, only $4 million or 2.8 per cent was used for the purchase of undeveloped land.[20] The majority of funds went toward the purchase or development of residential accommodation.

Urban fringe land must be purchased by developers at prices reflecting expected revenues from urban uses. This investment must then be financed until the land becomes ripe for development. Since the original investment, and hence the holding cost, reflects the potential for urban use, any offsetting revenues during the holding period from interim agricultural uses are small in relative terms. Because of the magnitude of initial investment outlays, high holding costs and lengthy delays encountered in the land planning approval process, the urban land development industry has in recent years come to be dominated by large corporations. A number of large foreign-controlled corporations such as Genstar, Costain and MEPC are active in the industry as well as large Canadian firms such as Cadillac Fairview, Campeau Corporation and S.B. McLaughlin Associates Ltd.

Expansion beyond the domestic market for development firms based abroad requires foreign investment because of the nature of the product sold. Unlike most other products, land development services or rental dwellings cannot be exported. The finished product of the development process can only be sold in foreign markets through an investment of capital, management skills and technology in the foreign market.

These firms, of course, benefit from their market expansion. A larger market means a larger base from which to choose new initiatives. In addition, the diversification made possible by operating in several countries reduces overall business risks of the corporation.[21] Capital required for the expansion of these firms comes from retained earnings and the issuing of both debt and equity in Canada and abroad. Once the Canadian subsidiary becomes profitable, its retained earnings can also be used for expansion.

Problems?

Several concerns have been raised regarding the foreign ownership of Canadian urban fringe land. First, the claim is made that foreign owners produce developments alien to the Canadian way of life. Second, it is argued that foreign firms, because they require a lower rate of return, pay relatively high prices for Canadian properties which in turn leads to high housing costs for Canadian consumers. High housing prices in Canada have also been attributed to speculation and monopolistic behaviour by foreign firms. A final criticism, which is also levied at foreign investment in Canadian recreational and agricultural lands, is that land is a basic resource to Canada and, therefore, should not be in foreign hands. The first two criticisms are primarily economic, while the last concerns the question of national identity.

Shape of development

Foreign developers could prejudicially alter the shape of the Canadian environment if they have development concepts which are inferior to those used by Canadian developers.[22] Regarding this point, the Ontario Select Committee on Economic and Cultural Nationalism has concluded:

> "There is little evidence, for example, that Canadian-owned developers do or would behave any differently (than foreign developers) as regards the nature of design of residential and commercial developments. In any case, and as the Committee has noted elsewhere in its studies, some Canadian corporations and especially Canadian banks, have been persistent employers of foreign design services in their major buildings."[23]

Thus, it appears that criticism regarding foreign development standards is unwarranted. In any event, this type of criticism ignores the fact that the development of land does not occur in a vacuum. Before actual construction can begin, the developer must have his plans approved by the local planning authority. Through this approval process development designs which are inappropriate to the local area would be rejected or revised.[24] As well, if foreign development standards were inferior, the consumer would be unlikely to purchase their output.

Price effects

The second concern over foreign ownership of Canadian urban fringe land is the price effect. The argument is that foreign participation in the urban fringe land market increases the price of developed properties, especially housing, to the disadvantage of Canadian consumers.

There is little information on the price effect of foreign urban fringe land investments but in the case of developed rental properties numerous incidents have been reported in the press of foreigners paying relatively inflated prices. Donald has asserted that this has occurred because foreign investors have underestimated the costs of property management.[25] It is, however, generally argued that these inflated prices have been paid because the foreign investor is willing to accept a lower rate of return than his Canadian counterpart. Although there is no empirical evidence to suggest that foreign investors, in general, are satisfied with a relatively low rate of return, there are two reasons which might suggest that this is possible. First, the foreign investor may have access to lower-cost funds than the Canadian investor and second he may feel that Canadian investment offers the benefit of risk reduction through diversification.[26]

On the other hand, the foreign investor may actually require a higher rate of return than the Canadian investor because, unlike the local investor, he suffers an exchange rate risk when converting his investment proceeds from Canadian dollars into his own currency. The net result of these conflicting pressures on expected rates of return is unclear.

Assuming foreign investors do pay inflated prices for urban fringe land, what effect does this have on rents and housing prices? If it is indeed true that the foreign investor requires a lower rate of return than the Canadian investor, no increases in rents or housing prices need result. The investor, be he foreign or Canadian, examines the expected net revenue stream of his prospective purchase, discounts it at his required rate of return and offers a price which reflects the discount rate and expected rental stream.† In the case of a required rate of return that is low by Canadian standards, the price he offers will be high. The high purchase price is the result of the relatively low rate of return, not the result of an anticipated increase in the income stream. In other words, the foreign purchaser is willing to accept the same revenue flow from rents. If foreigners can be found who are willing to pay top dollar to Canadians selling fringe land or developed properties and at the same time to provide accommodation to Canadian tenants at competitive prices, Canadians would seem to come out winners on all counts.

If, on the other hand, the Donald hypothesis is correct, the foreign investor will attempt to increase rents or output prices to compensate for the over-valuing of the property. It is unlikely, however, that these rent increases will be possible. This is because any one foreign investor supplies a very small portion of the market and must act as a price taker

†Editors' Note: For a discussion of property valuation and bid price, see the first essay in this volume, by Professor David Nowlan.

rather than a price leader. Indirect effects on price may result where foreign purchases trigger optimistic expectations regarding property values. If this were the case, the sellers of developed properties would only accept the inflated prices for properties. These increased prices would in turn have to be passed on to the consumer in the form of increased rents and residential lot prices. In the long run, these higher prices would induce firms to increase the rate of production of both developed rental properties and residential lots. The increase in supply would, of course, lower sales prices of both types of property. The net result, in terms of both price and quantity, depends on the extent to which this supply response is curbed by either pressures to restrict output in markets where only a few sellers operate, restrictions resulting from delays in the development approval process, or technical constraints on output.

The Alberta Select Committee of the Legislative Assembly has concluded:

> "The Committee is of the opinion that the price of residential land is affected more by such factors as monopolies, lack of competition, interference with the supply of residential lots (by restrictive municipal practices in the name of good planning) and the lack of funds for servicing residential lots, than by land purchases by non-Canadians."[27]

Rather than foreign developers being the cause of high housing prices, monopolies and local government planning controls seem to be the culprits.†

†Editors' Note: The comments here notwithstanding, the evidence produced elsewhere in this book, particularly by Markusen and Scheffman, does not support the contention that monopoly power has been the cause of high housing prices.

Foreign owners — developers or speculators?

The second criticism levied at foreign investors in urban real estate is that they do not develop their properties and are only interested in speculative profits. Speculation in this sense is taken to mean the holding of undeveloped properties for resale. This type of activity is not carried out solely by foreigners. Canadians, as well, engage in speculative activities. Thus, if the objective of government is to curb land speculation, the appropriate policy is the introduction of a speculation tax that applies to both foreigners and residents alike.†

A similar situation exists where the objective of public policy is to ensure a competitive, as opposed to a monopolistic, development industry. Restrictions regarding the foreign ownership of land will not ensure that land markets become competitive because Canadian firms possessing market power would not be affected by such legislation. In fact, it is likely that their market power would be increased because of restrictions regarding the entry of foreign firms. That is, the competition provided by foreign firms would be eliminated. As in the case of speculation, the policy instrument used to promote competition in land markets should be applied to all, rather than a select group only.

Balance of payments effects

Finally, consider the role of foreign investment in Canadian land in terms of transfer of technology and balance of payments effects. The activities of multinational land development firms in Canada produce benefits by introducing in Canada technological and managerial innovations developed abroad. Costs in terms of creation of a dependency on foreign-based research would seem to be minimal.

†Editors' Note: For a discussion of speculation, see the paper by Smith and Carr in this volume. See also L.B. Smith, "The Ontario Land Speculation Tax: An Anatomy of an Unearned Increment Land Tax," *Land Economics*, February, 1976.

Investment of foreign funds in Canadian land provides an offset to deficits incurred on current accounts. The Economic Council of Canada has concluded that substantial amounts of foreign investment may be required if the Canadian economy is to grow at levels similar to other nations and remain competitive in world markets.[28] If a portion of this is to consist of direct investment, the basic issue is: what sectors of the Canadian economy should be open to this investment? Real estate, rather than being an area of concern, is probably one of the safest areas. Unlike oil or minerals, real estate cannot be exported. Unlike manufacturing, an investment in real estate is a relatively passive investment. Elaborate local and regional government planning and control ensure that citizens through their voting power have a voice in determining how land is used. Given this situation, what controls have, in fact, been placed on the foreign ownership of Canadian land and what has been their effect?

III. THE ECONOMIC IMPLICATIONS OF CANADIAN LEGISLATION FOR THE FOREIGN OWNERSHIP OF LAND

As a result of public attitudes, the federal government and various provincial governments have adopted policies and legislation which monitor or restrict the acquisition of Canadian land by foreign individuals and firms. Table 1 presents a summary of this diverse legislation. Several provinces, notably British Columbia, Alberta and Manitoba, prohibit the granting of Crown land to non-Canadian citizens. Others, such as Ontario and New Brunswick, give preference to Canadian citizens in the granting of Crown land. The effect of such restrictions is to lower the demand for Crown land and thus permit increased accessibility to Canadians. If the lower demand results in lower prices, the economic welfare of Canadians purchasing or leasing Crown land will be enhanced at the expense of taxpayers in general.[29]

Foreign ownership restrictions

Two provinces, Prince Edward Island and Saskatchewan, restrict the sale of privately-owned land to non-residents (including Canadian citizens) of their respective provinces. As is noted in Table 1, non-residents of Prince Edward Island can purchase privately-owned land provided they obtain consent from the Lieutenant Governor in Council. During the period from January 1, 1972 to December 31, 1974, consent was granted for approximately 80 per cent of the acreage which came under review. In Saskatchewan, on the other hand, non-residents can purchase land provided that the total assessed value of properties held by the non-resident individual does not esceed $15,000. Despite these exemptions, the legislation in both provinces will at least partially eliminate non-residents from the market, resulting in some lessening in the price of land. Because of this, the welfare of residents who are prospective purchasers of land will be increased at the expense of land sellers.

In Prince Edward Island, properties less than ten acres or those with less than 330 feet of shore frontage are exempt from the legislation. This results in the creation of two distinct land markets, the exempt market and the regulated market. Average prices in the former will tend to be higher because no restrictions on non-resident purchases are imposed. Sellers will thus have an incentive to subdivide their properties in order to take advantage of higher prices in the exempt market. However, a moratorium on subdivisions is currently in effect in Prince Edward Island which prevents such activity.

While the results of these restrictions are evident in the case of recreational land, they may be subject to an important modification where farmland is involved. The demand for farmland is derived from the value of the agricultural products which can be produced. Given constant agricultural product prices, a fall in the price of farmland will increase the profitability of farming. This will provide an incentive for Canadians to enter into farming, demand farmland and thus tend to reduce the decline in the price of farmland. Only if there are impediments to the flow of investment funds into farmland or if Canadian farmers require a

TABLE 1
Summary of Canadian Legislative Action With Regards to Foreign Ownership of Land

Governing Body	Name of Act or Most Recent Amendment	Description
Newfoundland		No restrictions currently in effect
Prince Edward Island	An Act to Amend the Real Property Act, 1972.	Non-residents of Prince Edward Island cannot acquire property of 10 acres or more or shore frontage of five chains (330 ft.) or more without permission from the Lieutenant Governor in Council.
Nova Scotia	An Act to Provide for the Disclosure of Land Holdings by Non-Residents and Certain Corporations, 1969.	Non-residents of Nova Scotia are required to register their land holdings with the Registrar of Land Holdings.
New Brunswick		No restrictions, but preference is given to residents in the lease of Crown land for recreational purposes.
Quebec	An Act Respecting Duties on Transfer of Land, 1976.	Non-residents of Canada are required to pay a tax of 33% on acquiring land. The Act does, however, contain a series of exemptions.
Ontario	The Land Transfer Act, 1974.	Non-residents of Canada are required to pay a tax of 20% of the value of the property when acquiring land (residents are required to pay a transfer tax of less than one percent). Numerous exemptions are contained in the Act.
	The Public Lands Act, 1970.	Cottage lots on Crown Land can be leased to non-Canadians only after they have been made available to Canadians for one year.
Manitoba	The Crown Lands Act, 1970.	Restricts the granting of Crown land including ranch and farm grazing permits and certain timber cutting rights to Canadian citizens.

Saskatchewan	Saskatchewan Farm Ownership Act, 1974.	Non-resident individuals of Saskatchewan are limited to agricultural land holdings with an assessed value of not greater than $15,000. In 1974, farmlands were assessed at levels from 10 to 20 percent of market value.
Alberta	Amendments to the Public Lands Act, 1973.	Restricts the granting of Crown Land to Canadian citizens.
	Amendment to the Alberta Land Titles Act, 1975.	A declaration is required as to whether a property purchaser is a non-Canadian or acting on behalf of a non-Canadian.
British Columbia	Lands Act 1970.	Restricts the granting of Crown Land to Canadian citizens.
	Amendments to the Land Registry Act.	A declaration of Citizenship is required to become a registered owner of land.
Government of Canada	Foreign Investment Review Act, 1973.	Provides for a review of takeovers of existing business enterprises or certain types of new business initiatives by non-eligible persons (non-eligible persons include those who are not Canadian citizens) with the purpose of preventing such acquisitions when they fail to offer significant benefit to Canada. Acquisitions of lands which are considered acquisitions of business enterprises would be subject to review.
	Amendment to the Canadian Citizenship Act, 1976.	Allows individual Provinces the right to prohibit the sale of land to aliens.

NOTE: The objective of this Table is to provide a very general summary of the legislations regarding alien land ownership in Canada. Such a summary, of course, cannot reflect a precise legal interpretation of the provisions of the legislation. Those who desire the legal rigour as well as more information regarding exemptions and definitional questions should consult the legislation itself.

SOURCE: Federal Committee on Foreign Ownership of Land, ***Report to the First Ministers,*** Information Canada, Ottawa, 1975. ***Foreign Investment in Land — Alternative Controls,*** proceedings of a seminar sponsored by the Faculty of Commerce and Business Administration, June 1976.

McFayden, Stuart, "The Control of Foreign Ownership of Canadian Real Estate", ***Canadian Public Policy,*** Vol. II, No. 1, Winter 1976, pages 65-77.

Manitoba Department of Agriculture. ***In Search of a Land Policy for Manitoba,*** undated.

Ricketts, Mark. "Quebec limits foreign land ownership", ***Financial Post,*** October 9, 1976, p. P-8.

higher rate of return than foreign farmers operating in Canada, will the transfer restrictions significantly decrease the price of agricultural land.

Ontario and Quebec have Acts which impose discriminatory taxes on aliens acquiring land. Both Acts, however, contain a series of exemptions and deferrals depending on the purchaser and nature of the transaction. In Ontario, the overall effect of the exemptions is to focus the tax on the alien purchase of rural and urban fringe lands as well as income and rental properties.[30] In Quebec, the legislation is intended to focus on land speculation.

Generally speaking, both Acts increase the welfare of Canadian land purchasers at the expense of current landowners. This is because the taxes tend to decrease the demand by potential foreign purchasers, which in turn results in a lowering of land prices in general.

Unfortunately, because the value of urban fringe raw land is determined by expected future residential lot prices, rather than the converse, it would appear that these savings will not be passed on to the consumers of final output.

Transfer taxes

Transfer taxes are, however, a more economically efficient device for restricting alien ownership than the outright restrictions discussed previously, since the alien whose bid exceeds the highest Canadian bid by 20 per cent in Ontario or 33 per cent in Quebec is still able to purchase the land. Bid prices for both Canadians and aliens are a function of expected net income as well as the rate of return required from the investment. If the rate of return net of transfer tax does not fall below the alien's required rate of return, a transfer tax will not prevent alien land acquisition.

For example, if it is expected that a given parcel of land will yield a net income of $120 per year to perpetuity and Canadian investors require a 12 per cent rate of return, they will bid $1,000 for the parcel. If alien investors require a 9.99 per cent rate of return, they will be prepared to bid up to $1,201.20, inclusive of tax, for the parcel.[31] Under Ontario's 20 per cent transfer tax, aliens would not be excluded from the market because they would be willing to purchase the parcel from the owner for $1,001 and pay the transfer tax of $200.20. The welfare of Canadian purchasers would be unaffected, the welfare of land sellers would be decreased to the extent that they could have obtained more than $1,001 from the sale of land in the absence of tax, and the welfare of Ontario residents in general would be increased because government revenues increased by $200.20.

If the same situation were subject to the 33 per cent Quebec transfer tax, alien purchasers would be forced from the market because their bid of $1,201.20 would not be sufficiently high to outbid Canadian purchasers. Under the 33 per cent tax, alien purchasers would have to bid $1,333 to purchase the land. The beneficiary of this higher tax would be Canadian purchasers of land, since the tax eliminates foreign demanders from the market. The welfare of land sellers is decreased and there are no revenue effects for the government.

The situation is further complicated when leverage is considered. Land transactions typically occur with downpayments which are a small percentage of total property value. Transfer taxes of 20 or 33 per cent are significant proportions of total value and they are sums which cannot be mortgage financed. Therefore, whereas an alien might be prepared to bid $120,000, inclusive of tax, for a $100,000 property available on a 10 per cent downpayment basis, he might still be deterred by the additional cash outlay for tax. This outlay raises the required initial capital from $12,000 to $30,000 in the case of a 20 per cent tax.

Foreign Investment Review Act

The major federal legislation regarding the alien acquisition of land is the Foreign Investment Review Act. This legislation provides for the review of takeovers of existing Canadian business enterprises or certain new business initiatives by non-eligible persons (including non-Canadians and corporations controlled by non-Canadians) to ensure that such activities offer significant benefits to Canada.[32] This legislation is applicable to land transactions because of the broad definition of the term business as "any undertaking or enterprise carried out in anticipation of profit."[33] Guidelines concerning real estate businesses issued by the Department of Industry, Trade and Commerce indicate that acquisitions will *tend* to be associated with the acquisition of a business and thus subject to review where the seller is a corporation, is active in relation to the property, or changes the nature of its activities as a result of the sale.[34] On the other hand, acquisitions where the purchaser uses an entirely different skill in relation to the property than did the vendor *tend not* to be associated with the acquisition of business. Generally speaking, the higher the value of the property, the greater the likelihood that its transfer will be considered the acquisition of a business and thus subject to review.

Transactions subject to review are evaluated with regards to the following criteria outlined in section 2(2) of the Foreign Investment Review Act:

a. 'the effect of the acquisition. . .on the level and nature of economic activity in Canada';

b. 'the degree and significance of participation by Canadians in the business enterprise';

c. 'the effect of the acquisition. . .on productivity in Canada';

d. 'the effect. . .on competition in Canada'; and

e. 'the compatibility of the acquisition. . .with national industrial and economic policies. . .taking into consideration industrial and economic policy objectives enunciated by the government or legislature of any province likely to be significantly effected. . .'

A positive benefit to Canada must be demonstrated before approval would be given. Thus, acquisitions which have a neutral effect on these criteria would be rejected.

It is unlikely that the Foreign Investment Review Act is relevant to the purchase of recreational land inasmuch as recreational land is purchased for personal use rather than in anticipation of profit.[35] Acquisitions of farmland would appear to be the acquisition of a business enterprise and thus subject to review. Whether or not such acquisitions would be approved depends on the specific nature of the transaction. In the only reported proposal of this nature, approval was given to Sparkford Estates Ltd. (British controlled) to acquire the Rocking Chair cattle ranch at Cawston, B.C.

Uncertainty exists as to whether or not the acquisition of urban fringe land for development purposes is subject to review under the Foreign Investment Review Act. No cases of this nature have been publicly reported and the guidelines mentioned previously are not conclusive. However, if such acquisitions are subject to review, it is likely that they would provide significant benefit to Canada and thus be approved. It is easily demonstrated that the purchase of land for development purposes would create increased employment in the construction industry, increased economic activity in general and increases in the supply of housing or developed commercial or industrial properties, depending on the nature of the proposed development.

However, when such transactions are reviewable, the review procedure imposes higher costs on foreign development firms. These costs take the form of compliance costs, costs of uncertainty and possibly higher land costs because of the intervention of additional Canadian intermediaries. Whether or not these costs can be passed on to the consumer depends on the dominance of foreign firms in the particular city in question. In markets where foreign firms are sufficiently dominant, higher land prices to the Canadian consumer would result. In markets where Canadian firms play an important role, no price increases would generally be expected.

Canadian Citizenship Act

The final legislation of relevance is the recent amendments to section 24 of the Canadian Citizenship Act. These amendments allow individual provinces to prohibit the sale of land to non-Canadians as they deem necessary.[36] Previously, section 24 gave aliens the same rights as Canadian citizens in acquiring real property.

In a 1975 judgment by the Supreme Court of Canada, the Prince Edward Island legislation regarding the acquisition of land by non-residents (see Table 1) was upheld. However, confusion existed as to whether or not provinces had the right to prohibit the alien acquisition of privately-owned land or were forced to legislate against all non-residents including Canadian citizens to circumvent section 24 of the Canadian Citizenship Act.[37] The recent amendments to the Citizenship Act serve to clarify the situation. It is too early to determine if new initiatives will be forthcoming from the provinces as a result of these amendments. Provincial policies will no doubt be influenced by the local situation and local concerns.

IV. OVERALL CONCLUSIONS OF THE ECONOMIC IMPACT OF FOREIGN OWNERSHIP OF CANADIAN LAND

Are foreigners responsible for the land and housing price increases experienced in Canada over the last several years? Do foreign landowners misuse their property? Are their developments inferior by Canadian standards? Have foreign landowners been responsible for the decline of the local farm community?

Careful examination suggests that the answer to the preceding questions is 'no'. In fact, the opposite can be concluded, that is, foreign investment on the present scale appears to provide benefits which more than offset the costs. Price effects do not appear significant and foreigners do contribute as consumers to the local community. They appear to manage their land as efficiently as Canadians and they serve as a conduit for technological innovations in both the agricultural and land development industries. If the scale of foreign investment in Canadian land were to greatly increase, this balance of benefits and costs could well be upset as price effects and non-economic considerations such as loss of a 'basic resource' become more important.

Additional prohibitions or regulatory measures are costly in terms of both administrative and compliance costs and in terms of potential retaliatory measures. Adequate monitoring of the scale of foreign land investment in Canada coupled with further investigation of the costs and benefits associated with these investments appears to be the best policy stance.

Notes

[1]Statistics Canada, *Corporations and Labour Unions Returns Act*, Catalogue 61-210, 1972.

[2]J. Alex Murray and Lawrence Leduc, *A Cross-Sectional Analysis of Canadian Public Attitudes Toward U.S. Equity Investment in Canada*, Ontario Economic Council, Working Paper No. 2/75, p. 14.

[3]These criticisms have been raised in numerous press reports and in popular magazines. A particularly scathing attack on foreign ownership of Canadian land is Maurice Cutler, "Foreign Use and Canadian Control of Our Land and Resources," *Canadian Geographic Journal*, Vol. 90 (4, 5, 6), Vol. 91 (1 and 2), 1975, pp. 4-19, 18-33, 34-48, 19-41.

[4]*Caveat on Non-Resident Ownership Prince Edward Island*, Land Registration and Information Service, Land Statistics Division, Occasional Paper No. 1, March 1974. Canadians not resident in Prince Edward Island own an additional 46,240 acres of land in the province.

[5]Estimates based on Nova Scotia Department of Lands and Forests Statistics, June 1974.

[6]Estimates made by the Department of Municipal Affairs, Province of New Brunswick.

[7]Kell Antoft, *Matters Related to Non-resident Land Ownership in Nova Scotia*, Discussion Paper No. 71-02, Institute of Public Affairs, Dalhousie University, Halifax, Canada, 1971.

[8]If the potential Canadian purchaser is, in fact, outbid by the foreigner his welfare is lessened only in the sense that he is less well off than he could have expected to have been, had the foreign buyer not intervened.

[9]Estimates based on Nova Scotia Department of Lands and Forests Statistics, June 1974.

[10]Alternatively, recognizing that both the costs of local property taxes and the benefits of local government services may be capitalized in land values, it can be argued that the foreigner buys at a price reflecting the capitalized value of both streams. In this case, the foreigner will have paid, at time of purchase, the capitalized value of the benefits of local government services but he will be unable to use the full complement of these services.

[11] *In Search of a Land Policy for Manitoba*, Manitoba Department of Agriculture, undated.

[12]This figure is the result of a 20-municipality survey conducted by the Resource Economics Branch of Alberta Agriculture.

[13]Jacob Brown, *A Study of Purchases and Ownership of Saskatchewan Farm Lands by Citizens and Companies of the United States of America to December 31, 1970*, Research Report RR:72-11, University of Saskatchewan, Saskatoon, June, 1972.

[14] *Report of Select Committee on the Ownership of Agricultural Lands*, Legislative Assembly of Saskatchewan, March, 1973.

[15]As reported in the Ottawa Citizen, Wednesday, September 8, 1976. It should be noted that this figure does not provide any information on the rate of increase or decrease in land holdings by foreigners because it is likely that foreigners were sellers as well as purchasers of properties.

[16]Brown, *op. cit.*, p. 10.

[17] *Ibid.*, p. 13.

[18] *Ibid.*, p. 9.

[19]See Gerald Knowlton, "Comments on Legislation Restricting Alien Ownership of Land," in *Foreign Investment in Land - Alternative Controls.* Proceedings of a seminar sponsored by the Faculty of Commerce and Business Administration, the University of British Columbia, June, 1976.

[20]P.S. Ross and Partners, "Impact of Foreign Investment in Commercial and Multiple Family Residential Real Estate in the Greater Vancouver Area," prepared for the Real Estate Board of Greater Vancouver, March, 1974.

[21]The large Canadian-controlled development firms such as Cadillac Fairview and S.B. McLaughlin also operate in foreign markets.

[22]For example, the British developer may use dwelling insulation standards which are suitable for the temperate climate in Britain but inadequate in the harsher climate experienced in many Canadian centres.

[23]Foreign Ownership of Ontario Real Estate, *Interim Report of the Select Committee on Economic and Cultural Nationalism*, Queen's Printer for Ontario, 1973, p. 32.

[24]It is interesting to note that British nationals may have exerted a far greater influence on urban development patterns in Canada through their participation as Canadian municipal planners in the planning process than through their ownership powers.

[25]John Donald, "The Influence of Foreign Investors on Canadian Real Estate," *Canadian Business*, June, 1975, p. 56.

[26]The access-to-capital question is a difficult question. A foreign-owned firm such as Genstar would have access to funds at a cheaper rate than a small local development firm. However, large Canadian firms such as Campeau and Cadillac Fairview enjoy a similar advantage. Favourable access to credit is not a function of nationality, but rather of credit rating.

[27]Alberta, Select Committee of the Legislative Assembly, 1973.

[28]Economic Council of Canada, *Twelfth Annual Review:Options for Growth*, Ottawa, 1975, Chapter 6.

[29]Decreased demand may have little or no effect on the price of Crown land, depending on the pricing strategies employed by the various provincial governments.

[30]Land developers are exempt in the acquisition of urban fringe properties.

[31]Even if aliens accept lower rates of return than Canadian investors, they will not be adverse to accepting the higher rates of returns sought by Canadian investors. Thus, if there is only one alien firm operating in the market, his offer price would be only slightly higher than the potential Canadian purchaser's, say $1,001. However, in cases where more than one alien firm is operating, the alien firms will compete against each other thereby increasing the price of land to $1,201.20.

[32]For a more detailed discussion of the provisions of the Foreign Investment Review Act, see Robert Hobart and Stuart McFadyen, "Federal Legislation on Foreign Ownership: Foreign Investment Controls and Real Estate," in *Foreign Investment in Land - Alternative Controls*, proceedings of a seminar sponsored by the Faculty of Commerce and Business Administration, University of British Columbia, June, 1976.

[33]Foreign Investment Review Act, section 3(1).

[34]The guidelines are not, however, legally binding.

[35]Exceptions would include the acquisition of hunting and fishing lodges for commercial purposes.

[36]One important exception is where the acquisition has been reviewed and approved under the provisions of the Foreign Investment Review Act.

[37]Excellent legal analysis of both sides of the debate are available in Ken Lysyk, "Controls on Foreign Investment in Land: Constitutional Aspects," and John Spencer, "The Alien Landowner in Canada," both included in *Foreign Investment in Land - Alternative Controls*, proceedings from a seminar sponsored by the Faculty of Commerce and Business Administration, University of British Columbia, June, 1976.

Housing and Land Prices in Canada and the U.S.

MICHAEL A. GOLDBERG
Professor and Chairman
Urban Land Economics Division
Faculty of Commerce and Business Administration
University of British Columbia

THE AUTHOR

Michael A. Goldberg was born in Brooklyn, New York in 1941. He received his Bachelor of Arts degree in economics (cum laude) from Brooklyn College in 1962. His postgraduate work was done at the University of California (Berkeley), where he received his M.A. (1965) and Ph.D. (1968) degrees in economics. He joined the University of British Columbia in 1968, and now holds the title of Professor and Chairman of the Urban Land Economics Division in the Faculty of Commerce and Business Administration. He has been a consultant to various federal and regional agencies in both the U.S. and Canada on subjects dealing with urban land economics, urban transportation planning and zoning and land use controls.

Dr. Goldberg is author of numerous publications, including: "Transportation, Urban Land Values and Rents: A Synthesis," published in *Land Economics*, Vol. 46, no. 2, May 1970; "Ecology and Planning" (with C.S. Holling), *Journal of the American Institute of Planners*, July 1971; "An Evaluation of the Interaction between Urban Transport and Land Use Systems," *Land Economics*, Vol. 48, No. 4, November, 1972; "Simulation, Synthesis and Urban Public Decision-Making," *Management Science*, Vol. 20, No. 4, December, 1973, Part II; "On the Inefficiency of Being Efficient," *Environment and Planning A*, Vol. 7, No. 4, December, 1975; "Residential Developer Behavior 1975: Additional Empirical Findings," (with D.D. Ulinder), *Land Economics*, Vol. 52, No. 3, August, 1976; *Recent Perspectives in Urban Land Economics: Essays in Honour of Richard U. Ratcliff and Paul F. Wendt*, (Editor), (Vancouver: Urban Land Economics Division, Faculty of Commerce University of British Columbia, 1976).

Housing and Land Prices in Canada and the U.S.

MICHAEL A. GOLDBERG
Professor and Chairman
Urban Land Economics Division
Faculty of Commerce and Business Administration
University of British Columbia

I. SOME CIRCUMSTANTIAL EVIDENCE, AND CONCEPTUAL MUSINGS: AN INTRODUCTORY OVERVIEW

Are there REALLY any price differences?

By the time this essay is published the character of the recent Canadian housing crisis may have changed significantly from one of high prices and perceived shortages to one of sluggishness and maintaining the value of the housing stock that the Canadian public only recently has gone into hock to purchase and support. This is a point I will close on.

Doubtless much of the discontent with Canadian housing prices during the past several years stems from implied comparisons with U.S. cities to the immediate south. This is not completely illogical since in most instances the closest city for comparison is south of the border and not within Canada. British Columbians look to the state of Washington, Manitobans to Minnesota and Torontonians to the U.S. midwest and north-east. Cablevision and other north-south regional communication vehicles reinforce the tendencies to make this sort of comparison.

Since recent evidence shows that housing prices relative to incomes in Canada are not high, then the notion that housing prices are not only high, but too high must come from elsewhere.[1] Thus, this Canadian-U.S. comparison and analysis.

The September, 1976 issue of *House and Home* speaks about "Why a house priced at $37,500 in Ohio sells for $65,000 in Toronto." The *Vancouver Sun* on December 11, 1976 compares a $59,900 house in Winnipeg with a "similar but slightly larger home in suburban Minneapolis at perhaps as much as $50,000" (p. 13). The October 17, 1976 edition of the *Seattle Post-Intelligencer* advertised similar suburban tract homes for prices ranging from $29,500, 30 minutes by freeway from Seattle, to $42,650 in an adjacent suburb. The next week, the October 23, 1976 edition of the *Vancouver Sun* advertised similar houses in similar terms with dissimilar prices ranging from a 'low' of $53,815 to a high of $69,000 depending on location and extras. One ad did approach Seattle prices. There was a semi-detached unit advertised in Squamish *only* 50 minutes by winding road from downtown Vancouver. The price: a modest $38,361.

At first look, it appears that there really are quite staggering differences between housing prices in Canadian cities and the U.S. cities directly to the south of them. The question looms, *why?*

This study is a first step in the direction of providing an answer. The analysis proceeds by drawing out of a standard explanation of how housing and land markets function (presented in detail in Appendix A), a list of causal factors that might be expected to be in some way associated with the apparently higher prices in Canada vis-a-vis the United States. We then track down these factors and measurements of them in a real life comparison. The bulk of the search is concentrated in a rather detailed comparison of the Seattle, Washington and Vancouver, British Columbia metropolitan regions. Although we have selected a specific city-to-city comparison we have, where possible, drawn out the implications for the general case of housing and land prices in Canada and the U.S.

Having tracked down and identified the culprits, we return to suggest policies that are appropriate to the situation.

The chase begins

The focus of this book and our essay is the price of land. However, as is shown in the Appendix, the price of land is determined by the price of housing. Accordingly, we can get at the determinants of land price inflation and differences between land prices in different areas by examining the housing market.

Fifteen years ago, house prices in Canada and the United States were roughly equivalent. Since that time house prices in Canada could have grown relative to those in the United States for one of three reasons: either demand grew more rapidly with similar increases in supply in the two countries; or demand grew at roughly equivalent paces and supply failed to keep pace in Canada; or lastly, elements of both these phenomena could have been occurring.

In the following sections we focus most of our attention on the demand side of the market. We have been led to do this by two considerations. First of all, the currently observed differences between Canadian and U.S. housing prices are of relatively recent vintage. Secondly, the theory of the housing market outlined in the Appendix suggests that in relatively short periods of time such as we are dealing with, housing prices are preponderantly influenced by demand factors. In addition, a pre-emptive look at the data suggested that our quarry was not to be found on the supply side (see Section II of this paper).

Elusive factors on the demand side

Intuitively we can see that anything that increases demand either in the short run, or relative to supply in the long run, will increase price. What sorts of things increase demand? Changes in the total number of households will certainly affect demand. Increases in households through migration will increase demand. Alternatively, even with a constant number of households but with rising household incomes, house prices will generally rise. More liberal mortgage credit, other things remaining constant, will increase house purchasing power and thus tend to drive up prices in the short run. Special tax treatment will also increase demand

and prices. For example, the fact that the capital gains on principal residences are tax exempt in Canada makes housing an attractive investment relative to other assets, which are taxed, and tends to increase demand. In the U.S. roughly similar capital gains treatment, together with a federal tax credit on mortgage interest and property taxes also serve to stimulate housing demand, and thus prices, in the short run (and in the longer run, too, if a corresponding supply increase is not forthcoming).

Two-sided story

Just as demand increases can lead to price increases, so can demand decreases lead to price decreases. Tightening mortgage credit, out-migration and declining household formation can all lead to declines in demand and therefore price. Particular policies which can lead to such decreases in demand include freeway construction which attracts central city households to suburban locations, therefore lowering the price of central city housing stocks. In addition, discrimination by mortgage lenders against properties in certain areas (such as U.S. inner core city areas) can lead to declining effective demand and therefore declines in price. Racial discrimination can also lead to declining prices by restricting demand to certain groups. It should be noted, however, that increases and decreases in demand need not have symmetrical effects on price.

Increases in demand in the longer run will coax out increases in supply so that the longer-run price picture depends to some considerable extent upon the cost of providing these additional supplies of housing. Decreases in demand, however, will have a depressing effect on price since the stock is fixed (even in the long run if no building occurs) and decreases in demand must lead to decreases in price unless there are wholesale abandonments of the stock so that declines in the stock through abandonments and demolitions keep pace with declines in demand.

Given this intuitive introduction to some of the factors that influence the market price, we can now examine these factors in the U.S. and Canada and in Seattle and Vancouver to begin to piece together the various elements of the puzzle.

We look first at the overall Canada-U.S. situation to see if there are any obvious candidates to include in a more detailed analysis.

II. A LOOK AT SOME 'FACTS'

An empirical look at Canadian and U.S. housing market performance

As is traditional in economic analyses, we will split the market into demand and supply elements to begin to isolate some of the factors which can account for the perceived price differences. Starting with demand components we see from Table 1 that over the period 1950 to 1974 the number of U.S. households increased from 42.9 million to 69.9 million or by nearly 65 per cent, while over roughly the same period the number of Canadian households increased from 3.4 million to 7.0 million, or by more than 100 per cent. The rate of household formation is thus an obvious candidate

TABLE 1
Population

	Total	Age Group 25-54	Age Group 25-54 as a % of Total	Households
UNITED STATES (thousands except percentages)				
1950..........	152,271	63,126	42	42,857
1960..........	180,671	67,718	38	53,021
1970..........	204,879	71,745	35	63,450
1974..........	211,909	76,414	36	69,859

Source: *Statistical Abstract of the U.S. 1975*

	Total	Age Group 25-54	Age Group 25-54 as a % of Total	Households
CANADA				
1951..........	14,009,409	5,448,984	39	3,409,295
1961..........	18,238,247	6,749,469	37	4,554,736
1971..........	21,568,310	7,707,520	36	6,041,302
1976..........	22,598,016	—	—	7,045,400

Source: *Census of Canada* 1951, 1961, 1971; Cat. No. 98-1951, 92-535, 92-715, 93-531, 93-702

Statistics Canada's Estimate of 1976 Population

Household and Family Projections for Canada and Provinces; Cat. No. 91-517

cause for price differences. On the other hand, from Table 2 we see that incomes and the percentage of incomes spent on housing in the two countries parallel each other quite closely. Thus, purchasing power on a national scale is roughly equivalent and should not be a source of great significance for explaining the price differences—although as we shall see, inter-regional income differentials may be important.

Another potential source of price differences could be preferences for accessibility—that is, preferences for housing close to the employment centre or urban core. If Canadians prefer access (or need access because of lower auto usage) then they will be willing to pay more for housing than Americans do. In essence, Americans must discount the amount they can pay for houses because they absorb higher transportation costs so that their composite purchase of housing plus transport will contain relatively more transport and less housing. Table 2 provides some supporting evi-

TABLE 2
Incomes & Expenditures

	P.D.I. Per Capita	Housing Expenditures as a % of Total P.D.I.	User-Operated Transportation Expenditures as a % of Total P.D.I.
UNITED STATES (billions except per capita and percentages)			
1960	1,937	13.20	11.37
1965	2,436	13.42	11.50
1970	3,376	13.14	10.45
1973	4,295	12.88	11.35
1974	4,623	—	—

Source: *Statistical Abstract of the U.S. 1975*

	P.D.I. Per Capita	Housing Expenditures as a % of Total P.D.I.	User-Operated Transportation Expenditures as a % of Total P.D.I.
CANADA (millions except per capita and percentages)			
1961	1,475	13.77	10.01
1966	2,303	13.08	10.85
1971	2,769	14.54	10.09
1974	4,121	—	—
1975	4,734	12.87	10.23

Source: Statistics Canada. *National Income & Expenditure Accounts* 1961-1975, Cat. No. 13-201

dence for this view as does Table 3 which compares automobiles in operation for selected years from 1953 to 1975. The significance of this table is that during the period (the 1950s) when the eventual shape of cities of the 1970s was being formed by transport and land use decisions, the U.S. had 70 per cent greater per capita automobile usage than Canada. Thus the demand for freeways was greater and freeways were built on a massive scale across the country (roughly $300 billion being spent between 1956 and 1976).[2]

TABLE 3
Automobiles in Operation

	United States Automobiles (thousands)	United States Automobiles Per Capita	Canada Automobiles (thousands)	Canada Automobiles Per Capita
1975..........	95,241	.45	7,074	.31
1960..........	57,103	.32	3,255	.18
1954..........	38,828	.24	—	—
1953..........	—	—	2,044	.14

Source: *Ward's 1976 Automotive Yearbook*
Automotive Industries Statistical Issue, March 1962
Statistics Canada *Household Facilities and Equipment*, Cat. no. 64-202

The effects of such massive urban transportation expenditures can be illustrated by Figure 1 which shows the relationship between city centre distance and house prices. House prices decline with distance from the city centre (e.g. with declines in accessibility).[3] However, it is postulated (and later demonstrated with regard to Seattle) that this so-called rent gradient is much steeper in Canada, implying that people prefer or require housing closer to the urban core because of the absence of freeways. Thus, house prices are higher than in the U.S. for close-in locations and lower for more remote areas of metropolitan regions which in the U.S. are within a commuting zone but which in Canada are still in agricultural or lower-density semi-urban uses.

Later, when looking at Seattle and Vancouver, we will see this confirmed and reinforced by much higher transit patronage in Vancouver. Thus, we can add preference for access to our candidate list of plausible explanations for housing price differentials.

FIGURE 1
Price-Distance Gradient

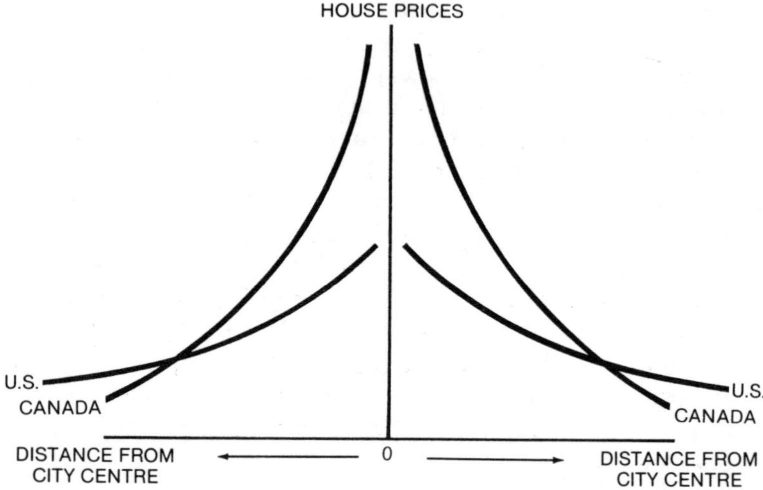

This diagram illustrates the relationship between the location of housing (distance from city centre) and its price. In the U.S., the curve is flat indicating that there is little premium for close-to-centre housing because access to the suburbs is easy and quick. In Canada, close-to-centre housing rates a high premium because there are fewer access routes and the effective supply of land is therefore smaller. Empirical verification of the price-distance relationship can be found in Table 16.

Another important factor to be considered is the availability of money and mortgage credit. Table 4 illustrates the fact that in the 1970s money supply and mortgages in force have increased at considerably faster rates in Canada as compared to the U.S. In Canada between 1960 and 1974 the money supply increased by 150 per cent while in the U.S. it increased by only 100 per cent. Similarly, mortgages outstanding increased nearly six-fold during the period in Canada whereas they did not even triple in the U.S. The availability of mortgage credit becomes a leading contender as a primary cause of price differentials. Moreover, as can be seen from Table 5, the Canadian mortgage market was reasonably competitive on the supply side with no major source of credit having more than 21 per cent of the stock of mortgages and none having less than 9 per cent. In the U.S., in comparison, Savings and Loans and Life Companies hold more than three-quarters of the mortgages. This higher degree of concentration implies that mortgage credit could be less widely available.[4]

TABLE 4
Money Supply & Mortgages Outstanding

	Money Supply (1)	Mortgages Outstanding
UNITED STATES (billions)		
1960	144	270
1965	171	326
1970	221	452
1974	284	687

(1) Money Supply = Currency plus Demand Deposits

Source: *Statistical Abstract of the U.S. 1975*

	Money Supply (1)	Mortgages Outstanding
CANADA (billions)		
1960	6,189	9,289
1965	—	18,264
1970	9,699	30,119
1974	15,306	53,824

(1) Money Supply = Currency plus Demand Deposits

Source: *Bank of Canada Review 1975*
Canadian Housing Statistics 1975

TABLE 5
Holders of Residential Mortgages

Total	Commercial Banks $	%	Savings Banks $	%	Savings & Loans	%	Insurance Companies	%	Pension Funds	%	Finance Companies	%	Other	%
UNITED STATES 1974 (billions)														
370.2	82.4	22	45.0	12	202.3	55	22.4	6	2.7	.8	10.8	3	5.3	1.5

Source: *Statistical Abstract of U.S. 1975*

Total	Chartered Banks	%	Trust Companies	%	Loan Companies	%	Credit Unions	%	Life Companies	%	Other	%
CANADA 1975 (millions)												
50,516	7,716	15	10,500	21	6,890	14	4,750	9	10,300	21	10,000	20

Source: *Canadian Housing Statistics 1975*

To tidy up some details on the demand side, it should be noted that in spite of higher rates for mortgages in Canada (11.81 per cent compared to 8.92 per cent in 1975, for example) consumers are willing to go into debt to own houses.[5] Thus, increased mortgage indebtedness is not due to lower mortgage rates but rather to something inherent in the Canadian demand for housing and mortgages, such as the trade-off of transport costs for access.

It could also be argued that Canadians spend more because more of them are employed but the approximately equivalent rate of unemployment lays aside this potential source of differences in demand.[6] Similarly, it could be said that Canadians have different expenditure patterns and therefore higher demand comes from spending higher proportions of income on housing. Table 6 lays this potential argument to rest. Finally, it might be alleged that higher house prices in Canada are merely the result of general inflation rates being higher, but this argument too can be disposed of in light of the generally equal rates of inflation.[7]

On the demand side we can tentatively conclude, and set aside for further analysis with reference to Seattle and Vancouver, that relatively easier access to mortgage finance

TABLE 6
Urban Family Expenditures

	Urban United States			Urban Canada		
	Housing Expenditure[1]	Total Budget	Housing Expenditure as Percentage of Total Budget	Housing Expenditure[1]	Average Income	Housing Expenditure as Percentage of Total Budget
	$	$		$	$	
1974...	3,236	14,333	22.6	3,306	13,500	24.5
1973...	2,810	12,262	22.9	—	—	—
1972...	2,810	11,446	24.6	—	—	—
1971...	—	—	—	2,886	11,500	25.1
1970...	2,501	10,664	23.5	—	—	—
1969...	—	—	—	2,638	10,500	25.1

Source: *U.S. Statistical Abstract*
Statistics Canada, *Urban Family Expenditure,* Cat. No. 62-541(b), 62-540 and 62-537

[1] Includes shelter costs, household furnishings and household operation.

and differences in the trade-off between transportation and housing can explain much of the difference that exists in house prices between Canada and the U.S. One last potential candidate for explaining price differences is racial discrimination and discriminatory lending practices. The effect of discrimination where demand, especially for existing central city housing, is driven down by lending practices restricting mortgage credit is to lower housing prices compared to non-discriminatory situations. A transport policy based on freeways, and racial discrimination in outlying areas, reinforces this pattern by allowing central city middle income residents to 'escape from the city' to the suburbs. In other words, they withdraw their demand, the demand curve falls, and prices are lower than if they had stayed and/or if financial institutions would buoy up demand through mortgage loans on central city housing stock. Such discrimination has been documented in numerous U.S. markets but has not yet been shown to be a factor in Canadian cities.[8]

TABLE 7
Stock of Housing

	Total Units	Total Occupied Units	Single Detached Units	S.D. Units as a % of Total	Multiple Units	M. Units as a % of Total
UNITED STATES						
1950	45,983,398	42,826,281	29,115,698	63	16,552,482	36
1960	58,326,357	53,023,875	40,103,346	69	17,444,873	30
1970	68,679,038	63,449,747	44,800,846	65	23,878,346	35

Source: *U.S. Census of Housing* 1950, 1960, 1970

	Total Units	Total Occupied Units	Single Detached Units	S.D. Units as a % of Total	Multiple Units	M. Units as a % of Total
CANADA						
1951	3,585,128	3,409,295	2,275,615	67	1,123,220	33
1961	4,577,211	4,554,493	2,978,501	65	1,156,031	34
1971	6,259,000	6,034,505	3,591,770	60	2,378,635	39

Source: *Census of Canada* 1951, 1961, 1971; Statistics Canada, Cat. No. 98-1951F, 93-523, 93-727

Meanwhile back on the supply side. . .

So far we have shown that the demand side factors of household formation, mortgage credit and access preference could lead to significant price increases *assuming* no change in the stock of units. Let's look now at the supply side of the market in both Canada and the U.S. to see if supply kept pace with demand.

Table 7 gives us some limited insights into supply by providing data on housing stocks in the U.S. and Canada. Housing stocks in the U.S. increased by 17.7 per cent from 1960 to 1970 while in Canada they increased by 36.7 per cent from 1961 to 1971. This compares with a 19.7 per cent increase in households over the period in the U.S. and a 32.5 per cent increase in households in Canada. Thus, supply did keep pace with demand in both countries. More importantly, we can see from Table 8 that Canada's housing industry significantly outperformed the U.S. housing industry in terms of the relative output and stability of the output of housing units. On a per capita basis Canada has been building significantly more housing than has the U.S. during the period 1960 to 1975.

Based on these data, therefore, we would have to conclude that supply has at least kept pace with the increase in the number of households in Canada compared with the U.S. Moreover, in recent times (since 1970) Canada has significantly outproduced the U.S. in relative terms. Accordingly, we must look somewhere other than deficiencies in supply to explain the relatively higher prices of houses in Canada. Thus, we turn to examine two specific housing markets, Seattle and Vancouver, to narrow the range of alternative explanations, since ultimately housing markets are local in character.

TABLE 8
Housing Starts

	Total Units	Single Detached Units	Multiple Units
UNITED STATES (thousands)			
1960	1,296	1,009	287
1961	1,365	989	376
1962	1,492	996	496
1963	1,642	1,022	620
1964	1,562	973	589
1965	1,510	965	545
1966	1,196	780	416
1967	1,322	845	477
1968	1,548	901	647
1969	1,500	811	689
1970	1,467	815	652
1971	2,084	1,153	931
1972	2,378	1,311	1,067
1973	2,057	1,133	924
1974	1,353	889	464
1975	1,171	896	275
TOTAL	24,943	15,488	9,455

Source: *Housing and Urban Development Trends,* 1974, 1971, 1970.
Construction Review, 1976

	Total Units Started	Single Detached Units	Multiple Units
CANADA			
1960	108,858	67,171	41,687
1961	125,577	76,430	49,147
1962	130,095	74,443	55,652
1963	148,624	77,158	71,466
1964	165,658	77,079	88,579
1965	166,565	75,441	91,124
1966	134,474	70,642	62,832
1967	164,123	72,534	91,589
1968	196,878	75,339	121,539
1969	210,415	78,404	132,011
1970	190,528	70,749	119,779
1971	233,653	98,056	135,597
1972	249,914	115,570	134,344
1973	268,529	131,552	136,977
1974	222,123	122,143	99,980
1975	231,456	123,929	107,527
TOTAL	2,946,470	1,406,640	1,539,830

Source: *Canadian Housing Statistics 1975;* Table 9

III. SEATTLE AND VANCOUVER UNDER THE MICROSCOPE

Housing markets are highly localized, and if we are to understand house price differentials we must really explore specific markets. Thus, the following detailed look.

Seattle and Vancouver should be similar if we are going to make the kinds of comparisons talked about earlier. They are. Both are of approximately the same age and size. Both are port cities, with constraining topography. Primary products, particularly lumber and wood products, form an important segment of the economic base of the regions. Climates and proximity to each other (150 miles) round out a summary list of their similarities.They are alike enough to allow us to take a more detailed look.

Again, starting from the beginning, are there really any price differences of importance between these cities? If there are, did our cursory view of national differences yield any leads?

Price differences

Table 9 compares housing prices in Seattle and Vancouver. First, it should be noted that the sales information is based upon sales through the multiple listing services (MLS) in Vancouver and upon sample sales for Seattle. These MLS sales in Vancouver have been shown to be biased downward (i.e. provide an underestimate) by having a larger proportion of lower-priced houses than would a truly representative sample of all sales. The Seattle data are not biased, however, and represent a good measure of house prices in the Seattle region. Thus, if anything, Table 9 is downward biased for Vancouver prices and relatively unbiased for Seattle.

It is apparent from Table 9 that house prices are significantly different in the two metropolitan regions. This is particularly striking since as recently as 1971 house prices were higher in Seattle. However, since 1971 the MLS data show that Vancouver prices rose by 160 per cent while house prices in Seattle increased by only 34 per cent. Since these dramatic price differentials have occurred during a five year period and since this is a 'short-run' situation, it is quite legitimate to rely on the assumption that, in relative terms, the demand side of the market has been the principal source of the price variation.

TABLE 9
Housing Prices and Price Indices

	Vancouver Sales Price MLS Ave.	Index (67 = 100)	Seattle Sales Price	Index (67 = 100)
1960 ...	$13,105	73	$19,757	87
1961 ...	12,348	69	19,984	88
1962 ...	12,158	68	20,892	92
1963 ...	12,636	71	21,120	93
1964 ...	13,202	74	21,347	94
1965 ...	13,964	78	21,347	94
1966 ...	15,202	85	22,028	97
1967 ...	17,836	100	22,709	100
1968 ...	20,595	115	23,390	103
1969 ...	23,939	134	26,343	116
1970 ...	24,239	136	26,297	116
1971 ...	26,471	148	26,343	116
1972 ...	31,465	176	27,251	120
1973 ...	41,505	232	28,160	124
1974 ...	57,861	324	30,430	134
1975 ...	64,471	370	32,702	144
1976 ...	68,900	386	35,200	155

Source: *Real Estate Trends in Metro Vancouver*
Real Estate Research Report

TABLE 10
Sample 1976 Residential Lot Values

	METRO SEATTLE		METRO VANCOUVER	
	Per Sq. Ft.	Lot	Per Sq. Ft.	Lot
High Value Central City Residential Lot	$1.65	$37,400	$12.62	$100,000
Medium Value Central City Residential Lot ..	.59	13,372	5.05	40,000
High Value Suburban Residential Lot	.87	19,700	4.73	37,500
Medium Value Suburban Residential Lot	.47	10,700	4.17	33,000

Source: *Real Estate Research Report, Spring 1976*
Real Estate Trends in Metro Vancouver 1976

DEMAND

Population and income differences

Looking first at demand we see some striking differences and striking similarities. First, over the period 1950 to 1976 population increased by just under 100 per cent in Seattle. In Vancouver from 1951 to 1976 the equivalent figure was roughly 120 per cent (see Table 11). [Actually Seattle grew by 95 per cent in 26 years while Vancouver increased by 121 per cent in 25 years, hardly a dramatic difference.][9] Thus, population growth would not seem to be a source of the dramatic price differences, though surely a contributory factor in the absence of corresponding increases in supply.[10]

We must look elsewhere for demand differences. Income is a logical place to turn. Unfortunately, there are no data available for recent years on incomes by metropolitan area. From the most recent data for states and provinces it is evident that from 1961 to 1975 in the state of Washington incomes increased by 153 per cent.[11] In British Columbia from 1961 to 1975 incomes per capita increased by 230 per cent.

TABLE 11
Population

	Total Population	Age Group 25-54	Age Group 25-54 as a % of total	Households
METRO SEATTLE				
1950......	732,992	324,575	44	213,575
1960......	1,107,213	428,692	39	359,814
1970......	1,421,869	463,089	33	418,431
1976......	1,425,800	—	—	—

Source: *U.S. Census of Population,* 1950, 1960, 1970
Washington State Office of Policy Planning.

Source: *U.S. Census of Housing,* 1950, 1960, 1970

	Total Population	Age Group 25-54	Age Group 25-54 as a % of total	Households
METRO VANCOUVER				
1951......	530,728	227,408	43	153,975
1961......	790,165	316,618	40	228,596
1971......	1,082,350	408,765	38	346,215
1976......	1,178,000*	—	—	—

Source: *Census of Canada,* 1951, 1961, 1971; Statistics Canada, Cat. No. 98-1951-M5, 95-537, 95-728, 95-758, 93-531, 93-702

* Preliminary Estimate

Moreover, from 1970 to 1975 incomes per capita in B.C. increased by 84 per cent, while the corresponding figure for Washington is only 53 per cent over the period.

It seems safe to conclude initially that while population growth was not a very likely cause of price increases, income growth was.[12] This conclusion is further supported by unemployment rates in the U.S., Canada, British Columbia and Seattle. Since 1969 (the year of the Boeing lay-off) unemployment rates in B.C. have been significantly lower than in Seattle, particularly during the years 1970 to 1972. Since 1972, B.C. rates have remained a steady 0.6 per cent below Seattle rates. This should be reinforced by the fact that B.C. rates in general are higher than corresponding unemployment rates in the GVRD,[13] so that using B.C. as a comparison understates the differences in unemployment between the GVRD and the Seattle metropolitan area.

Tax and travel differences

Other potential causes of price differences in housing between Seattle and Vancouver include property taxes and the preference for accessibility. Effectively, Seattle property tax rates are twice the corresponding Vancouver rates. These tax differences are striking and can account for substantial price differences by themselves when capitalized into house prices. The tax question is a difficult one, however, since Vancouver data do not reflect the B.C. homeowner grants. Similarly, U.S. data do not reflect the fact that local property taxes are deductible expenses for federal income tax purposes.

A final substantial source of demand differences (and therefore a source of price differences) is the travel behaviour of Vancouverites as opposed to Seattlites. Measurements confirm that Seattle has nearly four times the number of lane miles of highway that Vancouver has (1,539 lane miles versus 405 lane miles). The Vancouver region encompasses 1,000 square miles [only 630 square miles (approx.) if you exclude the parts of the region over 1200′ in altitude]. This compares with 4,200 square miles in the Seattle-Everett Standard Metropolitan Area (SMA) which is our definition of metropolitan Seattle. Thus, the Vancouver region is much denser. Higher density will lead to higher land prices which in turn result from higher house prices (e.g. greater willingness to pay high house prices for houses on smaller lots). For instance, when the Seattle Real Estate Research Report presents information on suburban lot prices their standard-sized lot is 20,000 square feet. When the Real Estate Board of Vancouver in its Real Estate Trends in Metropolitan Vancouver talks about suburban standard lots they are using 66' x 120' or 7,920 square feet as a standard.[14]

Additional support for this relatively greater preference for access and therefore density in Vancouver as opposed to Seattle is provided by data on transit use in the two metropolitan areas. Analysis of this information reveals that although the transport systems are essentially the same size, the Vancouver system has been consistently carrying about twice as many passengers since the mid-1960s. Moreover, recent planning in Vancouver has been aimed at transit almost exclusively, including ferries and light rapid transit while in Seattle they are in the midst of yet another great freeway debate.[15]

Evidence on accessibility that confirms the above impressions is gained from a comparison of actual travel time contours for the two cities. In general, these comparisons show that the Seattle commuter can travel significantly greater distances while spending the same amount of time en route as a Vancouver commuter. In other words, significantly more land is within, say, 20 minutes travel time from the city centre in Seattle.

Summary of demand differences

The picture that emerges from these empirical explorations is that population is not likely to be an explanatory factor in our search for the 'causes' of price differentials. However, greater increases in incomes in Vancouver are (contrary to the impression gained from the national comparisons) the cause. Moreover, the previously alluded to preference of Canadians for centrality and density is borne out by the information presented above. Such preferences will cause Canadian land bids to be higher than the equivalent land bids in the U.S. This combined with the absence of freeways constrains Canadian and Vancouver urban development. People trade-off transportation costs for access and bid up house prices close-in and therefore land prices close-in. In the U.S. the situation seems reversed where suburban locations are preferred, leading to lower central city land prices and higher suburban prices than in Canada where suburban lands are still in farm use and therefore at farm values plus some speculative increment for possible conversion for urban uses in the future. Income differences and accessibility preferences therefore seem to be where our search for explanations of price differentials has taken us.

These 'explanations' will hold if we can show that there was not an offsetting supply restriction in Vancouver. Therefore we must look at the supply side of the market.

SUPPLY

From census data (reported in Table 12) we discover that from 1950 to 1970 total occupied units increased by exactly 100 per cent in Seattle and correspondingly by 125 per cent in Vancouver from 1951 to 1971. This takes us up to 1970-71 which is when house price differentials really began to become evident. What has happened since then is of real concern, since it is alleged by many that house prices have gone

TABLE 12
Stock of Housing

	Totals Units	Total Occupied Units	Single Detached Units	S.D. Units as a % of Total	Multiple Units	M. Units as a % of Total	Owner Occupied Units	O.O. Units as a % of Total
METRO SEATTLE								
1950..	252,396	236,258	173,588	74	77,746	33	149,382	63
1960..	392,656	359,814	285,299	79	102,696	29	240,180	67
1970..	513,208	473,222	360,970	76	138,770	29	306,930	65

Source: *Census of Housing,* 1950, 1960, 1970.

	Totals Units	Total Occupied Units	Single Detached Units	S.D. Units as a % of Total	Multiple Units	M. Units as a % of Total	Owner Occupied Units	O.O. Units as a % of Total
METRO VANCOUVER								
1951..	—	153,981	114,510	74	32,330	21	105,445	69
1961..	229,670	228,598	171,620	75	47,630	21	159,414	70
1971..	—	345,875	216,445	63	127,200	37	203,515	59

Source: *Census of Canada,* 1951, 1961, 1971; Statistics Canada, Cat. No. 98-151M-5, 95-537, 95-728

TABLE 13
Housing Starts

	Total Units	Single Detached Units	Multiple Units
METRO SEATTLE			
1960	7,434	6,218	1,216
1961	8,874	7,159	1,715
1962	12,721	8,709	4,012
1963	11,480	7,355	4,125
1964	7,452	4,409	3,043
1965	8,269	5,436	2,833
1966	13,293	7,458	5,835
1967	24,137	9,967	14,170
1968	23,377	10,349	13,028
1969	13,924	6,359	7,565
1970	9,598	5,274	9,324
1971	5,681	4,374	1,307
1972	6,157	4,890	1,267
1973	6,990	4,942	2,048
1974	7,626	5,496	2,130
1975	11,493	7,616	3,877

Source: *Real Estate Research Report*

	Total Units	Single Detached Units	Multiple Units
METRO VANCOUVER			
1960	—	—	—
1961	—	—	—
1962	7,387	3,607	3,780
1963	8,941	3,874	5,067
1964	12,791	4,219	8,572
1965	11,684	4,095	7,589
1966	9,138	4,465	4,673
1967	13,896	6,328	7,568
1968	15,690	5,658	10,032
1969	17,690	5,165	12,525
1970	13,437	4,832	8,605
1971	15,444	5,674	9,770
1972	14,126	6,023	8,103
1973	14,953	7,088	7,865
1974	12,037	5,451	6,586
1975	11,832	5,762	6,070

Source: *Real Estate Trends in Metro Vancouver*

up in Vancouver because of government interference and supply restrictions. Table 13 refutes this argument convincingly. Between 1970 and 1975, Vancouver started 60,300 dwelling units of all types. During the same period Seattle registered only 47,500 dwelling starts. Thus, even with essentially stagnant population growth in the two metropolitan areas, we still see that Vancouver started 27 per cent more units than Seattle. Supply not only responded admirably but as we can see from Table 14 perhaps it over-

TABLE 14
Completed But Unoccupied New Single Family Units

	Metro Seattle	Metro Vancouver
	(Spring)	(June)
1965	888	171
1966	684	256
1967	877	323
1968	960	485
1969	1,431	328
1970	1,396	482
1971	579	230
1972	609	249
1973	619	277
1974	633	510
1975	716	876
1976	783	1,193

Source: *Real Estate Research Report,* Spring 1976
Real Estate Trends in Metro Vancouver, 1976, 1970

Completed But Unoccupied New Condominium/Multi-Family Units

	Metro Seattle Condominium Units	Metro Vancouver Multi-Family Units
	(Spring)	(June)
1976	806	1,517 (October, 1976)
1975	1,067	1,498
1974	—	375
1973	—	586
1972	—	587
1971	—	964
1970	—	546

Source: *Real Estate Research Report,* Fall 1976
Real Estate Trends in Metro Vancouver, 1976

responded, leading to significant unsold inventories. Table 14 also includes information on condominiums which were reported by the Central Mortgage and Housing Corporation to number nearly 2,000 unsold units at the end of 1976, with unsold single detached units reaching 1,200 units.[16] It appears that there has not been any supply shortage but rather some demand shortage in recent months (a result which is, incidentally, fully consistent with the model of stock and flows presented in the Appendix).

One last area which must be noted for completeness is rental housing. For both Vancouver and Canada vacancy rates have been significantly lower than in Seattle and the U.S. However, since 1973 rents have been controlled and lower average vacancy rates therefore have not contributed to increased prices. A shortage of rental accommodation probably did drive many people into the condominium market, however, and doubtless helped create the short-term overdemand which led to our current oversupply.

So much for data and concepts. What can we conclude?

IV. CONCLUSIONS, UNANSWERED QUESTIONS AND POSSIBLE EXTENSIONS

Popular myths relating to housing prices in Canada and the United States have been both supported and refuted by the evidence that appears above. Data for Seattle and Vancouver support the belief that house prices do differ.

Other myths that have been presented in the media and by housing industry and public officials, and which purport to explain (more properly blame) these differences, have been refuted. The myth that Canadian housing supply is sluggish and unresponsive to demand has been shown to be untrue. More generally, laying the blame on government restrictions on supply can be set aside as a factor in the relatively higher house prices that have prevailed in Vancouver (and Canada) as opposed to Seattle (and the U.S.). Rather, demand factors seem to be working. Household formation, money supply, mortgage availability, incomes and the preference for access all seem to lend credence to the argument that during the recent period (since 1970) demand factors grew much more rapidly in Canada than in the U.S. Thus, despite relatively greater production in Canada, house prices rose more rapidly and to a relatively greater extent, pointing the finger at demand rather than supply as the likely cause of the observed house price differentials. Table 15 summarizes demand and supply factors from 1950 to the present. The data appear as annual percentage compounded growth rates to reduce the data to a common comparative base.

To summarize these findings:

- Excess demand, through rapid increases in demand, appears as the major culprit in raising Canadian house prices above U.S. levels.

- Supply grew very vigorously during this period of price appreciation, lending little credence to the argument that supply restrictions and 'government interference' caused the problem.

- Despite the local nature of real property markets, the data imply that national policies, particularly monetary and mortgage policy, fueled the price spiral in Canada. Moreover, national transportation policy (particularly freeway construction) in the U.S. did much to affect local property markets by providing fringe lands with access similar to the central city areas. This essentially served to 'dump' large quantities of suburban land on the urban land market, decreasing the value of the standing stock of housing in central areas and increasing the value in suburban areas. Thus, while national policy in Canada was fueling demand, U.S. transportation policy was decreasing the demand for central cities by dumping large acreages on the market through freeway construction. Canadian policy increased demand without a national urban transportation policy and thus increased price in the short run, while U.S. policy decreased demand and therefore price.

TABLE 15

NOTES:

1. **Rates of Population Growth** (Compounded Annual Rate)

1.1 UNITED STATES	— Total Population	50/74 -	1.39%
		60/74 -	1.15%
		70/74 -	.85%
	— Age Group 25 - 54	50/74 -	.80%
		60/74 -	.87%
		70/74 -	1.59%
	— Households	50/74 -	2.06%
		60/74 -	1.99%
		70/74 -	2.43%
1.2 CANADA	— Total Population	51/76 -	1.93%
		65/76 -	1.44%
		71/76 -	.94%
	— Age Group 25 - 54	51/71 -	1.75%
		61/71 -	1.34%
	— Households	51/76 -	2.95%
		61/76 -	2.95%
		71/76 -	3.12%
1.3 METRO SEATTLE	— Total Population	50/76 -	2.59%
		60/76 -	1.59%
		70/76 -	.05%
	— Age Group 25 - 54	50/70 -	1.79%
		60/70 -	.77%
	— Households	50/70 -	3.42%
		60/70 -	1.52%
1.4 METRO VANCOUVER	— Total Population	51/76 -	3.24%
		61/76 -	2.70%
		71/76 -	1.71%
	— Age Group 25 - 54	51/71 -	2.90%
		61/71 -	2.59%
	— Households	51/71 -	4.13%
		61/71 -	4.24%

2. **Rates of Growth of Stock of Housing (Comp. Annual Rate)**

2.1 UNITED STATES	— Total	50/70 -	2.39%
		60/70 -	2.62%
2.2 CANADA	— Total	51/71 -	2.90%
		61/71 -	2.85%
2.3 SEATTLE	— Total	50/70 -	3.53%
		60/70 -	2.78%
2.4 VANCOUVER	— Total	51/71 -	4.13%
		61/71 -	4.23%

3. **Rates of Growth of Money Supply and Mortgages Outstanding**

3.1 UNITED STATES	— Money Supply	60/74 - 4.97% 65/74 - 5.80% 70/74 - 6.47%
	— Mortgages Outstanding	60/74 - 6.90% 65/74 - 8.64% 70/74 - 11.03%
3.2 CANADA	— Money Supply	60/74 - 6.68% 70/74 - 12.08%
	— Mortgages Outstanding	60/74 - 13.37% 65/74 - 12.76% 70/74 - 15.62%

4. **Rates of Growth of P.D. Income and P.D.I./Capita**

4.1 UNITED STATES	— P.D. Income	60/73 - 7.57% 65/73 - 8.42% 70/73 - 9.32%
	— P.D. Income/CAP.	60/74 - 6.41% 65/74 - 7.38% 70/74 - 8.18% 73/74 - 7.64%
4.2 CANADA	— P.D. Income	61/75 - 10.07% 66/75 - 11.12% 71/75 - 14.62%
	— P.D. Income/CAP.	61/75 - 8.69% 66/75 - 8.34% 71/75 - 14.35% 74/75 - 14.88%

5. **Rates of Growth of Housing Prices**

5.1 SEATTLE	60/70 - 2.90% 60/76 - 3.68% 70/76 - 4.98%
5.2 VANCOUVER	60/70 - 6.34% 60/76 - 10.93% 70/76 - 19.02%

The land value/transportation cost relationship that depicts land values as declining with distance (or access) from the central city is presented graphically in Figure 2. U.S. transportation policy has served to increase access of outlying areas and therefore their land values at the expense of the existing central locations, tending to flatten out the land value curve. Canadian policy of transit improvement and little freeway construction has resulted in a relatively steeper curve. It is not surprising therefore to find land values much higher in Canadian central cities than in corresponding U.S. cities, holding everything else constant (such as income, population and households and money supply).

Unanswered, unasked, and annoying questions

Demand elements appear to be the source of price differences. In one sense our search is over. However, in more fundamental ways these findings imply that the real search has not yet begun. What search? The search for viable real property markets, and livable cities. Has our poking into house prices helped to begin this more basic safari to track the liveable city? I think so.

Some previously unasked questions can point the way. Do we really want low price housing? Is low price housing related to liveability? In comparing Canadian and U.S. cities were we really comparing apples with apples, or grapes and prunes? Do higher prices necessarily imply government interference, inefficiency and imperfections in the Canadian urban system? More to the point, are Canadian urban institutions really inferior to their U.S. analogues or alternatively is the U.S. the 'model' of urban development that Canada really wants to follow?

Sketching out answers to these questions starts us on the road to knowledge about the Canadian urban system. It is knowledge of that system which we should be seeking since housing, important as it may be, is in the end only an element in urban living and enjoyment.

FIGURE 2
Price-Distance Gradient

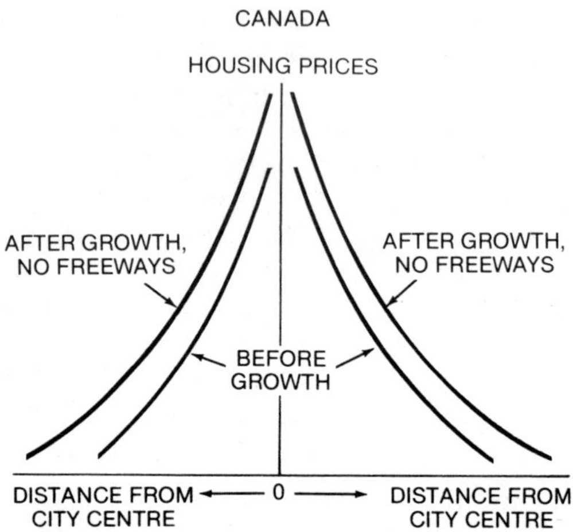

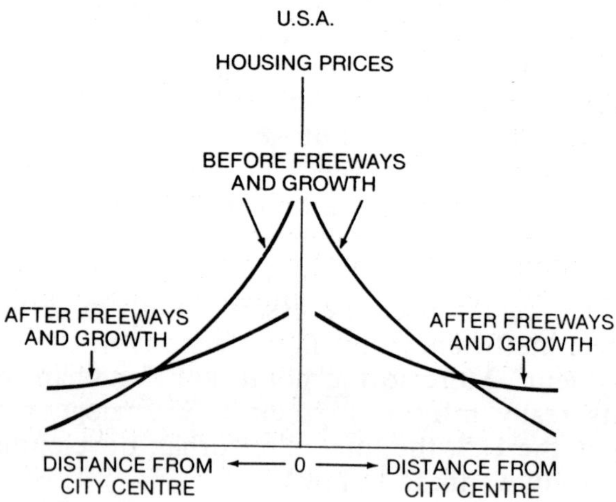

These figures illustrate the impact of freeways on the price-distance gradient in the U.S. compared with Canada. Freeways increase the effective supply of land within a given travelling time distance from the city centre and hence reduce the price of all land within that travelling time zone. In Canada, fewer freeways have been built and as a consequence, the increased demand for close-to-centre land occasioned by population growth has resulted in a bidding up of the price of land a given distance from the centre.

In Canada nearly 70 per cent of the households own their dwellings.[17] For most households home ownership represents the bulk of household assets. Driving down house prices eats into the value of these assets and would be, I suspect, significantly more unpopular than high prices for the 30 per cent who do not own dwelling units. The old adage that everyone wants expensive wheat for the farmer and cheap bread for the consumer cannot hold. We cannot have simultaneously low prices for house buyers and high prices for house sellers. In addition to being politically unworkable, a low housing price policy is counterproductive since in the longer run it would lead to more spending on housing and more wasteful construction of large units. Recent high prices should have taught us that housing, land, and housing materials are in short supply. They are scarce resources. As such they should be treated with care not frittered away through prodigal policies of making housing cheaper.[18] High prices from both an economic and environmental point of view, while unpleasant, are warranted if we are to maintain a reasonable quality of living in a world of finite resources.

High prices also reflect the high level of demand for Canadian urban living places. Unlike U.S. cities, Canadian core areas are much in demand for living and command premium prices. Rosedale in Toronto, Westmount and Outremont in Montreal, and Shaughnessy in Vancouver, are all within 5 minutes of the absolute centres of their respective urban cores. Instead of bemoaning high prices in Canadian cities, why not glory in the knowledge that Canadian core areas are in demand, are healthy, and are actively sought after? High price and high environmental quality go together and it is completely logical to expect that the high quality of Canadian urban areas will be reflected in high prices.

This raises the question of whether Canadian and U.S. cities are comparable. I think not. Canadian cities are compact, continually being renewed by private homeowners and investors and are stable, slowly evolving entities. U.S. cities, on the other hand, have been bombarded during the past 30 years by a series of 'facilitating government policies' such as

TABLE 16
Residential Lot Prices
(price per square foot)

Metro Seattle		Metro Vancouver	
University-Ravenna	$1.48	Kerrisdale	$9.09-10.10
Laurelhurst	4.11	Shaughnessy	9.52-11.11
Broadmoor	0.63	Oakridge	9.39
Mountlake-Capital Hill	1.10	Point Grey/Dunbar	6.50- 9.17
Washington Park-Denny Blaine	1.02	South Van/Cambie	5.83- 8.33
Mount Baker	0.43	Killarney	6.30- 8.15
Beacon Hill	0.35	Grand view	8.59- 9.34
West Seattle	0.79	Burnaby South	4.72- 5.14
Queen Anne	1.10	New Westminster	4.17- 5.00
Magnolia	2.42	Central Lonsdale	5.83
Ballard	1.65	Deep Cove	4.16- 5.28
Green Lake	1.48	British Properties	2.98- 3.44
Broadview	1.45	Ambleside/Dundarave	6.33- 6.67
Bellevue	0.87	Coquitlam	3.47- 3.79
Kiagvah	0.59	Pt. Coquitlam	3.19- 3.65
Kent	0.56	Richmond (new home)	5.42- 5.83
Des Moines	0.37	Surrey (North & Central)	3.19- 3.28
		North Delta	3.33
		Tsawwassen	3.66- 4.04
		Langley	3.33- 4.03

Distance (miles)	Price (as % of central city price)	Distance (miles)	Price (as % of central city price)
0	100%	0	100%
22	79%	10	67%
50	54%	12.5	61%
		20.5	43%

Vancouver per square foot prices calculated using the lot widths stated in R.T.M.V. and a depth of 120′. Where a range of lot sizes and lot prices were given, the smaller size was applied to the lower price and the larger to the higher.

Sources: *Real Estate Research Report,* Spring 1976.
Real Estate Trends in Metro Vancouver, 1976.

urban renewal, freeway construction and public housing (to give just a sampling). Such 'facilitation' of urban development in the suburbs and urban redevelopment in central areas has had an incredibly destabilizing impact on private investment in U.S. cities, on the composition of central city residents, and on the quality of the urban environment. While the gas stations might be the same on U.S. and Canadian street corners, the cities are fundamentally different in their vitality, stability, and liveability. Conclusion: comparisons are odious.

If comparisons are unwarranted why continue to make them? My suspicion is that much of the motivation underlying the present volume on land policy also underlies the Canadian propensity to compare. Basically, Canada must be doing something, if not everything, wrong. Higher housing and land prices must reflect incompetence, government interference, and terrible imperfections in the housing and land markets which prevent supply from efficiently and effectively meeting demand. I do not hold this opinion. On the contrary I feel the opposite is the case, that high prices reflect the success of our urban policies and non-policies, such as fragmented local zoning and building by-laws. Instead, I see examples of terribly powerful interventions by governments in the United States which act to lower the price of housing through introducing, or allowing to be introduced into the system, a number of imperfections and distortions which are largely absent so far as we know in Canada. Give me an example, the reader is doubtless saying. Here are several.

The British North America Act (the core of the Canadian Constitution) effectively prevents the Government of Canada from taking any direct role in urban development. As a result, Canadian cities are not dotted with federally built highways, public housing projects, and urban renewal. They are also not saddled with the operating costs of the 'free' capital grants that were available to cities under the U.S. Constitution. Because of its awesome ability to raise revenue and spend money the U.S. federal government during the past century has gotten directly involved in urban transportation, renewal, and development. It has also made massive contributions to local school systems. Canadians often whine about the inability of the provinces to come to agreement with the federal government on such 'give-aways'. As a result, Canadian cities have had to grow out of local and provincial tax revenues and private investment. Such growth has been less spectacular than U.S. growth. It has also been spectacularly less expensive. Canadian cities are not on the verge of bankruptcy.[19]

Without a large federal presence Canadian cities have grown on a pay-as-you-go basis. Local property markets and municipal growth controls together dictated urban form. Canadian urban development was evolutionary.

'South of the border' the story has been, and continues to be, different. Massive injections of highway funds put suburban landowners and developers in oligopoly positions in relation to central city real property. Provision of vast quantities of suburban land on urban land markets depresses prices in the central city and raises prices in the previously inaccessible suburbs. Urban renewal and freeway development together remove a great deal of the physical stock of structures in U.S. cities, lessening their attractiveness and livability and further depressing the demand for and hence, price of, core dwelling places. Since these federal policies are large in scale and have relatively short implementation periods, the pace of change is rapid. New areas develop virtually overnight while central city neighbourhoods decay as quickly. Change verges on a revolutionary, not evolutionary, scale. Such large-scale and rapid 'innovation' results in significant disruption of central city and suburban neighbourhoods, travel patterns and most importantly, expectations. Central city expectations become gloomy in the knowledge that additional transportation 'improvements' will erode the demand for central city neighbourhoods and therefore depress prices. The size of these urban investments by the U.S. government are such that disruption of orderly urban growth occurs and uncertainty about future patterns of urban development are introduced.

Racial discrimination and mortgage market discrimination against central older areas (so-called red-lining) do not improve the picture. They introduce more uncertainty, and the prospect of even gloomier future events. In such a setting is it any wonder that U.S. house prices are lower? Where Canadians bid up house prices because of the stability of neighbourhoods and the likelihood of capital gains, Americans discount (bid down) the value of the standing stock of housing because of prospects of large scale government intervention that will further erode the value of central city properties and lead to capital losses. With negative expectations, people will offer central city stock for sale 'to get out while the getting is good' and thus paradoxically drive down prices and expectations further. The absence of private urban renewal expenditures surely is evidence of the poor investment climate in U.S. central cities. Public funds have bred uncertainty and the need for more and larger public redevelopment investment. In Canada the situation is reversed where a healthy climate free of large-scale government expenditures led to abundant private investment which is surely a symptom of investor confidence. This confidence breeds more investment and further confidence. Both are positive feedbacks: one leading to healthier cities, the other to sicker ones.[20]

Therefore, instead of typifying Canadian house prices as being much higher than the U.S. house prices, I would advocate turning the situation around and viewing U.S. house prices as being depressed. Why are they depressed? Because of large-scale government interventions which lead to disruptions in the normal evolution of the urban areas into which they are introduced. Disruptions heighten uncertainty which further lowers demand for housing stocks, which are fixed in the short run, and depresses prices. Red-lining, racial discrimination and the bad image of American cities darken the gloom. Less uncertainty in Canadian cities derives from the slower, more evolutionary character of urban development and implies higher prices.

On reflection, it is not the Canadian housing situation that bears looking into: it is the U.S. housing market that warrants closer attention.[21] Perhaps a dose of Canadian sluggishness typified by small scale and minimally effective local policies is called for. Might not Canada be the appropriate model for future U.S. non-involvement in cities.

The story is as complete as we can make it given limitations in data, time and print. It is my opinion as a result of these explorations that high prices signal healthy cities not government and industry bumbling. To reinforce this opinion I want to pick up on a point made at the outset where I posited that the question facing housing policymakers when this volume hits the streets is more likely to involve falling prices and an excess of vacant new units than rising prices and shortages. The latest data from the Greater Vancouver Real Estate Board show that for the first time since they have been keeping an MLS price index (roughly 3 years) it has fallen.[22] Moreover, the latest edition of the C.M.H.C. housing statistics for B.C. shows the number of newly completed and unoccupied units to still be rising. How can we possibly deal with this new crisis of excess stocks and falling prices? Look South? I doubt it. How about just looking, and while we focus our eyes the market will move the product to consumers, prices will rise and we will be off chasing our tales of Canadian blundering while living in what is perhaps the world's highest quality urban environment. Just let's keep those blunders coming. Let's continue to make haste slowly.

APPENDIX A — HOUSE AND LAND PRICE DETERMINATION

All models (e.g. conceptual frameworks) are abstractions from, and simplifications of, reality. A 'good' model is one that allows us to distill the essence of a process, such as the market for housing and urban land, in a sufficiently simple way that we can use both to explore the likely impacts of a variety of changes (instead of 'experimenting' with the real world) and as an aid in analyzing changes that have already occurred.

The art in constructing models is to keep them simple while realistic. We can achieve this end by making realistic assumptions. The model presented here makes a number of simplifying assumptions which are quite plausible and the simplicity of the model allows us to use it in a number of situations to explore the mechanisms by which housing and therefore land prices are derived from market situations.

Figure 1 is a graphical representation of the model we will be using. It comprises two quite different components: the left hand portion represents the total stock of housing; the right hand portion represents the flow of new units onto the housing market. Thus its name: A Stock-Flow Model of Housing Price Determination. This model underlies much of the discussion in the paper.

The stock component (Figure 1a) states that the quantity of housing in the *short run* (say less than 3 to 5 years) is fixed because housing is both durable and immobile. The durability implies that at any given point in time the supply of housing is dominated by the houses already in existence (the stock). The stock has grown over the years as a result of the construction of new units, which because of their durability, accumulate over time. As a result, the stock of houses that has accumulated through successive additions of new units tends to be large relative to the addition of new units in any one year (the flow). For instance, the stock of housing in the Greater Vancouver Regional District (GVRD) is currently approximately 400,000 units. Preliminary estimates show that 1976 was a near record year for new construction in the GVRD with somewhere between 16,000

FIGURE 1
A Stock-Flow Model of Housing Price Determination

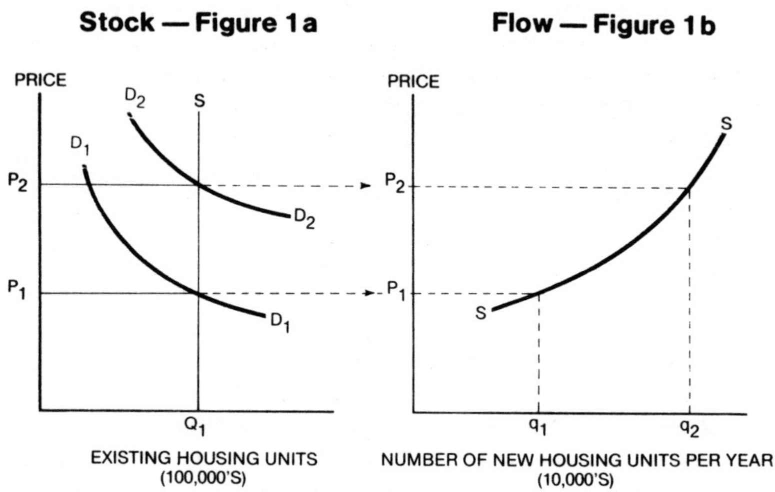

The number of housing units in existence at any point in time (the stock) is determined by the accumulation of housing units as a result of past construction. Due to the inflexibility of the supply under changing circumstances, fluctuations in demand are reflected in price fluctuations.

The number of housing units added to the stock during a given year (the flow) is responsive to price. The higher the price is, the larger will be the production of new units. The price at which new units can be sold is determined by the supply of and demand for existing housing.

and 20,000 new units being (e.g. 4 to 5 per cent of the standing stock).

To represent the fact that the supply of housing units is fixed in the short run, Figure 1a depicts the supply of housing units as being vertical. We call such a supply condition inelastic (e.g. there is no change in supply as we change price). Supply is inelastic because in the short run the maximum possible number of additions to it (new construction) is small (4-5 per cent) relative to the stock.

Under such circumstances we can see that, since changes in supply are assumed away in the short run, changes in demand will lead to changes in price as demand moves up and down along the inelastic supply curve. This can be seen as we shift demand upward from D_1D_1 to D_2D_2 price shifts from P_1 to P_2 and there is no change in supply.

Looking initially only at Figure 1a we can say that given an immobile (e.g. we can't move additional units in or out in the short run to shift supply) and durable (e.g. large stock relative to new construction) supply, price is solely determined by demand fluctuations since changes in supply are not possible in the short run. This gives us some insights into how prices are determined by the relationship between demand and supply, but it does not shed any light on how additional units are brought on to the market. To explore the so-called flow dimension of the stock-flow model we turn to Figure 1b which depicts the supply curve for new units. We can see immediately that this supply curve is relatively elastic with respect to price compared to the inelastic stock supply. Thus, more new units will be built as prices rise to coax more builders and more units onto the market. This supply curve of new units slopes upward to the right to reflect this responsiveness to price. At higher prices, higher production levels (flows of new units) will be achieved.

Having presented the two components of the stock-flow model we need to establish a link between them. This link is provided by price. The price of housing is determined in the stock portion of the model where total demand equals total supply (e.g. the stock). This price then goes on to determine the level of new construction activity from the flow portion of the model.

We are therefore assuming that price is determined outside the flow portion of the model and that new construction merely responds to predetermined prices. The question immediately arises as to the reasonableness of this assumption. Let's examine the pricing behaviour of builders to demonstrate the reasonableness of this assumption.

Builders and developers do in fact work backwards from market price to costs and profits. We can see that at price P_1 developers will build q_1 new units. They determine their level of output by starting with the price, and *subtracting* from it the various costs of construction (labour, materials, financing, and overhead), a normal profit and the amount that they can afford to pay for land. Thus, price is related to costs by starting with price as given, subtracting costs and seeing if a normal profit awaits at the end. Land prices are therefore residuals.

As demand increases in Figure 1 and price increases to P_2 we see that there is now an increase in construction activity to q_2. In addition, in the short run we see that other costs remain the same except for profits and land. Immediately after the price rise, developers holding land purchased at the former lower price, will experience an increase in profit. However, as this increase in profit is perceived by other developers they will jointly bid for the land since land is the key ingredient in earning this higher profit. Since in the short run land is fixed in supply, the increased search for land to build higher priced homes (e.g. P_2 vs. P_1) bids up the price of land and erodes the profits. Thus, at P_2 we find that all increases in price have been absorbed by increased land prices since other costs remain the same. Using a numerical example to illustrate:

	Year 1	Year 2	% Change
House price	$50,000	$60,000	20%
Building costs (incl. normal profit)	40,000	40,000	0
Maximum bid for the land	$10,000	$20,000	50%

This simple example summarizes the shift from P_1 to P_2 illustrated by Figure 1. It also depicts the important concept that the costs of development are subtracted from the price to *derive* a bid for the land. As a result the demand for land is referred to as a *derived demand* as distinct from a pure demand for a commodity like apples which are demanded for their consumption. The demand for land (and for other so-called factors of production like machinery and factories) is derived from the uses to which it can be put. The greater the value is of the use to which the land can be put, the higher the demand is for the land and, given its fixity of supply in the short run, the higher therefore is its price.

This then is the result that we were aiming for with this model. The price of land is derived from the price of housing. In the short run with the stock of houses and land fixed, it is the price of housing that determines the price of residential land. Costs of land to developers, or to individuals who want to have houses custom built, therefore cannot affect price, they can only be affected by price. In this short-run situation the distinction between price (determined by total demand and total supply-stock) and cost is critical. Price can vary widely from cost. Witness pet rocks whose cost of production was minimal yet whose price was 'outrageous' in comparison with the costs of inputs (e.g. rocks).

Given the foregoing analysis, the problem of land prices which this volume addresses, can be translated with minimal loss of reality into the problem of house prices. Accordingly, the analysis in the paper concentrates upon housing prices since they determine land prices under conditions of changing demand in the short run and not vice versa.

To summarize, we go back to one of the first land economists, David Ricardo, the British economist (and financier), who posed the question, "Is the price of corn high because the price of land is high, *or* is the price of land high because the price of corn is high?" The preceding analysis is analogous to Ricardo's reasoning done in 1819 where he concluded that corn prices (e.g. houses in our model) determine land prices and not the other way around. We can, therefore, focus our attention on those factors that influence housing prices since other things remaining constant, land prices will follow directly.[1]

[1]For an elaboration of this point of view see *Housing: It's Your Move, ibid.* The concept of derived demand is central to the argument and the interested reader is referred to Paul A. Samuelson and Anthony D. Scott, *Economics: Fourth Canadian Edition* (Toronto: McGraw Hill, Ryerson), 1975, for a discussion of the concept. Chapters 28-31 (pages 512-569) deal with payments to factors of production and are particularly relevant. For empirical evidence suggesting that during periods of rising prices developers are relatively unconcerned about land costs, see Michael A. Goldberg and Daniel D. Ulinder, "Residential Developer Behaviour: 1975," *Housing: It's Your Move*, Volume II, *op. cit.*, pp. 241-382.

Acknowledgements

This study could not have been completed without the assistance, guidance, and criticism of Mr. Jim Cox, my co-worker in collecting and analysing the data used in this report. His encouragement, careful analyses, energy and independence allowed me to finish this essay. Jim Cox must take much of the credit for what is of value here. As always, I as author, accept readily, whatever blame may result from the analyses and musings contained herein.

A number of other people also made this task much easier. Mr. Albert Crossetti of the Seattle City Planning Department gave freely of his time and provided us with data and background information on the housing situation in the Seattle area. Mr. Tom McGrath of McGrath Homes, gave us invaluable insights into the development of housing in Seattle as compared to Vancouver. Finally, Mr. Bob Schindler of the Puget Sound Council of Governments provided us with information on transportation for the Seattle region.

To all of the above, and to others who were generous in their help in teaching us about a 'foreign' city, go my thanks and hopes that the present effort may provide some alternative views and solutions to the thorny problems facing urban areas in North America.

Notes

[1]Housing Study Team, *Housing: It's Your Move*, (Vancouver, B.C.: Urban Land Economics Division, Faculty of Commerce and Business Administration, University of British Columbia), Volumes I and II, 1976.

[2]Wilfred Owen, *The Accessible City* (Washington, D.C.: Brookings Institution), 1972.

[3]John F. Kain has done a great deal of work in this area. See his recent study with John M. Quigley, *Housing Markets and Racial Discrimination*, (New York: National Bureau of Economic Research), 1975, for a summary of this work and its most current extensions.

[4]Institutional differences between the U.S. and Canada bear directly on the housing situation we are studying, since differences in the availability of mortgage credit can lead to very significant differences in effective demand for housing and therefore very different housing prices. First, it should be noted that changes to the National Housing Act during the past decade have allowed considerably more flexibility in government insured mortgage loans. Since 1969 the N.H.A. lending rate has been allowed to float so that N.H.A. insured mortgages are an attractive asset and are able to compete in capital markets for their share. Also in 1969, the 5-year renewal clause was introduced federally. The 1967 revision of the Bank Act also had significant implications for the availability of mortgage funds. Before this revision chartered banks could not lend at rates in excess of 6 per cent. Since 1960 mortgage rates exceeded that level and the chartered banks had to remove themselves as sources of mortgage credit. With the 1967 revisions the banks came back into the market with a vengeance. In 1967, chartered banks held $840 million in mortgages or roughly 3.5 per cent of the stock of outstanding mortgages. In 1975 bank holdings rose to $7,716 million or roughly 12.5 per cent of the stock of mortgages. These institutional changes toward greater flexibility allow market responsiveness of mortgage rates so that funds have flowed into the mortgage market as a result. These changes combined with easy money policies and generally buoyant economic growth certainly were a major, if not the major, contributor to nation-wide housing price increases. Lawrence B. Smith makes a series of related points about demand stimuli in his paper, *Anatomy of A Crisis: Canadian Housing Policy in the 1970's*, Fraser Institute, 1977.

While Canada was pursuing policies designed to ease the flow of mortgage funds and to remove institutional restrictions on flows of funds in capital markets, the U.S. was going in a different direction. Since the mid-1960s deposit rate ceilings on passbook savings accounts were imposed on thrift institutions by the Federal Reserve Board (Regulation Q). In periods of high interest rates and tight credit, such as those in the late 1960s and early 1970s, the thrift institutions (and life insurance companies as well) experienced significant difficulties in attracting and even in holding funds. Mortgage credit became very tight, not so much in terms of rates (which were influenced by deposit rate ceilings) but in terms of availability. Restricted availability of mortgage funds in the U.S. combined with the Milton Friedman era of tight money would have had the effect of lowering the effective demand for housing and therefore its price.

The skeptical reader might still raise some questions about the relative efficiency of Canadian and U.S. mortgage markets and institutions: For instance:

1. If capital markets became more efficient in Canada why did Canadian mortgage rates remain well above U.S. mortgage rates?

2. If capital markets became more efficient, allowing for increased flows of funds into mortgage markets, are there empirical results that demonstrate that mortgage rates are now low relative to other rates in Canada and the U.S.? In essence, if more mortgage money flowed into the mortgage market as a result of easing previously existing imperfections, why haven't yield spreads dropped between mortgages and other financial assets?

In both questions the questioner is ignoring, I believe, a number of institutional and demand factors. First, mortgage rates in Canada are likely to remain well above mortgage rates in the U.S. because the U.S. mortgage market is highly imperfect due to deposit rate ceilings and the large role played by government through the Federal National Mortgage Association (FNMA or Fannie Mae) and the Government National Mortgage Association (GNMA or Ginnie Mae). Regulation 'Q' governing passbook savings interest rates effectively keeps down the cost of capital for thrift institutions and by providing thrift institutions with a slightly higher passbook rate than banks allows them a slight edge in attracting capital from individual savers. Since these institutions are in addition restricted to residential mortgage loans for their assets, we can see that they cannot respond to normal market pressures and borrow at higher rates during high interest periods, nor can they lend on other assets when mortgages are unattractive. The present spread on deposit ceilings is 0.25 per cent, with banks allowed to pay 5.00 per cent and thrift institutions 5.25 per cent. With such low costs of capital compared to Canadian mortgage lenders and with such restrictions on their assets, it is not at all surprising that Canadian mortgage rates are higher than U.S. rates.

A more general question should be addressed here as well: does it make any sense for mortgage rates to be below existing prime rates? I think not. First, mortgages are much riskier assets than loans to Canadian General Electric or Imperial Oil. Thus, rates should reflect risk. This risk is not fully covered by mortgage insurance schemes since they, in general, protect the capital of the lender and do not cover foreclosure costs and interest foregone during foreclosure. Second, mortgages are expensive in terms of transactions costs to lenders. Witness the objections to the Borrowers and Depositors Protection Act which would allow prepayment at any time. Finally, mortgages are relatively illiquid and some premium must be tacked on for this. However, this premium I do not think is very substantial since it is estimated that nearly $2 billion of N.H.A. insured mortgages were estimated to have been sold abroad during 1976. Thus, in Canada at any rate, because of the relatively high yields that mortgages provide as a result of reasonably perfect capital markets, there is a market for mortgages as an investment. This secondary market should not be confused with the U.S. secondary market under Fannie Mae and Ginnie Mae which have been shown time and again (by Oliver Jones and Leo Grebler most notably) to be subsidies by the federal government of an imperfect mortgage market. Fannie Mae and Ginnie Mae primarily buy mortgages to pump up the liquidity of the thrift institutions since they have restricted sources of funds during times of tight credit. The low interest rates on U.S. mortgages are a major source of their mortgage problems since mortgages cannot compete unassisted with other financial assets as they can in Canada. Once again, I feel strongly that looking at U.S. secondary markets, and U.S. mortgage interest rates as guides to our policies is inappropriate and likely to lead to very wrong conclusions. So much for why U.S. rates are lower, and why U.S. secondary markets do not hold the answer to lowering Canadian mortgages rates. Our high rates have solved our mortgage credit problems because they have attracted funds into the mortgage market and provided for abundant, broadly based, mortgage funds.

The second aspect of these questions deals with yield spreads between mortgages and other financial assets. It is asked why such spreads haven't dropped given the supposed increases in market efficiency that I have been suggesting. The question assumes that demand for mortgages is constant. In such a situation, removing restrictions on mortgages would attract funds and lower yield spreads and rates. However, I have also been suggesting that demand for mortgages was increasing very rapidly during the early 1970s as a result of rapid increases in incomes which allowed people to borrow larger sums and also encouraged them to incur higher debt amounts than they would normally, since such debt would only be a burden in the very short run given that incomes would continue to rise. Thus, increases in the demand for mortgage funds would compensate for increases in supply keeping up interest rates.

Another factor also comes into play. During the early 1970s, as mortgage loan amounts rose dramatically because of the foregoing reasoning, debt/service ratios became limiting factors on loans. In other words, debt/service ratios approached their maximum amounts, thus exposing lending institutions to increased risk of default through inability to meet mortgage payments out of cash flow. Financial institutions would require some risk premium as a result which would further prevent yield spreads from narrowing. The wisdom of such a risk premium is borne out by the dramatic increase in defaults during 1976 compared to 1975 as expected salary increases failed to materialize. Thus, for a number of reasons, I feel that there is no inconsistency between greater efficiency in the mortgage market and constant yield spreads and high mortgage interest rates.

In summary, it appears that Canadian moves toward freer capital and mortgage markets did much to reinforce the economic growth trends since 1970 to increase the supply of mortgage funds, increase effective demand for housing, and in the face of a relatively inelastic supply of housing in the short run, drive up the price. In the U.S. credit was not so abundant and institutional restrictions aggravated tight money policies to limit effective demand for housing and therefore limit its price rise. For more detail on Canadian mortgage markets see James E. Hatch, *The Canadian Mortgage Market*, (Toronto: Queen's Printer, for the Ministry of the Treasury of Ontario), 1975. For the U.S. mortgage situation see Franco Modigliani and Donald Lessard, Editors, *New Mortgage Designs for Stable Housing in an Inflationary Environment*, (Boston: Federal Reserve Bank of Boston), 1975.

[5]For confirmation of residential mortgage interest rates see *Canadian Housing Statistics 1975* and *Statistical Abstract of the United States 1975*.

[6]For confirmation of unemployment rates see *The Labour Force* S.C. Cat. No. 71-001A, *1973 Labour Force Statistics*, and *Real Estate Research Report*, Spring, 1976.

[7]For Consumer Prices Indexes see *Canadian Housing Statistics 1975* and *Statistical Abstract of the United States 1975.*

[8]The U.S. Senate *Banking, Housing and Urban Affairs Committee* has published the proceedings from four days of hearings that it held regarding the *Home Mortgage Disclosure Act of 1975.* These hearings are available from the U.S. Government Printing Office in Washington, D.C. The hearings were held May 5-8, 1975 and much attention was directed toward red-lining and other discriminatory lending practices. The perniciousness of red-lining by thrift institutions is that thrift institutions represent virtually the only use of savings for small savers. Central city residents, to the extent that they are poorer, are thus in the position of lending money to thrift institutions at reduced rates due to deposit rate ceilings, and then not being able to borrow back these funds in the form of mortgages due to red-lining and discriminatory lending practices by the thrift institutions, which as we have seen represent a major source of mortgage funds in the U.S.

[9]In 1960-61 the U.S. had 9.9 times as many people as did Canada. During the period 1960 to 1975, however, the U.S. built only 8.5 times as many housing units. Comparing U.S. population figures for 1974 and those for Canada in 1976 (instead of for 1960 and 1961 as earlier) we see that the ratio has dropped to 9.4 times the Canadian population which still implies that Canada has had relatively more housebuilding activity.

[10]See Stanley W. Hamilton, "Measuring Change in House Prices," in Michael A. Goldberg (editor), *Recent Perspectives in Urban Land Economics: Essays in Honour of Richard U. Ratcliff and Paul F. Wendt,* (Vancouver: Urban Land Economics Division, Faculty of Commerce and Business Administration, University of British Columbia), 1976, pp. 64-83.

[11]For personal income per capita information see *Statistical Abstract of the United States 1975* and *National Income and Expenditure Accounts,* S.C. Cat. No. 13-201.

[12]Growth in households is an important factor in the demand for housing. Unfortunately, we do not yet have the preliminary estimates for households from the 1976 census. Preliminary population estimates, however, imply that there has been a rapid increase in household formation between 1971 and 1976 and a dramatic decrease in household size. This implication follows from the virtually stagnant population growth during the period of most buoyant demand for housing as evidenced by our house price increases, low vacancy rates and high levels of housing starts.

[13]The monthly *Bulletins of Economic Activity* published by the B.C. Department of Economic Development present regional unemployment data monthly for B.C. and corroborate this point.

[14]See for Vancouver, *Real Estate Trends in Metropolitan Vancouver,* 1976 (Vancouver Real Estate Board of Greater Vancouver), 1976; and for Seattle see *Real Estate Research Report,* Vol. 27, No. 1, Spring, 1976 (Seattle: Seattle Real Estate Research Committee), 1976.

[15]Recent transportation planning in Vancouver has centred on the development of additional bus lines (both diesel and electric), improvement of service on existing lines, the introduction of a passenger ferry system to open Summer, 1977, across Burrard Inlet, and the reintroduction of street cars, now *light rapid transit* (LRT), on

old rights-of-way of the B.C. Electric Railway. There are no freeways planned, and only one vehicular route is being proposed seriously for expansion; the addition of a Fraser River crossing at Annacis Island to ease congestion at the Deas Tunnel to the southern municipalities. In Seattle, earnest efforts are being made concerning transit and more efficient use of existing bridges through carpooling and reduced tolls for carpools. However, a major debate is presently underway concerning the construction of another bridge across Lake Washington to accommodate Interstate 90. If this project goes ahead extensive freeway construction will take place in Seattle to link I-90 with existing north-south I-5. Thus, freeway planning is far from dead yet in Seattle and the outcome of the debate over I-90 will have far-reaching consequences for the future form and viability of Seattle's core area. This is an instance where Seattle might profitably learn from the Vancouver experience where no freeways have yet been built through the city. Without additional freeways, perhaps inner areas have a chance at naturally renewing themselves. With additional freeways their chances pale.

[16]Central Mortgage and Housing Corporation, *British Columbia Region Housing Statistics*, October, 1976 (Ottawa: Central Mortgage and Housing Corporation).

[17]Statistics Canada, *1971 Census of Canada*, (Ottawa: Statistics Canada).

[18]For this reason I believe that the Assisted Home Ownership Program is likely to prove to be the most important housing policy innovation during the past decade because it has begun the slow process of changing expectations about housing from large single-detached units to smaller, denser and more economical units. While every Canadian may have the right to adequate housing, at an affordable price, it is not at all obvious that *adequate* must mean two thousand square feet of living space, with carpets, dishwasher and basement. AHOP has signalled a new era of adequate housing, which appears to be much more consistent with the land, labour and capital resources at our disposal. The program has been successful from the point of view of housing supply, there being 47,739 units started since 1973 when the program really got off the ground. As long as the units meet N.H.A. building code requirements they are acceptable under the program. It is up to the developer to decide whether to build a posh small unit or a minimally furnished larger one. Thus, even though C.M.H.C. does set a maximum price for A.H.O.P. units by geographic region, they leave it up to the market to determine the details. Once again, the Canadian government has moved toward private sector suppliers of housing, as it had done earlier with mortgage funds. The general trend as a result is quite clearly away from direct participation in markets and more toward influencing market parameters indirectly such as through AHOP.

[19]Much abuse is hurled at local municipalities that have moved toward very high servicing standards and the imposition of impost fees for off-site impacts of developments. Such local policies seem completely rational and well founded. They essentially represent pay-as-you-go policies for urban development. Demanding high quality infra-structure investments in streets, oversize sewers, curbs, paved lands, and buried utilities mean that these investments will have low maintenance costs and high reliability. This ensures that future public funds needed to operate these capital outlays will be small and accounted for at the outset. In the U.S., however, the give-aways were not properly accounted for and are now placing serious strains on municipal operating and capital budgets as the 'free' capital ages and requires

additional expenditure. High standards, dubbed 'cadillac services' by detractors, make economic sense (cents?). Impost charges which pass on increasing marginal costs of growth to those who impose the costs also make sense. By demanding high quality capital investment from developers, and by getting revenues for the general fund, municipalities can ensure low property taxes and high levels of service. It is not strange therefore to see such significant differences in property taxes as we have seen between Canada and the U.S.

[20]To strengthen this point it should be noted that the bulk of urban renewal schemes in Canada have been privately financed. Moreover, *urban renewal* as it existed in the U.S. never came to play a very large part in Canadian federal policy. In 1969 as a result of the *Hellyer Task Force on Housing*, the urban renewal provisions of the N.H.A. were removed and replaced later with neighbourhood improvement and rehabilitation schemes. Thus, urban renewal policies were in force from the 1964 revisions of N.H.A. until their demise in 1969. Once again the story in the U.S. was very different since the urban renewal program was large and well established before World War II. The scale and and insensitivity of urban renewal programs incurred the wrath of both citizens and researchers during the 1960s and these programs have largely been phased out or downplayed. The important point for our arguments here is that the myth of private enterprise in the U.S. concerning housing is just that; a myth. Similarly, the myth that Canadian governments have been intervening in urban land and housing markets also is subject to question. The private sector has contributed most of the funds and ideas to Canadian urban redevelopment, while in the U.S. just the reverse is true. For more information on urban redevelopment in Canada see Robert Collier, *Contemporary Cathedrals*, (Toronto: Harvest House), 1975. For an introduction to U.S. urban renewal see Jewel Bellush and Murray Hausknecht, Editors, *Urban Renewal: People, Politics and Planning*, (Garden City, N.Y.: Anchor Books), 1967.

[21]In this regard it should be noted that much of U.S. housing policy in the past has been built on the notion of providing reasonably priced new housing to allow middle income households to move out of the existing housing stock and thus free it up for lower income households. This so-called 'filtering' mechanism has either implicitly or explicitly been a pillar of U.S. housing policy in the post-war period. No wonder that U.S. prices are lower. So much policy is aimed at dumping existing stocks on the market to keep prices low and encourage lower income households into them. The result has been in part the dying U.S. central city. In Canada as we have noted, the aim has been toward stimulating demand so that housing prices have stayed high and the cities livable. There is not time here to get into the filtering debate other than to cite Gary Sands' recent paper which does set out the questions quite clearly. See Gary Sands, "Housing Turnover: Assessing Its Relevance to Public Policy," *Journal of the American Institute of Planners*, Volume 42, No. 4, October, 1976, pp. 419-426.

[22]*Vancouver Realtor*, Volume 14, No. 1, January, 1977, pp. 2-5

References

Bellush, Jewel and Murray Hausknecht (Editors) *Urban Renewal: People, Politics and Planning* (Garden City, N.Y.: Anchor Books, 1967).

Canada, Ministry of Transport, *Federal Task Force on Housing and Urban Development* (Honourable Paul Hellyer, Chairman) (Ottawa: Queen's Printer, 1969).

Central Mortgage and Housing Cooperation, *Canadian Housing Statistics* (Ottawa: Central Mortgage and Housing Corperation, various years).

Collier, Robert, *Contemporary Cathedrals* (Toronto: Harvest House, 1975).

Eldredge, H. Wentworth (Editor), *Taming Megalopolis* (Garden City, N.Y., Anchor Books, 1967).

Goldberg, Michael A. and Michael Y. Seelig, *Planning - The ASPO Magazine* "Canadian Cities: The Right Deed for the Wrong Reasons", 41(3): 8-13

Goldberg, Michael A. (Editor), *Recent Perspectives in Urban Land Economics: Essays in Honour of Richard U. Ratcliff and Paul F. Wendt* (Vancouver: Urban Land Economics Division, Faculty of Commerce and Business Administration, University of British Columbia, 1976).

Hardwick, Walter G., *Vancouver* (Don Mills: Collier-Macmillan Canada, Ltd., 1974).

Hatch, James E., *The Canadian Mortgage Market* (Toronto: Queen's Printer for Ministry of the Treasury, 1975).

Housing Study Team, *Housing: It's Your Move*, Volumes I and II (Vancouver: Urban Land Economics Division, Faculty of Commerce and Business Administration, University of British Columbia, 1976).

Jones, Oliver and Loe Grebler, *The Secondary Mortgage Market: Its Purpose and Potential*, (Los Angeles: Real Estate Research Program, University of California, 1961).

Kain, John F. and John M. Quigley, *Housing Markets and Racial Discrimination: A Microeconomic Analysis* (New York: National Bureau of Economic Research, 1975).

Modigliani, Franco and Donald Lessard (Editors), *New Mortgage Designs for Stable Housing in An Inflationary Environment* (Boston: Federal Reserve Bank of Boston, 1975).

Real Estate Board of Greater Vancouver, *Real Estate Trends in Metropolitan Vancouver* (Vancouver: Real Estate Board of Greater Vancouver, various years).

Sands, Gary, "Housing Turnover: Assessing Its Relevance to Public Policy," *Journal of the American Institute of Planners*, Volume 42, No. 4, October, 1976, pp. 419-426.

Seattle Real Estate Research Committee, *Real Estate Research Report* (Seattle: Seattle Real Estate Research Committee, various years).

Simmons, James and Robert Simmons, *Urban Canada* (Toronto: Copp-Clark Publishing, 1969).

Fraser Institute Books in Print

FRIEDMAN ON GALBRAITH
. . . and on curing the British Disease

Why is it that the economic mind behind the Prime Minister has few, if any, followers in the economics profession? Why is it that John Kenneth Galbraith's theories have become widely accepted when there is a total lack of support for them? Is Galbraith a *scientist* or a *missionary*? Milton Friedman, Nobel Laureate in Economics 1976, addresses these and other questions about Galbraith as economist and prophet in this Fraser Institute book. Whatever the reader's view of Galbraith, this book by Friedman is must reading. It is said that Canada and other countries are on the same path as Britain—to some, the *British Disease* is the logical ending of Galbraith's story. In the second essay in this book, Professor Friedman outlines a cure for the British Disease: the principles that Friedman develops in this essay are of immediate Canadian interest as they point out the necessity to adopt gradualist corrective policies *now* before the more jarring policies currently required in the U.K. are necessary here.

66 Pages • $3.95 paperback • ISBN 0-88975-015-7

★ ★ ★

WHICH WAY AHEAD?
Canada after Wage and Price Control

Fifteen well-informed Canadian economists assess the controls programme, suggest the reasons why it should be ended, and propose policies that should be adopted after controls end—**policies to give Canada a healthy and internationally competitive economy—policies for restraint in the public sector—policies to meet the critical double-headed challenge of low inflation and full employment.** Contributors include Jack Carr, Tom Courchene, John Helliwell, David Laidler, Richard Lipsey, Michael Parkin, Simon Reisman, Grant Reuber and Michael Walker.

376 Pages • 5 Charts • 9 Tables • $4.95 paperback • ISBN 0-88975-010-6

★ ★ ★

THE ILLUSION OF WAGE AND PRICE CONTROL
Essays On Inflation, Its Causes And Its Cures

A look at the causes of inflation and an examination of responses to it in Canada, the United States and the United Kingdom. Contributors include Jack Carr, Michael Darby, Jackson Grayson, David Laidler, Michael Parkin, Robert Schuettinger and Michael Walker.

258 Pages • 16 Charts • 7 Tables
$5.95 paperback ISBN 0-88975-001-7 • $2.95 pocketbook ISBN 0-88975-005-X

★ ★ ★

HOW MUCH TAX DO YOU REALLY PAY?
Introducing The Canadian Consumer Tax Index

Have you ever stopped to think what you pay your federal, provincial, and municipal governments in taxes? Have you ever wondered how much hidden tax you pay on all of the things you buy? This Fraser Institute Guide asks and answers two basic questions: Q: Who pays for government? (A: You do!) and Q: How much do you pay? By reading this book, you will see for the first time how astronomically the Canadian CONSUMER TAX INDEX has risen over the past fifteen years. And if you want to, you can actually calculate how much tax you really pay and your real tax rate.

120 Pages • 6 Charts • 22 Tables • $2.95 paperback • ISBN 0-88975-004-1

ANATOMY OF A CRISIS
Canadian Housing Policy in the Seventies

In this book—a further title in the Fraser Institute Housing Series—Professor L. B. Smith, Associate Chairman of the Department of Political Economy at the University of Toronto, and one of Canada's leading urban economists, considers the content and objectives of Federal housing policies from 1935 to the present. His conclusions that **1) housing policy is more and more being used as a vehicle for redistributing income in Canada and 2) that this policy is at the same time destroying the private sector's incentive and ability to supply housing,** make the book required reading for everybody concerned with housing in Canada today. The book contains a comprehensive bibliography.

55 Pages • 7 Tables • $3.95 paperback • ISBN 0-88975-009-2

★ ★ ★

THE DO'S AND DON'TS OF HOUSING POLICY:
The Case of British Columbia

This book is the second in the Institute's on-going housing economics series, the first of which was: "Rent Control—A Popular Paradox". Economist Raymond Heung's book is a case study of housing in British Columbia. As well as taking vigorous issue with the methodology and conclusions of the 1975 Jaffary and Runge reports, (issued as a result of a B.C. government-funded Interdepartmental Study), the Heung book provides a useful and detailed framework for housing market analysis, together with an examination of the costs of adopting a housing allowance scheme for British Columbia. This scheme, guaranteeing access to basic accommodation for all residents in the province, would cost less than half as much as current government outlays on housing in the province. The book, written by a former staff member of the government study team, has a message applicable to every province. As such, it should be of interest to everyone concerned with Canadian housing economics.

145 Pages • 4 Charts • 28 Tables • $8.00 paperback • ISBN 0-88975-006-8

★ ★ ★

RENT CONTROL—A POPULAR PARADOX
Evidence On The Economic Effects Of Rent Control

Eleven essays on the economics of housing in Canada and on the effects of rent control in the United States, the United Kingdom, Austria, France and Sweden by F. A. Hayek, Milton Friedman, George Stigler, Bertrand de Jouvenel, F. W. Paish, F. G. Pennance, E. O. Olsen, Sven Rydenfelt and M. A. Walker.

230 Pages • 9 Charts • 28 Tables • $2.95 pocketbook • ISBN 0-88975-007-6

★ ★ ★

THE REAL COST OF THE BC MILK BOARD
A Case Study In Canadian Agricultural Policy

Two Simon Fraser University professors of economics, Herbert Grubel and Richard Schwindt, analyze the social cost of the B.C. milk marketing board, the impact of the milk quota system and the extent to which the Board transfers income from consumers to producers. Grubel and Schwindt develop an analytical framework that can be applied to marketing boards in general. Their study documents the consequences of marketing boards and has been published to stimulate public discussion of the important economic issues at stake.

78 Pages • 6 Charts • 6 Appendices • $3.95 paperback • ISBN 0-88975-013-0

To: The Secretary,
The Fraser Institute,
626 Bute Street,
Vancouver, British Columbia. V6E 3M1
Canada.

PUBLICATION ORDER FORM

Please send me:

__________ copies of ______________________________

__________ copies of ______________________________

__________ copies of ______________________________

Enclosed is payment in full of $__________ or credit card no.: Chargex # ----------------
Mastercharge # ------------------------------

Signature: ______________________________

Name: ______________________________
(please print)

Organization: ______________________________

Address: ______________________________

____

MEMBERSHIP REQUEST FORM

Dear Sir:

Please send me information on how I can become a member of the Fraser Institute.

Name: ______________________________

Title: ______________________________

Organization: ______________________________

Address: ______________________________

____